Karangarua

Unity Through Diversity in Transactional Analysis

Edited by Keith Tudor and Matt Bird

Tuwhera Open Access Books

ISBN: 978-1-99-101164-0

Published in 2025 by Tuwhera Open Access Books. Printed by IngramSpark.

Cover design: Charlotte Hāriata Mann (Tūhoe, Ngāti Kahungunu ki Wairoa, Neiafu Vava'u)

The cover design is inspired by the pākati carving pattern found in wharenui (Māori meeting houses), which represent the traditional storehouse of knowledge. Pākati is a pattern of triangular notches, often used in carving and tā moko, symbolising precision, process, and repetition in carving, and also associated with strength and resilience, the two joining points of which also represent unity and diversity.

ISBN (online): 978-1-99-101159-6

ISBN (print): 978-1-99-101164-0

Freely available online at https://tuwhera.aut.ac.nz/

Endorsements

This book is a powerful and timely collection of reflections, research, and practice that honours the theme of *Karangarua: Unity Through Diversity*, as explored during the 2024 Transactional Analysis (TA) Conference in Whanganui-a-Tara | Wellington, Aotearoa New Zealand. Each chapter is a unique response to a call across professional, cultural, spiritual, and personal realms, inviting readers into deeper relationship with themselves, with others, and with the evolving field of TA. The authors respond to the karanga to participate initially at the TA Conference and now in this volume with generosity and insight, creating a dialogue that is both intellectually rigorous and emotionally moving.

The concept of standing in dual relationship runs through the book as both metaphor and method. The contributors offer a weaving together of perspectives, grounded in TA theory and practice, and enriched by mātauranga Māori, neuroscience, philosophy, and lived experience. From the marae to the therapy room, from humour to working with bad men, from cultural scripting to creativity, this collection affirms that diversity is not a challenge to be managed, but a source of vitality, resilience, and transformation.

TA provides a shared language, a relational philosophy, and a set of tools that support reflection, dialogue, and growth. Yet the authors do not rest on tradition as they interrogate it, expand it, and reimagine it, in light of contemporary challenges. Whether exploring Japanese we-ness, Māori frameworks of wellbeing, or the discursively constructed criminal self, the authors affirm that TA must evolve to honour diverse ways of knowing and being. The challenge is not to dilute TA's theory, but to deepen it by listening to voices that have been marginalised, by embracing discomfort, and by holding space for transformation. This book is a wero – a challenge and an invitation to the TA community and beyond. It calls us to create spaces where psychological safety, cultural integrity, and relational depth are prioritised. It affirms that transformational learning and healing begin with relationship, and that unity through diversity is not only possible, but essential.

As we listen to the unique voices within this collection, we are reminded: e koekoe te tūī, e ketekete te kākā, e kūkū te kererū | The tūī, the kākā, and the kererū each make their own unique sound. Together, they form a chorus. Together, we must move forward.

Maria Haenga-Collins (Ngāti Porou, Te Aitanga a Māhaki, Ngāi Tahu, Pākehā), Lecturer, Auckland University of Technology, Aotearoa New Zealand

1

It is with great respect and admiration that I offer this endorsement of *Karangarua: Unity Through Diversity in Transactional Analysis*.

This volume stands as a testament to the depth, breadth, and evolving spirit of our international TA community. Originating from the 2024 international Transactional Analysis Conference held in Aotearoa New Zealand, it honours the spirit of karangarua – a Māori concept evoking the call and response that connects people across difference, and the courage to stand in two worlds at once.

In bringing these voices together, the editors have created a work that is both grounded and visionary – a meeting place of theory and culture, of personal story and professional insight. This book *Karangarua* reminds us that our unity as a community does not rest on uniformity, but on our willingness to listen, to learn, and to honour the many languages through which human understanding is expressed.

On behalf of the International Transactional Analysis Association, I commend this volume to readers everywhere. May it inspire continued dialogue, fresh scholarship, and the enduring spirit of respect that lies at the heart of our work.

Marguerite Sacco, President, International Transactional Analysis Association, South Africa

I really, really loved reading this. There are some scholarly articles and some very personal stories – and all bring a flavour of the uniqueness of the author(s) and their thinking and also the richness of their connectedness and the co-created event that gave birth to the book. I have learned something about Māori culture, the tikanga – customs and traditional values – and the natural assumption that every here-and-now relationship is both spiritual and physical and also reverberates with past and present relationships, and, when at the start of Paper 5, I read the translation of the tauparapara, meaning both incantation and beginning, I found myself in tears. We need more of that in the world.

Charlotte Sills, TSTA(P), Psychotherapist, Coach, Supervisor, Professor of Coaching, Hult Ashridge Executive Education, UK

Karangarua: Unity Through Diversity in Transactional Analysis captures what's most vital about the field of TA: real conversations, genuine connection, and the courage to learn across cultures. The voices assembled within these pages reflect a commitment to making our workplaces and communities more open and resilient, grounded in a deep respect for the unique perspectives each person brings.

These stories and frameworks aren't only theory; they offer practical pathways for leaders, coaches, and everyday practitioners to build authentic dialogue that bridges difference. By centring diversity as a source of wisdom, the book invites us all to challenge assumptions, widen our lens, and champion inclusion – not only as a value, but as a way forward.

Whether you're beginning your journey with TA or seeking fresh inspiration, *Karangarua* stands out as a resource that encourages reflection, sparks action, and builds unity through our shared – and varied – human experience.

Grace JM Lam, Founder & Director, SeraphCorp Institute, Singapore

I had the privilege of attending the Conference that gave rise to this book. It was my first TA conference, and a great experience, during which I met many of the people who have contributed to this. I am delighted to see this book published and am honoured to endorse it. These papers, written by passionate, friendly, hopeful, sincere, and intelligent people are surprisingly easy to read. It left me thinking big thoughts about my own mahi (work), and life, and the way things change and yet stay the same: we polish and improve as we go. This book is an informative and important resource for anyone supporting others in their journey to mauriora – a thriving life.

Briony Fiso (Ngā Puhi, Tuhoe, Te Whanau-a-Apanui, Ngāti Porou, Ngāti Kahungunu), Addictions and Mental Health Clinician, Te Rūnanga o Toa Rangatira, Porirua, Aotearoa New Zealand

Karangarua: Unity Through Diversity offers an extended attempt to develop a genuine bicultural engagement between Indigenous healing and Western psychotherapies in Aotearoa. A genuinely dual partnership is rare internationally, so this publication is much to be welcomed. The original initiative required the Conference to articulate many difficult issues, particularly around colonialism, social inequalities and marginalisation, but did this. The resulting diverse papers in this publication also speak within the larger

3

domain of international TA theory and practice. It's a brave and challenging enterprise, and contains much to commend it to a wide range of therapeutic communities.

Dr John Farnsworth, Registered Psychotherapist, Life Member, Association of Psychotherapists Aotearoa New Zealand, Ōtepoti | Dunedin, Aotearoa New Zealand

Forewords

It is with immense pride and gratitude that I write this foreword for *Karangarua: Unity Through Diversity in Transactional Analysis*, the first publication of its kind from Aotearoa New Zealand. This book represents a milestone in the history of our TA community – a moment where our local voices, stories, and scholarship come together to speak to the world.

Born out of the 2024 international Transactional Analysis Conference held in Te Whanganui-a-Tara | Wellington, *Karangarua* captures the spirit of that extraordinary gathering – a coming together of practitioners, teachers, and thinkers from across cultures, disciplines, and generations. The title, *Karangarua*, reminds us of the strength that arises when we stand in two worlds – the local and the global, the psychological and the social, Māori and Pākehā – and find relationship between them.

Within these pages, readers will find a rich diversity of voices exploring themes of bicultural engagement, spirituality, social justice, creativity, trauma, and learning. From reflections on wairua and whakapapa to innovative applications of TA in education, organisational life, counselling and psychotherapy, this collection reflects both the maturity and the vitality of TA in our region.

As co-president, with Mandy Lacy, of the Transactional Analysis Association of Aotearoa New Zealand, we and the whole Association celebrate this publication not only as a record of a remarkable Conference, but as a living expression of our Association's vision – to foster connection, respect, and curiosity in all our relationships – and thank Keith and Matt for their vision in bringing this embodiment of the Conference to fruition. May *Karangarua* inspire future generations of transactional analysts to continue the call – to stand together, and to honour unity through diversity.

Nō reira, tēnā koutou, tēnā koutou, tēnā tātou katoa.

Gerry Pyves, TSTA(P)
Co-President, Transactional Analysis Association of Aotearoa New Zealand

It is with great delight that I write this foreword for *Karangarua: Unity Through Diversity in Transactional Analysis*, which is not only a record of the 2024 international Conference but also designed to inspire future generations of TA practitioners in education, organisational life, counselling, and psychotherapy.

The Australian Transactional Analysis Association proudly supports the work of our colleagues in Aotearoa New Zealand; we believe our collaborative relationship brings great benefit to the members of both organisations. We look forward to sharing this inspiring collection of papers with all our members.

Patricia Hornsbury, MA (Counselling), ATAP
President, Australian Transactional Analysis Association

Contents

Tīmatanga kōrero | Introduction

Keith Tudor and Matt Bird

Karangarua | The call

E ngā waka, e ngā mana, e ngā hau e whā, karangatanga maha huri noa in ngā motu nei te mihi mahana atu ki a koutou katoa, tēnā koutou, tēnā koutou, tēnā koutou katoa. To the many talented and esteemed people who are propelled together by the four winds, spread throughout the islands, we greet you warmly, we greet you once, twice, three times.

We are delighted to be introducing this volume which you have – on your screen, printed out, or, if you have purchased the print on demand version, in your hands – that is, the book of papers from the international Transactional Analysis Conference, held in Te Whanganui-a-Tara | Wellington, Aotearoa New Zealand, in November 2024.

The Conference

The initiative for the Conference came from John Savage, a certified and teaching and supervising transactional analyst in Wellington who, in 2023, offered his services to the Transactional Analysis Association of Aotearoa New Zealand (TAAANZ) to run a TA conference. He asked Keith to head the scientific committee – to which Keith agreed, as long as he could work with Matt, who also agreed. The specific vision for the Conference came from discussions between John, the TAAANZ board, Keith and Matt, and then Shirley Rivers (Ngāi Takoto, Ngāpuhi, Te Waiōhua, Te Kawerau ā Maki) who gifted us the title Karangarua.

We then put out a call to the Conference and a call for papers:

> We have great pleasure in calling you (karanga) to this Conference, the title of which in te reo Māori (the Māori language) acknowledges the significance of the karanga or exchange of calls that forms part of the pōwhiri, a Māori welcoming ceremony, and also refers to people related through two different lines, and those standing in a double relationship. In what many of us experience as an increasingly conflictual world, it appears more important than ever to invite a focus on whanaungatanga (relationships) and our transactional analysis of them.

The themes of the Conference invite us to experience, think about and discuss how we do this – meeting, greeting, and seating – in a way that is respectful of both hosts and guests, while also acknowledging difference and diversity.

We also want to provide a space in which we can think about and discuss what happens when we don't do this so well, when relationships are ruptured in various ways, and how we can understand and intervene in disagreement, conflict, violence, and war. Thus, we are also calling for papers and workshop presentations on these themes. (TAAANZ, 2024)

As it was an international Conference, we – Keith and Matt – were keen to include overseas colleagues in the scientific committee and so invited Deepak Dhananjaya (India) and Grace Lam-Thomas (Singapore) to join us, to which they generously agreed.

Our call for abstracts from presenters represented an invitation to speak to the rich, diverse, and often painful aspects of the geopolitical landscape: divisive politics, systemic and structural violence, war, genocide, climate crisis, and innumerable atrocities that we, as a global TA community, face in our everyday lives and work. Both the organising committee and the scientific committee had a vision of colleagues here in Aotearoa New Zealand being joined by colleagues from overseas: all bringing theory and practice, ideas and actions with regard to how we navigate diversity in relationship, through unity (not to be confused with uniformity) as an aspiration in bridging individual, group, social, and political gaps, divides, and chasms. We were also aware that the last international conference in Aotearoa New Zealand had taken place, over 30 years ago, in 1992, also in November but in Auckland, with the theme of 'Partnership' (see Cartmel, 1992; Sherrard with Sevilla, 1992; and Appendix 1). Our vision was lofty. As the Māori whakataukī (proverb) puts it: Whāia te iti kahurangi, ki te tuohu koe, me he maunga teitei | Seek the treasure you value most dearly; if you bow your head, let it be to a lofty mountain. We had a good response and, after rigorous peer-reviews of submissions, we accepted 23 presentations (Table I.1), and were able to welcome over 60 participants, including those from Australia, Finland, India, Japan, The Netherlands, Slovenia, Sweden, and the United Kingdom.

Table I.1. Summary of the scientific programme of the international TA Conference.

Thursday 21st November 2024

11:00–12:30	Keynote. Karangarua – Standing in a double relationship Anna Fleming (Ngāpuhi, Ngāti Hine, Tūhoe) (Aotearoa New Zealand)			
13:30–15:00 Workshops	Creating an inspiring Adult learning environment. *Rhae Hooper* (Australia)	Let's talk ethics – and culture. *Jan Grant* (Australia), *Keiko Hoshino* (Japan), and *Anne Tucker* (Aotearoa New Zealand)	The metaphor of tukutuku: A process of diversity, knowledge, and connection. *Raewyn Knowles* (Aotearoa New Zealand)	Script cycles of organisation and individual in burnout. *Moniek Thunnissen* (The Netherlands)
15:30–16:30 Workshops	How to fly an airplane. *John Savage* (Aotearoa New Zealand)	Physis the integrator. *C. Suriyaprakash* (India)	Relationship to yourselves. *Evgenia Mikheeva* (Aotearoa New Zealand)	Working with Bad Men: TA approaches to the discursively constructed criminal self. *Seán Manning* (Aotearoa New Zealand)

Friday 22nd November 2024

9:00–10:30	Keynote. Goosebumps: Moments of truth in psychotherapy Jo Stuthridge (Aotearoa New Zealand)			
9:00–10:30 Workshops	Exploring we-ness across cultures. *Mariko Seki and Masumi Aonuma* (Japan)	How does change impact diversity? *Mandy Lacy* (Aotearoa New Zealand)	Self-compassion in supervision as a prevention of burnout *Maša Žvelc* (Slovenia)	Working co-creatively with trauma *Bèrit Fahlén* (Sweden) and *Bev Gibbons* (UK)
13:30–15:00 Workshops	The amputation of intuition. *Bev Gibbons* (UK)	Healthy symbiosis. *Debbie Robinson* (UK)	Reflections on TA in Aotearoa New Zealand from a Māori perspective. *TA Māori rōpū with Keith Tudor* (Aotearoa New Zealand)	

Saturday 23rd November 2024

9:00–10:30	Keynote. Karangarua – Being analytic and transactional, psychological and social, international and local Keith Tudor (Aotearoa New Zealand)			
9:00–10:30 Workshops	Many peoples, one nervous system. *Gerry Pyves* (Aotearoa New Zealand)	Observing self and ego states: Mindfulness and compassion in TA. *Gregor Žvelc* (Slovenia)	Positive games – Supporting the butterfly effect. *Paul Robinson* (UK)	War refugee script. *Sisko Torkkeli* (UK)
13:30–15:00 Workshops	Exploring the parallels between theory and practice in TA and Daoist martial arts. *Tony Conley* (Australia)	Embracing diversity through creativity. *Mandy Lacy* (Aotearoa New Zealand)	Reflective art space. *Raewyn Knowles* (Aotearoa New Zealand)	TA, laughter, and humour. *Johnathan Evans* (Aotearoa New Zealand)

The very week of the Conference came at the time of political action throughout Aotearoa during the Hīkoi mō te Tiriti (March for the Treaty [of Waitangi]), a context which is discussed in the first paper of this book (Te Amokura Griggs). The timing of the hīkoi in relation to the Conference represented so much of the vision and action we hoped to inspire, explore, and discuss. We witnessed a nation standing up for protecting the rights of all people of Aotearoa, and particularly those of tangata whenua (people of the land). Attending the final hīkoi to the steps of parliament was a deeply moving experience; I (Matt) accompanied an elder who had marched on those streets for social justice issues for over 50 years who, as we left, commented through tears that she 'always wants to walk on the right side of history'.

The book

Some weeks after the conclusion of the Conference a publishing company approached the scientific committee asking if we would be interested in creating a publication from the Conference presentations and workshops. We (Keith, Matt, Deepak, and Grace) discussed this; gauged the interest of presenters to submit papers – which was positive; and put forward a proposal to the TAAANZ Board, which agreed to fund the project. Although we decided not to pursue publishing the book with the original publisher, enthusiasm for the project remained; and we approached Tuwhera Open Access Publishing which agreed to publish the book as an open access publication, with an option of a print-on-demand book. We then invited all the presenters, including the keynote speakers, to submit papers, as a result of which, and, again, further to another peer-review process, are delighted to present 12 papers and a book review.

In the spirit of the Conference theme, embodied in by the pōwhiri (formal welcome), and given the context of the hīkoi arriving in Wellington just before the Conference, the first paper in the book, by Te Amokura Griggs (Te Hika o Papauma, Ngāti Apakura) sets the scene for the book by reflecting on the context of and the call to the Conference. This is followed by a paper from Shirley Rivers (Ngāi Takoto, Ngāpuhi, Te Waiōhua, Te Kawerau ā Maki), one of our original keynote speakers. Unfortunately, she was unable to attend the Conference herself due to ill-health, which, given that she had gifted us the theme 'Karangarua' and set the kaupapa (purpose) of the Conference, was a great loss – which is why we are particularly grateful that she accepted our invitation to contribute to the book – tēnā koe e hoa aroha | thank you, dear friend. In Shirley's absence at the Conference, we were very lucky to obtain the services of Anna Fleming (Ngāpuhi, Ngāti Hine, Tūhoe, Ingarangi), who stepped in at short notice, and delivered the first keynote speech on 'Karangarua – Standing in double relationship: Reciprocity and responsibility', and has also written it up as a paper – tēnā koe e hoa aroha.

The next four papers all respond quite specifically to the theme of the Conference in different ways and in different styles. Paper 4 is an extensive write-up by Raewyn Knowles of her very creative workshop 'Poutama tukutuku and transactional analysis: A process of diversity, knowledge, and connection through weaving wisdom', which invited the participants – and now invites the reader – in to experience and/or understand the tukutuku panel as a symbolic representation of collaboration or teamwork. Paper 5 is the third keynote speech given at the Conference on the theme of karangarua, which was given by Keith in which he outlines the call – and tensions – between being analytic and transactional, psychological and social, international and local. This is followed (in Paper 6) by a personal story from Bev Gibbons (who presented two workshops at the Conference) which she wrote in response to her experience of the Conference and coming to Aotearoa New Zealand. In Paper 7, which explores we-ness across cultures, Mariko Seki and Masumi Aonuma describe their response to the call to the Conference and their journey to and in attending both the Conference and the international exams that took place before the Conference. Subsequently, they and other colleagues have contributed to a chapter in a forthcoming book on issues of translation and interpretation at such international events (Aonoma et al., in press).

The next four papers are based on workshops and presentations offered at the Conference which, in some ways, link their subjects to the theme of the Conference and the invitation of the call for papers. Paper 8 discusses the mutually enriching and expanding aspects of creative expression and diversity, in which Mandy Lacy weaves TA theory, neuroscience, and creativity into a call for individual and collective exploration into creative processes. In Paper 9, Rhae Hooper explores education environments, drawing on TA philosophy and theory, and adult learning theory in examining ways in which adult learners and teachers can navigate diversity in a range of learning environments. In Paper 10, Seán Manning (with academic supervisors and co-authors Dave Nicholls and Elizabeth Day) provides an in-depth, articulate, and intriguing discussion on the discursive construction of the 'criminal self' through a sociopolitical lens, drawing on TA theory and three decades of group and individual psychotherapy work in men's prison systems, therapeutic communities, and a stopping-violence programme. The final paper in this tranche, Paper 11, offers a unique discussion on humour within TA. In it, Johnathan Evans provides a theoretical analysis of humour, drawing on TA and other psychotherapy theory, exploring the potential benefits and risks of the use of humour in practice.

As a scientific committee, we recommended to the organising committee that we had a bookstall at the Conference, which would – and did – represent the presence of the intellectual history and developments of and in TA. On the Thursday evening of the Conference. we held a launch of Keith's latest book on TA, *Transactional Analysis Proper – and Improper* (Routledge, 2025), a review of which by Deepak Dhananjaya also appears in this volume.

A significant part of the Conference was not only the influence of te Ao Māori on the kaupapa, planning, location, and venue of the Conference, but also the presence of Māori colleagues. In the year leading up to the Conference, a rōpū (group) of Māori colleagues – one qualified psychotherapist and a number of trainees, met regularly together online with two allies – had met with the purpose of bringing Māori in TA together, and of supporting the trainees to complete their training and qualification. At the Conference, the rōpū met together live for the first time, and as part of which presented themselves to the TA community and welcomed new Māori members. Given this, and Jemma Dymond's role as one of the first two Māori certified transactional analysts in the country – not least in contributing to a co-authored chapter about TA in and of Aotearoa New Zealand in another book (Dymond et al., in press) – we asked her for her reflections on the Conference which, appropriately, forms the last paper of this collection (Paper 13).

Finally, as this is an international book of papers from an international conference, we have included a glossary of Māori kupu (words) used in the text. Although these are generally explained in each of the papers that have used te reo Māori (the Māori language) (thus), we include this also for ease of reference, and have taken the opportunity to include some notes on the background to some of the words and concepts used. We thank Maria Haenga-Collins (Ngāti Porou, Te Aitanga a Māhaki, Ngāi Tahu), Raewyn Knowles, and Angie Strachan for their contributions to this.

Acknowledgements

It takes a professional village to raise a conference, and this is no less true of a book.

Firstly, we thank the Transactional Analysis Association of Aotearoa New Zealand and the Australian Transactional Analysis Association for organising, hosting, and supporting the 2024 international TA Conference, and the TAAANZ for funding the costs of producing this book in the two formats available to you, the reader: an open access book, free to download, and a print-on-demand version – tēnā kōrua | our thanks to both organisations.

Secondly, we thank the authors for sharing their work and especially for going the extra mile in converting workshop presentations into papers – tēnā koutou katoa | our thanks to you all.

Thirdly, we thank the peer reviewers for taking the time to ensure the integrity of the work and providing invaluable feedback – Lucie Belton, Traian Bossmayer, Deepak Dhananjaya, Diana Diaconu, Jemma Dymond, Anna Fleming (Ngāpuhi, Ngāti Hine, Tūhoe), Dr Maria Haenga-Collins (Ngāti Porou, Te Aitanga a Māhaki, Ngāi Tahu), Sian Haydon, Keiko Hoshino, Luke Oram, Fran Parkin, Julia Pool, Debbie Robinson, John Savage, Suriyaprakash Chendamaraikannan, Paul Robinson, and Moniek Thunnissen – tēnā koutou katoa.

Fourthly, we also thank those who provided endorsements for the book – John Farnsworth, Briony Fiso (Ngā Puhi, Tuhoe, Te Whanau-a-Apanui, Ngāti Porou, Ngāti Kahungunu), Maria Haenga-Collins (Ngāti Porou, Te Aitanga a Māhaki, Ngāi Tahu), Grace Lam-Thomas, Marguerite Sacco, and Professor Charlotte Sills – tēnā koutou katoa.

Fifthly, we thank all those who have been involved in the production of this book, especially Angie Strachan for her fine and prompt copy-editing, Charlotte Hāriata Mann (Tūhoe, Ngāti Kahungunu ki Wairoa, Neiafu Vava'u) for her cover design, and Donna Coventry and Thais Azevedo at Tuwhera Open Access Publishing at Auckland University of Technology – tēnā koutou katoa.

Lastly, we would like to thank each other.

I (Keith) am most grateful to Matt for accepting the offer I made him – hoping that he couldn't refuse! – to join me in editing this book. I have known Matt for a number of years and always have enjoyed his fine mind and, as I have got to know him more, his good sense of humour – and good company. I was keen to work with him, and also to encourage him to take his place as part of the next generation of transactional analysts in this country – as supervisors, trainers, writers, and editors. It's been an absolute pleasure to work with him, notwithstanding that, during the production of the book, we each had significant personal challenges, in the context of which, Matt has been both sensitive, supportive, robust, and resilient – kei te mihi nui ahau ki a koe, e hoa | my sincere thanks to you, my friend.

I (Matt) wish to thank Keith for his unrelenting passion, dedication, and mana in our TA community. When the invitation was made – which I sense he knew I would struggle to refuse – I felt both honoured and privileged to be asked, not solely for the unique opportunity, but for what the offer represented to me in being able to keep working alongside Keith. His generosity in inviting, encouraging, and mentoring the next generation of transactional analysts never ceases to amaze and inspire me. The editing process has been an enriching, and at times challenging, but, on the whole, inspiring learning journey. During the final group space of the Conference, I commented that I at times felt like I was 'standing on the shoulders of giants'. My heartfelt thanks go out to Keith, not only for the shoulders to stand on, but for the 'giant' encouraging me, and so many others, to walk alongside him. It has been an absolute pleasure and privilege working with you on this precious taonga – kei te mihi nui ahau hoki ki a koe, e hoa | my sincere thanks to you, my friend.

References

Aonuma, M., de Gioia, Jacolin, K., Seki, M., & Tudor, K. (in press). You say translation, we say interpretation: Reflections on cross-cultural transactions in transactional analysis. In G. Barrow, T. Newton, & K. Tudor, K. (Eds.). *Transactional analysis education: Transformation from the periphery*. Karnac.

Cartmel, G. (1992, December). Scientific programme expands on theme. *The Script*, *22*(10), 1, 7. https://membersarea.itaaworld.com/sites/default/files/itaa-pdfs/the-script/script-1992/DECEMBER%201992.pdf

Dymond, J. (Taranaki), Lacy, M., O'Reilly, M., Tawera, T. (Ngāi Tūhoe, Ngāti Awa, Ngāti Kahungunu, Tapuika, Tūhourangi), & Tudor, K. (in press). Transactional analysis in and of Aotearoa New Zealand. In G. Barrow, T. Newton, & K. Tudor, K. (Eds.). *Transactional analysis education: Transformation from the periphery*. Karnac.

Sherrard, E., with Sevilla, S. (1992, December). Marae experience sets tone for conference. *The Script*, *22*(10), 1, 7. https://membersarea.itaaworld.com/sites/default/files/itaa-pdfs/the-script/script-1992/DECEMBER%201992.pdf

Transactional Analysis Association of Aotearoa New Zealand. (2024). *Karangarua – Unity through diversity in relationship*. https://www.taaanz.nz/2024-international-conference

Keith Tudor, Ruatuna/Laingholm, Waitakere
Matt Bird, Ōtepoti
Aotearoa New Zealand

Paper 1

Horopaki me karanga | Context and call

Te Amokura Griggs (Te Hika o Papauma, Ngāti Apakura)

Abstract

In this paper, the author seeks to envision a pathway between understanding the impacts of colonisation through a transactional analysis lens. The theme of the Karangarua Conference centred on 'Unity through Diversity', provided a whaariki (ceremonial woven mat) upon which to develop self-awareness as well as enriching relationships in a therapeutic paradigm. This is achieved by reflections made between whakapapa (generational) settings and experiences with evolving developments, from the 1940s to now. The key findings revealed in the enhancement and strength of te Ao Māori (the Māori world) movements in contrast and self-awareness between these eras. This is achieved by providing a whānau lens to these developments over five generations. 'Ko wai au?' ('Who am I?') for a mokopuna will have a vastly strengthened view to that of her tīpuna, which will aspire into the future.

> Kia whakatōmuri te haere whakamua | I walk backwards into the future with my eyes fixed on my past.

The Māori framework for mental health is embedded within the four walls of a marae, in which mental health is dependent on hinengaro (two flowing waters of the mind); wairua (spirituality in te Ao Māori [the Māori world]); tinana (the physical aspect of self); and whānau (extended family), embedded in whakapapa (genealogy); on a foundation attached to whenua (the land) in which we are connected by tikanga (ways of being, our cultural norms), with(in) which we understand our connection, through creation (see also Paper 2).

Māori are over-represented in every facet of physical and mental health ailments as a consequence of systemic social and historic issues. Addressing illness or disease entails fixing every part of these systemic issues. Transactional analysis (TA) enables a person to be viewed – and to view themselves – within a complex social structure which affects their overall health.

In 2024, the Transactional Analysis Association of Aotearoa New Zealand (TAAANZ) and the Australian Transactional Analysis Association (ATAA) collaborated to organise the first TA conference to take place in Aotearoa New Zealand for some 15 years, which was held in Whanganui-a-Tara (Wellington). The theme was 'Karangarua – Unity through Diversity in Relationship', a theme that represented living in two worlds and realms, symbolic of the inter-connectedness of Māori in the physical and spiritual realms. The Conference further defined these paradigms as a relationship between people and their environment, for example, living in the Māori world and a Pākehā world (non-Māori world), or the world(s) of and between therapist and client.

My own journey with and in TA began in 2016 when, having completed a Bachelor of Addictions Studies, my DAPAANZ (Addiction Practitioners' Association Aotearoa New Zealand) supervisor suggested that I embark on further training in TA. I did this primarily with the Wellington Transactional Analysis Training Institute Ltd, and also attended several TA training residentials, completing my formal training in 2019, and, after some time out, am now actively preparing for my qualifying exam to become a certified transactional analyst.

My passion is to be able to support people in finding meaning in their lives, understanding how conscious and unconscious thoughts, and beliefs – about self and others – are formed. TA gave me that pathway which, to me, very much aligned to te Ao Māori. I applied this in an essay I wrote as part of my TA training, drawing on the Te Awhiowhio model (awhiowhio – whirlwind, tornado; Webber-Dreadon, 1999). This model provided a visual connection of the here-and-now, as well as back to the beginning of our Māori worldview of creation and on into the future. There are no boundaries or barriers between these times; at best, all is flowing and eternal.

As it turned out, the start of the TA Conference in Wellington began the day after a national hīkoi (march) to oppose the proposed *Principles of the Treaty of Waitangi Bill 2024 (94–1)* (Figure 1.1). This was an attempt to rewrite the founding document of our modern nation, *Te Tiriti o Waitangi* signed in 1840 (see Waitangi Tribunal, 2025). An earlier document – *He Whakaputanga o te Rangatira o Niu Tirene | The Declaration of the Independence of New Zealand* (Archives New Zealand, 2025), which had formalised our Māori nation, had been signed by Māori rangatira (chiefs) in 1835, a document that had been recognised by the then King of England (William IV).

The importance of the hīkoi was, for me, twofold.

Figures 1.1 and 1.2. The hīkoi arriving at the New Zealand Parliament, 19th November 2024. (Photos by Denis Came-Friar, and Matt Bird)

The first was that it represented the reality of the continuation or the flow of whakapapa (which also means blueprint and a depiction of our DNA [deoxyribonucleic acid]). As a nanny of seven mokopuna (grandchildren), this hīkoi was especially pertinent. My then youngest moko (grandchild) was attending the hīkoi. She was with her Dad (my son) and her Mama (who is of Welsh/English descent), and I have a lovely photo of her laying on the grounds of Parliament with her Dad (Figure 1.3). This was such a highlight, not least for the fact of her presence in a place that has, through colonial structures and law-making, impacted our lives and of Māori since 1854 when the settler parliament was founded. This image contrasts with her great-grandmother's life experience as a young Māori wahine (woman) trying to make sense of the absolute senselessness of her reality in Aotearoa in the 1940s, full of disorientation and confusion, representing a paradigm of colonisation including a denial of language and cultural practices.

My endeavour to honour my whakapapa and to maintain responsibility ensures the never-ending flow I refer to above. The fact that my two-year-old moko, at the start of her life, has spent a special moment talking with her Dad on the grounds of Parliament means that she will have a different experience to that of my nanny, my mum, and me, and that she will flourish and be informed and empowered in her mātauranga (knowledge) in which colonial constructs will not so freely permeate her sense of self.

Figure 1.3. Dechlan and Taeātea Nia Benioni. (Photo by author)

The second sense of importance of the hīkoi was linked to my excitement in knowing that I was going to attend this national – and international – TA Conference at which I would be engaging with many cultures and with people I had met previously and those I had yet to meet. My interest in attending was also to have an opportunity to learn new and inspiring developments in TA. This is the foundation on which my attendance at the Conference began.

So, on the morning of 21st of November 2024, we gathered on the foreshore of Whanganui-a-Tara, in front of Te Āti Awa/Taranaki Whānaui ki Te Upoko o Te Ika a Māui, standing under the shadow of the giant carved depiction of my tipuna (ancestor) Kupe. Kupe was a Polynesian explorer who, according to Māori oral history, was the first person to discover Aotearoa, the land of the long white cloud (Figure 1.3).

Figure 1.3. 'Statue of Kupe, Wellington Waterfront' by kiwi photo lover. Licensed under CC BY-SA 2.0.

Our welcome, the pōwhiri ceremony, was about to commence, formally to welcome all the Conference participants onto the whenua of Atiawa. This began with the karanga, the call of the kaikaranga (the caller) from the mana whenua (the hosts), to which there is a response from the manuhiri (visitors). These are the first voices in the ritual which is undertaken by wāhine (women) who are trained experts in this, and who, through the call and response, weave their voices, entwining motion and flow. As we thoughtfully proceeded to the front of the whare (ancestral house), the resounding calls acknowledge those who have passed before us. We are gathered; we move in motion as we meet each other, colleagues from afar and near. We take off our shoes and enter the whare. Complementing the first (female) voices, the kaikorero (male speakers) on both sides, that is, mana whenua and manuhiri, then acknowledge tangata whenua (the people of the land), and affirm the kaupapa (our purpose), that is, why we were gathering. This first ritual of encounter, encompassed within te Ao Māori, was followed by surrendering the tapu (sacredness) of the occasion by sharing kai (food), a process that makes us all noa (transported out of sacredness), which symbolises and acknowledges that the manuhiri are now one with tangata whenua (the people of the land).

References

Archives New Zealand. (2025). *He Whakaputanga o te Rangatiratanga o Nu Tireni | The Declaration of the Independence of New Zealand.* https://www.archives.govt.nz/discover-our-stories/the-declaration-of-independence-of-new-zealand

Principles of the Treaty of Waitangi Bill 2024 (94–1). https://www.legislation.govt.nz/bill/government/2024/0094/latest/whole.html

Waitangi Tribunal. (2025). *About the Treaty.* https://www.waitangitribunal.govt.nz/en/about/the-treaty/about-the-treaty

Webber-Dreadon, E. (1999). He taonga mo o matou tipuna (A gift handed down by our ancestors): An indigenous approach to social work supervision. *Social Work Review, 11*(4), 7–11.

Paper 2

Karangarua: Standing in a double relationship

Shirley Rivers (Ngāi Takoto, Ngāpuhi, Te Waiōhua, Te Kawerau ā Maki)

Abstract

Traditional Māori Society engaged seamlessly in the physical and the metaphysical realm of being. Both were natural environments to their wellbeing. Navigating these realms required knowledge of traditional Māori cultural constructs that guided engagements for Māori with each other and the wider environment. Understanding these constructs is fundamental for all practitioners working with Māori whānau. The impact of colonisation for Māori has seen the fracturing from traditional engagement in these two realms culminating in serious consequences for their health and wellbeing. Karangarua – how do I stand as a practitioner and navigate these two realms in my work with Māori whānau?

> The route to Māoritanga through abstract interpretation is a dead end. The way can only lie through a passionate, subjective approach. (Marsden, 1975)

Introduction

The notion that information can be objective fails to acknowledge that objectivity sits within a Western epistemology, privileging that ideology. All knowledge has a foundation of knowing that is grounded within certain values and beliefs. Western values are constantly in conflict with Indigenous values, where individual needs are in conflict with the needs of the collective and scientific thought is the polar opposite of spirituality. This paper is a journey of exploration to re-examine Māori tikanga practices as therapeutic resources for wellness within the contemporary colonial landscape.

Ko wai au? Who am I? This is a simple question, however, one that requires a complex response that invites peeling back the layers of personal, political, and problematic positions. In the context of Aotearoa New Zealand, in a colonial landscape that is influenced by the dominant Western culture and the discourses that have marginalised Māori, this question needs exploration. Colonisation has had significant consequences for the health and wellbeing of Māori in Aotearoa.

The lived experience of injustice, brutality, deprivation and marginalisation has been transmitted across multiple generations, aggravated by land loss, economic disparity, poverty, disease and racism that are reflected in diverse statistics of disparity and…. in health and wellbeing. (Moewaka Barnes & McCreanor, 2019, p. 23)

Māori spirituality (wairuatanga), customary practices, and beliefs on wellbeing were decimated as a consequence of colonisation. Legislation such as the *Tohunga Suppression Act 1907* denigrated the value of these practices while elevating and privileging Western medicine. The consequences for Māori meant being disconnected from vital practices that were core to their wellbeing.

Puao-te-ata-tu, the 1988 report of the Ministerial Advisory Committee on a Māori Perspective for the Department of Social Welfare, affirmed Māori processes of working with families and reclaiming their own systems of wellbeing. It was a strong karanga (call) for a te Ao Māori response to regenerate a pathway to healing. As an introduction and call to the theme of the 2024 international (TA) Conference in Wellington, this paper navigates through Māori ways of engaging and wellbeing.

Marae

An enduring focal point for Māori as a space for cultural engagement has been the marae (Mead, 2016). It has been – and is still – a space of ancestral connection, cultural maintenance, and colonial resistance. The marae has adapted to the political landscape, providing a vehicle for Māori to unite together, to engage in rituals that support our beliefs, and to debate the key political issues of the day (Walker, 1975). It seems sensible then to investigate the way Māori engage on a marae, and the protocols and practices with the view to gaining greater insights into their worldview.

Tikanga are guidelines that support the way Māori engage in the world (Barlow, 1991). Engagement on a marae is guided by tikanga. Tangata whenua (people of the marae) are obligated to care for manuwhiri (visitors) who come to the marae. All manuwhiri are formally welcomed on to the marae with a pōwhiri (welcoming ceremony). This formal process of pōwhiri acknowledges the tapu (restriction) status of the manuwhiri and the customary practices within the engagement that finish with hongi (the pressing of noses) and kai (food) that lifts the tapu and brings them to the status of noa (restriction lifted) (Tauroa & Tauroa, 1986).

Karanga

Karanga is the ceremonial call from the tangata whenua and is the first sound the manuwhiri hear when they are waiting at the tomokanga (marae gate). This call indicates that the process of pōwhiri has begun and that the manuwhiri can progress on to the marae (Mead, 2016). The purpose of the karanga is to welcome, celebrate, grieve, acknowledge, and converse with the wider realms of being. It is a call that connects the living (physical) and the spiritual (metaphysical) worlds and is a call that is heard through generations of whānau (families) across the country (Rewi, 2012, cited in Toki et al., 2022, p. 45).

Women give voice to the karanga (Mead, 2016). Their voice is the first that is heard on entering the marae and they have the responsibility of starting the process of formal encounter. The karanga begins with the invitation to the manuwhiri, as well as the spirits of ngā mate ō te wā (the recently deceased), to enter.

Haere mai ra	Come forward
Ngā manuwhiri tuarangi e	Visitors from afar
Haeremai, haeremai,	Welcome, welcome
Mauri mai o koutou tini mate	Bring with you the spirits of your dead
Kia mihia	That they may be greeted
Kia tangihia e	That they may be mourned
Piki mai, kake mai	Ascend on to our marae
Whakaekea mai te marae tapu	Ascend the sacred marae
O te iwi e	Of our people
Haeremai, haeremai, haeremai	Welcome, welcome, welcome.
(Tauroa & Tauroa, 1986, p. 50)	

The invitation to both the physical and spiritual realms emphasises not only the interconnectedness of these spaces, but also the essentialness of both in this engagement:

> The karanga is the first expression of welcome. It is the way by which the tangata whenua first make contact with the manuwhiri, across the physical space that exists between two groups. The karanga provides a safe word pathway, along which the manuwhiri may pass without fear. (Tauroa & Tauroa, 1986, p. 50)

The karanga is also a vehicle to externalise emotion, through the quiver of the voice and the well-spring of tears. These elements are all intertwined and represent the close relationship Māori have with both the living and the dead.

25

Karangarua

Karangarua – standing in a double relationship. More commonly, this term is used to describe whānau double connections. I am interested in extending the double relationship to explore how Māori engage seamlessly in the physical and the metaphysical realm of being. Both are natural environments to their wellbeing. The metaphysical realm of being not only acknowledges the ancestors that have passed on but also acknowledges the multiple atua (deity) that have shaped the physical realm: Ranginui (Sky father), Papatūānuku (Earth mother), and ngā Tama-ā-rangi (the children of Ranginui and Papatūānuku). These children include Tangaroa (the God of oceans and water), Tānemahuta (forests and bird life), Tūmatauenga (war), Tāwhirimātea (winds), and many more (Buck, 1929). These deities are present in the physical realm and provide not only physical nourishment but also spiritual.

With the impact of colonisation, Māori understanding of the spiritual realm has been marginalised (Moewaka Barnes & McCreanor, 2019). When Māori people present to health clinicians with physical ailments, it is also important to consider that they may (also) be understood spiritually, though this may not always be obvious to either the clinician or the whaiora (client) accessing these services. It requires knowledge by the clinician of cultural practices and the skills to create spaces for meaningful conversations.

For the clinician, the marae is once again a vehicle for understanding how to engage with whānau Māori. When visitors are called onto the marae, they make their way slowly into the physical space of the marae, stopping when they reach the marae ātea (Tauroa & Tauroa, 1986). This is the physical space that separates the tangata whenua from the manuwhiri, providing room to navigate the conversations of the day. Those conversations begin with confirming who is present, not only the living in physical form but also those living in the spiritual realm, the connections between the tangata whenua and the manuwhiri and the reason for the encounter (kaupapa).

The marae ātea is also a speculative space, where opportunities and possibilities are present (Walker, 1975). It provides each participant with the ability to observe from a distance, engage with openness and respond accordingly. It invites participants to pick up from the previous conversation or leave the previous conversation on the ātea, to lay there until the time is ready for both (groups of) participants to pick it up again.

The marae ātea requires formal debate, clarification of the kaupapa, and wider exploration of key information (Mead, 2016). Similarly, the clinician is inviting the whānau member to share who they are and what brings them to a particular meeting. Deeper conversations require both parties to clarify roles and responsibilities in order to ensure meaningful connections.

In Western thinking, time is measured in minutes or hours. For Māori, time is not linear (Durie, 2001), but, rather, is measured in the completion of the task or issue discussed. This is epitomised in the phrase mā te wā (it takes as long as it takes), which is used to denote the passage of time, and is used by Air New Zealand to farewell passengers when they depart from the plane. If people need to explore something in more detail, or to understand it in greater detail, then (more) time is taken. Opportunities for deeper understanding of the issue require time, and this is where the tension sits with the contemporary clinician who is tasked with time restrictions.

How do you invite conversations about wairua, about ancestors, about mountains who represent ancestors? This is where the marae ātea, or a transactional space, requires consideration. While the karanga denotes the beginning of the encounter process, what does the karanga look like in counselling, therapy, education, or consultation? The first karanga from tangata whenua, for example, a clinician, is an open invitation to manuwhiri to come in and to bring their ancestors with them. In the therapeutic process, this could begin with a karakia (entreaty to the deity) to pave the way for the work required in the session. A karakia seeks permission, ensuring that you have access to all the resources required for meaningful conversation (Paterson, 1992).

Karakia is followed by the whaikōrero (formal speech), which requires acknowledging who you are, that includes your whakapapa (genealogy). For the clinician, your whakapapa is your professional role, to be pono (true) to your role, open in obligations and naming of your tikanga (practice guidelines). The invitation is then given to the whānau member to respond, to begin the process of sharing their story. Ata haere, go cautiously; mā te wā, take the time needed to build a connection to your whānau member. This person is waewae tapu, a person who is new to your marae ātea, is here for the first time, and requires special acknowledgement and special attention.

This beginning process of whanaungatanga (connecting) for the whānau member will require encouragement from the clinician. Be invitational, curious, and reflective so that the story builds to provide a deeper understanding of who they are. Whakārongo (listen) with all your senses; with your taringa (ears) to what is being said; with your karu (eyes) as to what emotions are physically present; with your ngākau (heart) as to what emotions are being felt by you and the client; with your puku (intuition) as well as to what is not being said; and with wairua (spirituality) to what other intangible elements are present

27

in the story. When all these elements are present in the equivalent of your marae ātea, then true engagement can begin.

When wairua is invited into the marae ātea, the clinician must be cautious, ensuring that tikanga is in place to manage the tapu (restriction/prohibited) that is present. Tikanga practices will provide safety in this encounter to minimise risk, managing both the physical and spiritual elements. Risk is present in all encounters. Historically, whaikōrero was a blend of esoteric and metaphorical oratory that included 'political bluntness, diplomatic tact, artful expression and veiled illusion…. messages that are couched in a nexus of interacting relationships are more likely to be noticed' (Durie, 2001, p. 81).

The use of metaphors moves the discussion from the person to the issue, or from a post-modernist perspective, externalising the issue. When the focus is not on the person sharing the story, then tapu is acknowledged and managed. The invitation to explore how wairua is situated in the story can then be initiated by the clinician. Tīpuna (ancestors) who have passed on or significant whenua (land) sites can be invited into the story. These elements could provide deeper understanding on the issue in the story. The role of the clinician is to invite different ways of seeing the story, creating wider elements of knowing.

Within the whaikōrero processes, when speakers have concluded their speeches, a waiata (song) is always sung that compliments and elevates the speech and the speaker. The clinician's waiata could include the resources that support the whānau member to understand key elements of their story. Similarly, a koha (gift, usually money) is put down by the manuwhiri by their last speaker to acknowledge the mana of the marae. For the whānau member, their koha is their story. This gift is evolving throughout the session and enhanced by the clinician's use of their kōrero and waiata. The session is concluded with a hongi (pressing of noses) where the sharing of breath signifies a deeper connection for the tangata whenua and manuwhiri. It also moves the session from the manuwhiri being tapu to being noa (without restriction). While the session may have concluded, the connection is affirmed and acknowledged. Further work and engagement will happen in the future using the same structure.

When working with Māori clients to support their pathway to healing, a clinician must create space for karangarua – the physical and the spiritual relationship interwoven into a Māori worldview, interconnected and essential to wellbeing. The most obvious place to start is the cultural space that has survived colonial combat and transformed into the modern-day marae. The protocols and practices on the marae provide a framework for clinicians working to support Māori wellbeing. This framework begins with the karanga, the call for the two elements to be present in this encounter. The healthy engagement of these two elements provides an opportunity for wellbeing to exist.

References

Barlow, C. (1991). *Tikanga whakaaro*. Oxford University Press.

Buck, P. H. (1929). *The coming of the Maori*. Thomas Avery & Sons.

Durie, M. (2001). *Mauri ora: The dynamics of Māori health*. Oxford University Press.

Marsden, M. (1975). God, man and universe: A Māori view. In M. King (Ed.), *Te ao hurihuri: The world moves on* (pp. 143–164). Reed.

Mead, H. M. (2016). *Tikanga Māori: Living by Māori values* (Rev. ed.). Huia Publishers.

Moewaka Barnes, H., & McCreanor, T. (2019). Colonisation, hauora and whenua in Aotearoa. *Journal of the Royal Society of New Zealand, 49*(S1), 19–33. https://doi.org/10.1080/03036758.2019.1668439

Paterson, J. (1992). *Exploring Māori values*. Dunmore Press.

Tauroa, H., & Tauroa, P. (1986). *Te marae: A guide to customs and protocols*. Penguin.

Tohunga Suppression Act 1907. https://www.nzlii.org/nz/legis/hist_act/tsa19077ev1907n13353/

Toki, L., Cowie, T., Menzies, D., Joseph, R., & Fonoti, R. (2022). Karanga: Connecting to Papatūānuku. *Landscape Review, 19*(1). https://doi.org/10.34900/lr.v19i1.1193

Walker, R. (1975). Marae: A place to stand. In M. King (Ed.), *Te ao hurihuri: The world moves on* (pp. 21–30). Reed.

Paper 3

Karangarua – Standing in double relationship: Reciprocity and responsibility

Anna Fleming (Ngāpuhi, Ngāti Hine, Tūhoe, Ingarangi)

Abstract

Karanga is a call to relationship which also acknowledges the multiplicity of relationships and connections that bind us. The concept of karangarua, and of being in double relationship, has always been fundamental to Māori ideas of wellbeing. While disconnection practices have impacted how Māori interact with these ideas, they remain clinically significant with regard to prioritising positive health outcomes for Māori. This article discusses the concept of karangarua, and encourages us as clinicians to be aware of these relationships and connections, and particularly how these are experienced by the tangata whaiora that we work with.

Introduction

Karanga is the first voice of the hau kainga through the pōwhiri process, the indication that meeting and relating can begin. Karanga acknowledges the intersection of realms, the spiritual world and the physical world, to all elements of nature, inclusive and diverse (Toki et al., 2022). Karanga is reciprocal in nature. As the call from a female member of the home people echoes outwards, it is received and heard. While often reciprocated by another female member of the visiting party, karanga is a clear example of how different realms are connected and navigated. Karanga is not solely placed within the human realm, as it also includes the spiritual world and the natural world and the environment around us. In this way, the karanga begins the process of relationship, understanding ourselves within the context of our land, our experiences and everything around us.

The concept of karangarua and that of standing in double relationship is a familiar concept in te Ao Māori. Navigating diverse and distinct realms, and understanding the relationships between them is something that is fundamental to Māori. Māori have been aware of and supported by the relationships that exist between the physical and the metaphysical world, and the natural world and the human realm from the earliest time. However, the disconnection from these traditional realms through colonising and social practices have destabilised how Māori access and interact with these, which has led to negative impacts on health and wellbeing outcomes for Māori. In this kōrero, I explore some thoughts around the multiplicity of these connections and relationships, and how we might attend to them, specifically in the context of being practitioners of psychotherapy, though I am aware that there are other fields of application of transactional analysis.

The foundations of hauora

Thinking about Māori wellbeing begins by acknowledging that its foundations comprise a variety of sources. While some of these foundations are shared across population groups, there are some that are intrinsically Māori, and necessary when considering positive health outcomes for Māori peoples. As Mason Durie (2001) states, 'platforms for Māori health are constructed from land, language and whānau; from marae and hapū; from Rangi and Papa; from the ashes of colonisation; from adequate opportunity for cultural expression; and from being able to participate fully within society' (p. 33). Therefore, good Māori health extends beyond thinking about personal health outcomes and acknowledges the multiplicity of experiences and relationships that exist externally, historically, and socially for Māori.

Whakapapa is a key concept when thinking about positive connection and relatedness. Often translated into English as ancestry, a broader way of understanding this word in te reo Māori can mean to lay flat or to place in layers. This description again allows us to broaden our understanding to acknowledge the many connections that Māori have, and that whakapapa not only acknowledges our connection to our human ancestors, it also includes the connections that we have to our land, to the spirit world, and to all things that inhabit our universe.

As a psychotherapist, I am consistently thinking about the impact of these diverse connections and how this influences both the psychotherapeutic relationship and the experiences of the tangata whaiora who I support. The ongoing dominance of Western developmental and psychotherapeutic theories in our work has marginalised mātauranga Māori and, as Woodard (2014) states, the development of psychotherapy in Aotearoa flourished at the expense of Indigenous healers and healing practice. Understanding these historical factors and considering a more equitable approach to psychotherapy practice will impact the future development of our profession in Aotearoa.

Traditional realms

Wairua is a key concept when considering health or wellbeing for Māori. A definition of wairua is wai, meaning water and rua, meaning two (H. Kohu-Morgan, personal communication, 2017). These two waters can be seen as the interconnection of the spiritual world with the physical world. This connectedness also facilitates understanding of links from ourselves to the environment around us, and is a key factor of understanding the importance of connection.

These ideas of interconnection, holism, and balance are integral to Indigenous philosophies and ways of thinking, especially with regard to wairua. At a wider societal level, this relational way of thinking supports relationships between humans and the natural world, while, on an individual level, it calls for the acknowledgement of mind, body, and spirit, with each dimension interlinked and necessary in maintaining holistic health and wellbeing. A holistic view supports a balanced way of looking at the world through several lenses with a view to understand how to live well in, and with, the world.

As noted, whenua is also a key area of connection when thinking about hauora Māori. The definition of whenua has many meanings. It means land, in terms of the physical ground; however, whenua is also the word for placenta. When a baby is born, its placenta is buried in the ground, thus the whenua returns to the whenua. This is an example of how the different meanings of whenua are shared between the land, family, birth, and growth.

Papatūānuku (Earth Mother), along with Ranginui (Sky Father), were the first parents who gave birth to the different atua and to mankind. Each atua had responsibility for a different domain and were a key way in which Māori understood the natural world around them. According to Māori Marsden (2003), the double meaning of whenua as both placenta and land provided a constant reminder that we are 'born out of the womb of the primeval mother' (p. 45). Emphasis is given to the relationship between Papatūānuku and her children and whenua creating connectedness and reciprocal relationship between Māori and the land.

There is an interconnected and reciprocal relationship between Māori and whenua, in which the health of each depends on each other. Durie (1994) argues that Māori sought to belong in this relationship, rather than to take possession or ownership. Through relationship with whenua, Māori can engage in key concepts such as katiakitanga and rangatiratanga through the reciprocal requirements of the relationship. In this way,

Māori accept the responsibilities that come with being a guardian and the connections within the living worlds.

Whakapapa creates connections and relationships across all things including whenua. The phrase tangata whenua is described as people of the land, seeming to infer that a certain group are 'of' or occupy a certain place. Ailsa Smith (2004), however, states that the term tangata whenua

> has a deeper, more significant meaning of being 'composed of' the elements of that place through generations and centuries of occupation; for the people not only passed 'through' or over the land but the land passed 'through' and made up the substance of people both physically and metaphysically. (p. 13)

Colonised realms

To understand some of these concepts and relational structures emphasises and makes visible the different connections within te Ao Māori and the inclusion of them within good Māori health. Whāea Shirley encourages us with the idea of karangarua (Rivers, 2024) – how do we operate as practitioners in these two worlds, the physical and the metaphysical? Acknowledging these dualities is a fundamental part of te Ao Māori.

The processes of colonisation and urbanisation have drastically altered the way Māori interact with foundational structures (Fleming, 2018). Throughout the 19th and 20th centuries, Māori experienced significant land loss through settler purchase and occupation – see Sorrenson (1956) and McCreanor et al. (2006). Similarly, the process of urbanisation has led to many Māori being located away from their traditional homelands, with the movement toward major cities and towns meaning that tūrangawaewae and other identity markers are often located away from their primary residence. These losses and changes hold considerable impact as Māori become dislocated from ancestral connections and land attachments. On a practical level, Māori become obstructed from performing the kaitiaki tasks and responsibilities discussed above with regard to whenua. On a psychological level, Te Ngaruru (2008) speaks of the loss of performing reciprocal kaitiaki tasks with the land as compromising the mana of the people, which influences the psychological health of those affected and generations that follow. In this way these ongoing intergenerational and current disconnections create both physical and psychological obstacles which affect good individual and group health. Additionally, the *Tohunga Suppression Act 1907* set to legislate tohunga healing practice by imposing accrediting systems and penalty for those who continued to practice. This advanced the use of Western medicine as a treatment but was also a means of control (Fleming, 2018).

In the late 19th century, Māori began to respond to the consequences of colonisation. Māori groups and individuals became more involved in political and education systems in order to have access to governmental and societal processes. It continues to this day – the reclamation mahi of the 1970s and the more recent actions towards the *Principles of the Treaty of Waitangi Bill 2024* just this year are examples of responding to threats to tino rangatiratanga.

I also think of my and my whānau's experiences in these spaces. As the only daughter of a Ngāti Hine and Tūhoe mother and an English father who emigrated with his parents and siblings to Aotearoa in the early 1970s, I have experienced growing up in two realms. With dark skin and dark hair, I am probably visibly perceived as Māori, however my upbringing was very much influenced by my father's English heritage. I remember being placed in my primary school's Māori Cultural Group in the 1990s, which would now probably be known as a Kapa Haka group; however, I was not sure how to hold the poi or how to sing the songs. My reconnection to my taha Māori came as an adult, when I began to reconnect with some aunties and uncles, and then returned to my marae. Despite not having been there before, I can only say that the land felt familiar to me when I returned to it, and that there was a felt sense of my tūpuna whenever I was there. For me, the land itself was one of my strongest connectors.

A significant move for our whānau occurred when my Ngāti Hine based whānau relocated from rural Matawaia, to urban Māngere in Auckland, where my grandfather hoped he and his elder children could find employment. This move was successful as many of my aunties and uncles travelled daily to Onehunga, where they found work in the many factories based there. However, whānau members say that this move to Auckland was jarring: the traffic was overwhelming, and the smells and the noises different to what they were used to in Matawaia. My aunties and uncles also tell many stories of being smacked by teachers at school for speaking te reo Māori to the point that they became fearful to speak and instead would often stay silent. My aunty says that as a protective measure their parents encouraged their tamariki only to speak te reo Pākehā as soon as they left the front gate, though there was much confusion that came up for the tamariki around this.

Stories like these begin to illustrate some of the ways that iwi Māori have continued to navigate diverse realms. While historically, these realms or double relationships were grounded in mātauranga Māori, as processes such as colonisation and urbanisation began impacting the way Māori lived, this soon began to develop into requiring iwi Māori to be navigating a rapidly changing world.

A karanga to psychotherapy

Having its roots in Western modalities born in Europe and North America, traditional psychotherapy can easily be seen as a Western practice. One of my challenges for psychotherapy in Aotearoa is to become further engaged in the socio-political landscape and educated in the historical and contemporary processes which impact all our peoples and their experiences of good health and wellbeing. For me, psychotherapy is about taking the position of exploring and understanding the internal world in its relationships with the world around us. We are again reminded of karangarua and its invitation to stand in dual relationship – and, as practitioners, how we hold the internal worlds of the people we work with alongside the relationships they have with the world around them.

Finally, as I look to close this kōrero, I am thinking of Matua Haare Williams, a well-known kaumātua in te Ao Māori and the psychotherapy space, and a friend to Evan Sherrard, who I know was and still is highly regarded within transactional analysis in Aotearoa (see Tudor, 2017/2020; Williams, 2017/2020). Just last week, Matua Haare shared with me the following kōrero: 'Kei whea tōku mana, kei whea tōku rangatiratanga tui, tui tuia, ka rongo te pō, ka rongo te Ao ka āwatea e!' A translation for this is, 'Where does my standing come from, where does my chiefliness come from? It comes from the birds, it comes from the environment around, and, as the night moves to day a new dawn forms!' Matua and I spoke about the potential that each new day carries and the strength we can gather when we understand the possibilities in the connections that ground us each and every day.

Tēnā koutou katoa.

References

Durie, M. (1994). *Whaiora: Māori health development*. Oxford University Press.
Durie, M. (2001). *Mauri ora: The dynamics of Māori health*. Oxford University Press.
Fleming, A. H. (2018). Ngā tāpiritanga: Secure attachments from a Māori perspective. *Ata: Journal of Psychotherapy Aotearoa New Zealand, 22*(1), 23–36. https://doi.org/10.9791/ajpanz.2018.03

Marsden, M. (2003). The achievement of authentic being — God, man and universe. In T. A. C. Royal (Ed.), *The woven universe: Selected writings of Rev. Māori Marsden* (pp. 2–23). Estate of Māori Marsden.

McCreanor, T., Penney, L., Jensen, V., Witten, K., Kearns, R., & Moewaka Barnes, H. (2006). This is like my comfort zone: Senses of place and belonging within Oruāmo/Beachhaven, New Zealand. *New Zealand Geographer*, *62*(3), 196–207. https://doi.org/10.1111/j.1745-7939.2006.00070.x

Principles of the Treaty of Waitangi Bill 2024 (94–1). https://www.legislation.govt.nz/bill/government/2024/0094/latest/whole.html

Rivers, S. (2024). Karangarua – Standing in a double relationship. In K. Tudor & M. Bird (Eds.), *Karangarua: Unity through diversity in transactional analysis* (pp. x–xx). Tuwhera.

Smith, A. (2004). A Māori sense of place? – Taranaki waiata tangi and feelings for place. *New Zealand Geographer*, *60*(1), 12–17. https://doi.org/10.1111/j.1745-7939.2004.tb01700.x

Sorrenson, M. P. K. (1956). Land purchase methods and their effect on Māori population, 1865–1901. *The Journal of the Polynesian Society*, *65*(3).

Te Ngaruru, D. C. (2008). Whenua: The key to Māori health and well-being. *Kai Tiaki Nursing New Zealand*, *14*(5).

Toki, L., Cowie, T. M., Menzies, D., Joseph, R., & Fonoti, R. (2022). Karanga: Connecting to Papatūānuku. *Landscape Review*, *19*(1). https://doi.org/10.34900/lr.v19i1.1193

Tudor, K. (Ed.). (2020). *The book of Evan: The life and work of Evan McAra Sherrard*. Tuwhera Open Access Publishing. https://doi.org/10.24135/TOAB.2 (Original work published 2017)

Williams, H. (2020). Porporoaki: A bridge between two worlds. In K. Tudor (Ed.), *The life and work of Evan McAra Sherrard* (pp. 11–12). Tuwhera Open Access Publishing. https://doi.org/10.24135/TOAB.2 (Original work published 2017)

Woodard, W. (2014). Politics, Psychotherapy, and the 1907 Tohunga Suppression Act. *Psychotherapy and Politics International*, *12*(1), 39–48. https://doi.org/10.1002/ppi.1321

Paper 4

Poutama tukutuku and transactional analysis: A process of diversity, knowledge, and connection through weaving wisdom

Raewyn Knowles

Abstract

In this paper the author draws on the concept of the tukutuku panel as a symbolic representation of collaboration or teamwork. A form of Māori art and architecture, tukutuku panels are a traditional woven lattice that record various concepts and teachings. The tukutuku are also a symbol of cooperation and collective effort within a rōpū (group) and community. The reader is invited to reflect on the importance of collaboration and cultural appreciation through the lens of the tukutuku panels, in considering the potential unity through diversity within the psychotherapy community of Aotearoa New Zealand, though the implications of this theme extends beyond these islands. Images of tukutuku panels as created throughout the development of the workshop at the Conference, and subsequently this paper, are offered as a visual grounding of the process.

Introduction

The theme of the 2024 international TA Conference held in Wellington, karangarua – interpreted as 'unity through diversity' – prompted both personal and professional reflections on the integration of diverse knowledge systems within psychotherapeutic practice in Aotearoa New Zealand. As a tauiwi (non-Māori) psychotherapist working with clients from Māori, mixed-heritage, and various cultural backgrounds, I have found the exploration of identity and cultural context to be central to effective TA psychotherapy. Preparing for the Conference involved investigating how TA concepts can be meaningfully aligned with mātauranga Māori (Māori knowledge systems), particularly when addressing cultural narratives within the therapeutic space. I collaborated with whānau (family) and friends to create a tukutuku panel featuring the poutama design, symbolising the ascension of Tāne (a Māori God, the son of Papatūānuku [Earth Mother] and Ranginui [Sky Father]) from darkness into enlightenment. This pūrākau (narrative) resonates with TA's script theory and models of psychological development, offering rich metaphors for personal transformation. The process of weaving tukutuku became a relational, reflective, and embodied experience of bicultural engagement. It also served as a practical and symbolic expression of the karangarua theme.

My own exploration of this unfolded against the backdrop of significant sociopolitical developments in Aotearoa New Zealand. In late 2024, the proposed *Treaty Principles Bill* challenged the constitutional status of *Te Tiriti o Waitangi* ('*Te Tiriti*'), the foundational agreement between Māori and the British Crown. In response, the collective Te Toitū Te Tiriti led a nationwide mobilisation culminating in the Hīkoi mō te Tiriti (the March for Te Tiriti) in Wellington on 19th November, just two days before the Conference took place. This peaceful demonstration illustrated a shared commitment by Māori and non-Māori to uphold the original intent of *Te Tiriti* of co-governance (Article 1) and the protection of Māori sovereignty (Article 2) (Matike Mai Aotearoa, 2016; Mutu, 2019). Such efforts reflect the principle of unity through diversity, an intentional approach to peaceful relating (Köchler, 2012), and, thereby, reinforce the relevance of inclusive, Treaty-based frameworks for all domains of public life, including psychotherapy (Curtis et al., 2019; Paewai, 2024; Parekh, 2000).

Culturally safe and Treaty-honouring practice is foundational to professional competence (Psychotherapists Board of Aotearoa New Zealand, 2019). Psychotherapists must be able to integrate *Te Tiriti* obligations into their practice while valuing equity, diversity, and the unique worldview of Māori clients. The intention of this paper is to present how TA practitioners can engage with both TA and mātauranga Māori frameworks in a bicultural, relationally attuned manner. Although, as a psychotherapist, I focus on the application of these frameworks in the field of psychotherapy, such engagement applies to practitioners in all TA fields. In this context, karangarua speaks to the dual calls of Māori and Tauiwi worldviews, both of which can be held respectfully in service of client healing and autonomy (Tohiariki, 2024). Key Māori terms are introduced and briefly defined in the paper; a glossary is also provided at the end of the book (p. 202) to support deeper engagement.

This paper comprises five parts: firstly, some discussion of three core cultural concepts – of symbolism, collaboration through art, and kotahitanga (interwoven narratives); secondly, some description of three TA concepts – contracts, life scripts, and cultural integration; thirdly, a description of the workshop; fourthly; a discussion of integrating mātauranga Māori into TA practice; and, finally, some reflections on weaving wisdoms and a call to action (see Figure 4.1).

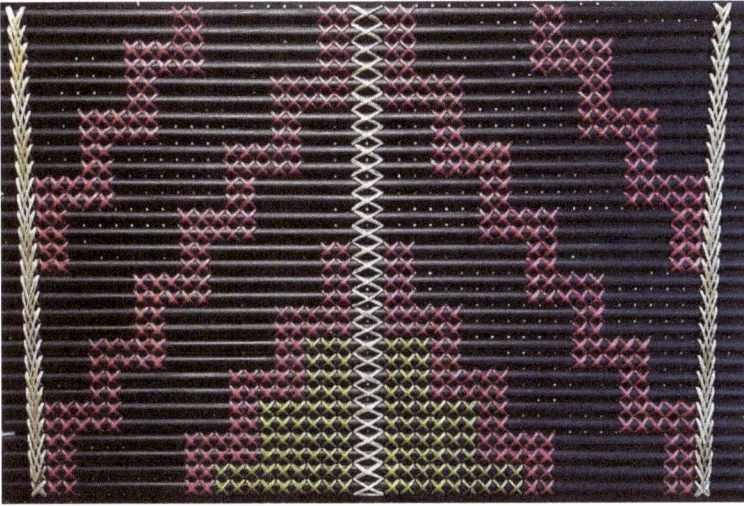

Figure 4.1. Pre-Conference Tukutuku (created by Raewyn Knowles, Bonnie Thocolich, Carissa Proffit, Leanne Thompson, Pirihira Karaitiana, Erana Tupe, Erana Thomspon, and Senga Ogle-Powell).[1]

Core cultural concepts: Symbolism, collaboration, and interwoven narratives

In this first part of the paper, I explore the symbolism of the poutama design as a pathway to knowledge; offer an example of the collaboration and art of weaving relationships and meaning; and a discussion of the concept of kotahitanga as an example of unity through diversity and shared purpose.

Symbolism: Poutama as a pathway to knowledge

The tukutuku panel, notably the poutama design, embodies layered metaphors of learning and transformation. Grounded in mātauranga Māori, the poutama carries cultural narratives that sustain identity across generations, aligning with the principles and intent of *Te Tiriti o Waitangi*. As Mahuika (2019) asserts: Indigenous knowledge systems and stories critically shape identity, wellbeing, and relationality, reinforcing values of unity, collective responsibility, and the transmission of ancestral knowledge.

The poutama design is imbued with the pūrākau of Tāne Mahuta, whose ascent to retrieve Ngā Kete o te Wānanga (the baskets of knowledge) articulates a profound

---

[1] All photographs in this chapter were taken by the author. Permission was provided by people captured in the image to use the photograph in the public domain.

narrative of learning and psychological transformation (Taonui, 2012). Tāne's journey, marked by the separation of Ranginui (Sky Father) and Papatūānuku (Earth Mother), opens a pathway for light, life, and knowledge. To access the baskets of profound wisdom, Tāne had to traverse celestial realms; encounter resistance from siblings; and demonstrate persistence, spiritual readiness, and relational awareness. Upon obtaining the knowledge, Tāne returned to disseminate it through the guardians (kaitiaki) and houses of learning (whare wānanga), often within meeting houses adorned by tukutuku which visually embody the journey and layers of knowledge embedded in the collective psyche (Taonui, 2012).

The narrative about Tāne symbolises multidimensional development: physical, mental, emotional, and spiritual. It emphasises relational intent: Tāne's purpose is not individual elevation, but the flourishing of te iwi (the people). His journey emphasises intergenerational responsibility, spiritual readiness, and collective flourishing. Thus, Tāne's ascent provides a relational template for identity, decision-making, and psychological becoming. The poutama – a striking stepped pattern – represents the ascent of Tāne-o-te-wānanga into the heavens in pursuit of elevated knowledge (Taonui, 2012; Te Ara, 2025). The stairway design signifies collective progression toward spiritual, intellectual, and cultural illumination.

Collaboration through art: Weaving relationships and meaning

Tukutuku creation is inherently communal. Each panel is a relational artifact, woven in collaboration, requiring weavers to work in close proximity, attuned to each other's actions and intentions. The process demands careful listening, shared pace, and mutual responsiveness. In this sense, the negative image created by each weaver mirrors the other, emphasising coordinated duality (Figure 4.2).

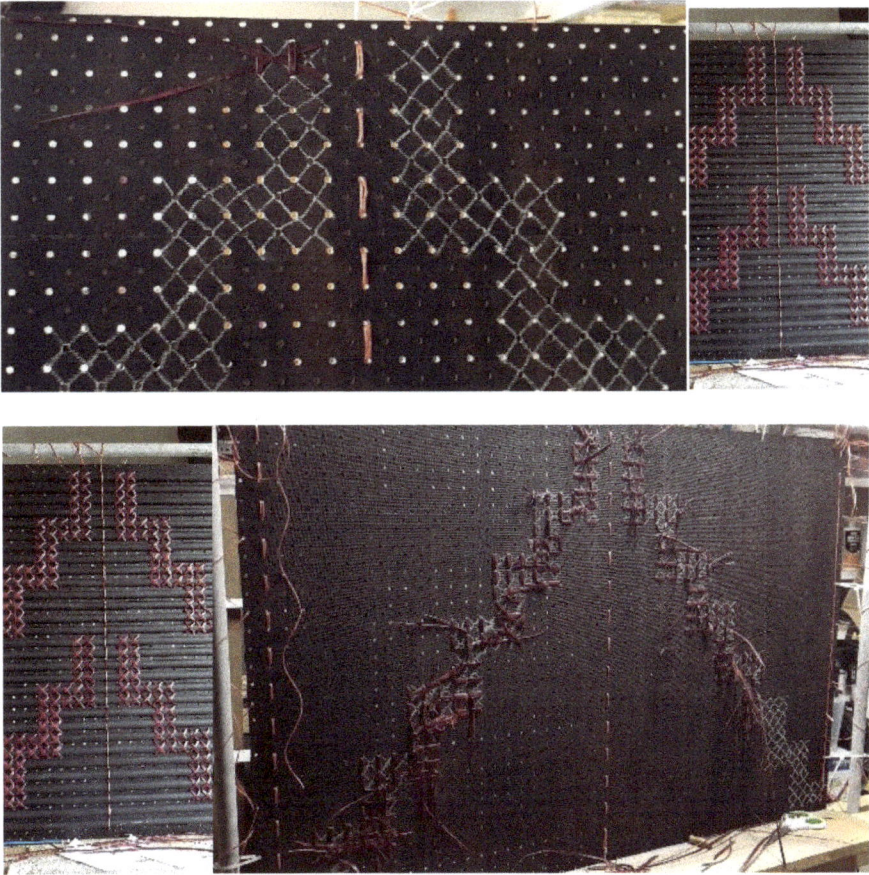

Figure 4.2. Creation of the tukutuku panel showing the negative image.

After researching the cultural meanings and processes of tukutuku, I wanted to create a panel grounded in respect for diversity. I recognised that guidance from a kaiako (teacher) and collaboration with a team of weavers were essential. Drawing on the expertise of a whānau kaumātua (elder), I chose the poutama design and embarked on the weaving journey, supported by nieces who had earlier participated in restoration projects at their local marae.

Together, we sourced and prepared materials – i.e., created frames, dyed harakeke (flax), and assembled tools – for a two-day wānanga (workshop) held in my garage (Figure 4.3). This iterative, communal process, carried out weekly over several months, produced a taonga (precious object) rich with symbolism and intention, while also nurturing relationships, collective creativity, and shared memories.

41

Figure 4.3. Preparing the flax and securing the dowl to painted boards.

Our preparation involved collaborative learning: exploring the iconographic significance of the patterns, painting the panels, and marking out the poutama design. As the threads intertwined, our conversations deepened. We shared laughter, tears, memories, and reflections on how this mahi (work) connected to our cultural identities and hopes (Figure 4.4).

Figure 4.4. Making a start on the panels.

Kotahitanga: Unity, collective identity, and shared purpose

Within the poutama, kotahitanga – unity, togetherness, and solidarity – emerges as a central Māori value, underscoring the strength of interconnection (Keane, 2012; Te Aka Māori Dictionary, n.d.). Kotahitanga encompasses historical, political, and cultural cohesiveness. Kawharu (1992a) frames kotahitanga as both value and force – a driving aspiration for collective authority and pan-tribal identity.

In the context of weaving, kotahitanga manifests through communal activity: people collaborate, share skills, and contribute to a common pattern and purpose – each contribution acknowledged and woven into the whole. This reflects a way of being-in-relationship that values inclusivity, mutual effort, and shared identity. In contemporary Aotearoa New Zealand, these values echo in political and social movements seeking inclusive unity. For example, community initiatives grounded in Treaty values advocate for collaboration without homogenising diversity – unity does not erase difference but respects plurality under shared principles (Community Waikato, 2025; Kawharu, 1992b).

Synthesis: Weaving culture, psychotherapy, and relational insight

By weaving together the conceptual strands – the symbolism of the poutama, Tāne's pūrākau, cultural scripting, and kotahitanga – an integrated framework emerges that foregrounds relationality, collective meaning, and transformation. In psychotherapeutic contexts, engaging clients with the tukutuku metaphor can facilitate exploration of cultural identity, script formation (Berne, 1961; Drego, 1983), and relational belonging (Minikin, 2024). Visual and embodied metaphors like weaving invite clients into transformative narratives – recognising their place within ancestral stories while choosing how to ascend, stitch by stitch, toward healing and autonomy. Additionally, kotahitanga offers a frame for relational integration – affirming that healing is a communal journey, where identities and stories are woven together for wholeness.

Figure 4.5 represents the three kete (baskets) of knowledge that Tāne brought back and which sit at the base of the pou or post that holds up the roof of the whare nui (meeting house), along with the two stones that represent the spiritual guardians of this knowledge, thereby, embodying the essence of kotahitanga.

Figure 4.5. The kete of knowledge and the stones of guardianship. (Image created by author.)

TA foundations: Contracts, scripts, and cultural integration

Founded by Eric Berne in the mid-20th century, TA is a framework for understanding psychological development, communication, and change. Some of its foundational concepts – therapeutic contracts (Berne, 1961; Steiner, 1971), life scripts (Cornell, 1988; Steiner 1974), and cultural scripting (Shivanath & Hiremath, 2003) – are particularly valuable in culturally attuned psychotherapy, especially within the bicultural context of Aotearoa New Zealand. Given the country's colonial legacy and the responsibilities enshrined in *Te Tiriti o Waitangi*, these concepts provide a critical lens through which to engage Māori clients with cultural integrity and therapeutic effectiveness (Norcross & Lambert, 2018).

Contracts: Foundation of ethical, collaborative practice
At the heart of TA is the concept of the 'contract' – an explicit bilateral agreement outlining a specific course of action to achieve a mutually identified goal (Berne, 1961) that structures the therapeutic alliance and reinforces client autonomy. Contracts ensure therapy is a co-created process, where both therapist and client are active participants. The client is positioned as capable of initiating, committing to, and sustaining change,

aligning with TA's foundational principle of autonomy. Steiner and Cassidy (1969) identify four critical components of a valid therapeutic contract, i.e.,

1. **Mutual consent** – Meaning that engagement must be voluntary for both parties.
2. **Valid consideration** – Meaning that each party must contribute: the therapist brings expertise and structure; the client brings commitment and engagement.
3. **Competency** – Meaning that both individuals must be capable of participation, operating from their Adult ego state.
4. **Lawful object** – Meaning that the contract must comply with legal and ethical standards.

More recently, Tudor (2025) contextualises contracts as structured, collaborative agreements between the therapist and the client, ensuring clarity, mutual understanding, and adherence to ethical practices.

In the context of Aotearoa New Zealand, contracts take on additional significance when viewed through the lens of *Te Tiriti o Waitangi*. Understood as a bilateral agreement between the British Crown and Māori Chiefs, a social contract grounded in mutual benefit, cooperation, and shared authority or co-governance (Matike Mai Aotearoa, 2016), the expectation of Māori was kotahitanga, reflecting a deep value placed on collaborative partnership and interdependence (Kawharu, 1992b). Although the Crown has often failed to uphold its side of the agreement, *Te Tiriti* remains a powerful ethical and political parallel to the therapist–client contract: both represent intentional relationships built on respect, reciprocity, and accountability.

Life scripts, pūrākau, and mātauranga Māori

Cornell (1988) conceptualises life scripts as 'self-defining and sometimes self-limiting psychological constructions of reality' (p. 281). These are not simply individual stories – they are relational and social artefacts formed through interaction with caregivers and cultural contexts. The formation of life scripts involves meaning-making in response to both nurturing and limiting messages, forming enduring patterns of belief and behaviour. In a mātauranga Māori framework, these ideas resonate strongly. Cultural scripting is inseparable from whakapapa (genealogy), tikanga (customary practices), and wairua (spirituality). A Māori client's internal narrative may be profoundly shaped by their ancestral stories, tribal values, and collective experiences, as well as connection to their whenua (land) (Fleming, 2018, 2020; Rua et al., 2017).

45

Here, pūrākau – ancestral narratives such as Tāne's ascent to retrieve Ngā Kete o te Wānanga – function as cultural templates for development, aspiration, and relational responsibility (Mikahere-Hall, 2013; Taonui, 2012). The poutama pattern symbolises this metaphorical ascent, reflecting progressive steps of learning, challenge, and spiritual development. When overlaid with TA theory, poutama becomes a metaphorical scaffold: the individual climbs toward self-knowledge and relational autonomy, supported by both ancestral values and therapeutic insight. Such metaphorical scaffolding enables the development of moral, technical, and aspirational selves (Drego, 1983). In this way, Māori clients may not be 'rescripting' in the Western psychological sense; rather, realigning with inherited cultural narratives that affirm collective belonging, purpose, and strength (Mikahere-Hall, 2013; Tohiariki, 2024).

Cultural scripting and the internalisation of collective experience

In TA theory, a 'life script' is an unconscious life plan formed in early childhood, shaped by the child's interpretations of familial messages and reinforced by later experiences (Berne, 1961; Cornell, 1988). Nested within cultural scripts that reflect societal expectations, values, and norms (Shivanath & Hiremath, 2003), they influence decision-making, emotional regulation, and relationships. Berne (1961) highlights the importance of folklore in transmitting cultural narratives, which Steiner (1974) extends by examining how scripts may carry oppressive cultural messages such as racism, classism, and sexism. These messages often operate covertly, shaping internal narratives that restrict autonomy and reinforce social hierarchies. Drego (1983) advances this understanding by introducing the concept of the Cultural Parent – the set of cultural norms and values internalised into the Parent ego state through three layers:

- Etiquette: socially accepted behaviours;
- Technicality: culturally sanctioned skills and knowledge;
- Character: internalised values, ideals, and aspirations.

This tripartite structure highlights how deeply culture influences individual psychological structures, often in ways that are invisible or taken for granted.

Shivanath and Hiremath (2003) propose a model of cultural scripting that identifies three intersecting layers: (1) **Family scripting**, or messages passed intergenerationally; (2) **Individual religious and cultural scripting**, reflecting ethnic, spiritual, or communal teachings; and (3) **Societal scripting**, encompassing the dominant ideologies of the broader culture (Figure 4.6).

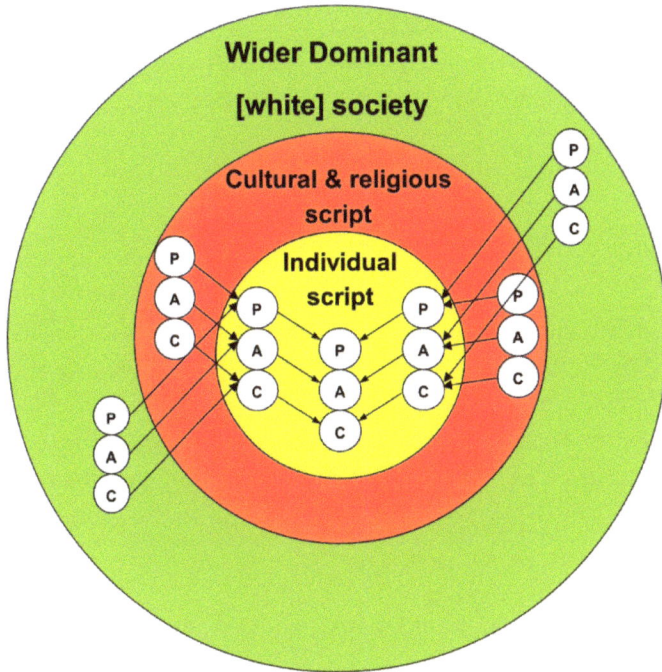

Figure 4.6. Cultural scripting influences (adapted from Shivanath & Hiremath, 2003, p. 174). Reproduced with permission from the copyright holder, Worth Publishing Ltd UK.

In Aotearoa New Zealand, societal scripting has historically privileged Pākehā norms and white, heteronormative values, while marginalising Māori ways of knowing and being. Cultural scripting, therefore, becomes both a vehicle for resilience and identity, and a source of internalised oppression that must be made conscious and challenged (Minikin, 2024; Tohiariki, 2024).

Shivanath and Hiremath (2003) further emphasise that cultural scripts are:
- internalised early and often unconsciously;
- reinforced by social institutions such as schools, media, religion, and government;
- embedded in collective behaviour and belief systems; and
- influence identity, relationships, and the perceived roles of individuals within their communities.

In this sense, cultural scripting shapes both how clients see themselves and how they perceive their options, obligations, and limitations within their cultural context. Baskerville (2022) refers to the transcultural and intersectionality impact on the formation of the identity of self, which is often an unconscious process with potential for bias for both client and therapist. Hence, cultural scripting must be accounted for in relation to power dynamics that might play out in the client's relationships, including that with their therapist.

The workshop

The Conference workshop invited TA practitioners to engage critically with cultural concepts alongside TA theory, deepening participants' understanding of how their own cultural narratives influence therapeutic practice, particularly when working with clients from different cultural backgrounds. By incorporating tukutuku, the workshop aimed to foster cultural reflection, relational collaboration, and appreciation for Indigenous knowledge systems.

Workshop objectives and design

The workshop was guided by three interrelated objectives: (1) to foster appreciation for cultural diversity and engagement with Indigenous metaphors, particularly tukutuku; (2) to prompt reflection on how participants' own cultural backgrounds inform their worldview and TA practice; and (3) to explore the potential for cultural unity within individuals and the broader TA community.

These goals were contextualised within the complex socio-political history of colonisation in New Zealand. *Te Tiriti o Waitangi* has been breached in numerous ways since it was signed in 1840. It was not until the establishment of the Waitangi Tribunal in 1975 (Waitangi Tribunal, n.d.) that formal mechanisms were introduced to address these violations (Matike Mai Aotearoa, 2016; Mutu, 2019). This historical background informed the workshop's ethical approach, particularly the emphasis on contracting for safety and self-care in potentially sensitive discussions. Participants were encouraged to engage at a level that felt appropriate for them, ensuring emotional safety within a diverse group.

The tukutuku process as cultural practice and metaphor

Central to the workshop was the use of tukutuku panels – traditional Māori woven latticework that is both artistic and symbolic – created in three distinct phases. The first involved a collaborative action research process with family and friends, serving as both a learning and relationship-building opportunity, where the foundations of the panel were established through a culturally respectful process (Figure 4.7). Contributions were allocated based on individual skills, interests, and availability. This collaborative construction necessitated clear communication and mutual understanding, especially since the pattern viewed from one side of the panel differed from the other. Thus, the weaving process itself became a metaphor for cross-cultural communication – requiring each person to hold their perspective while effectively engaging with another's.

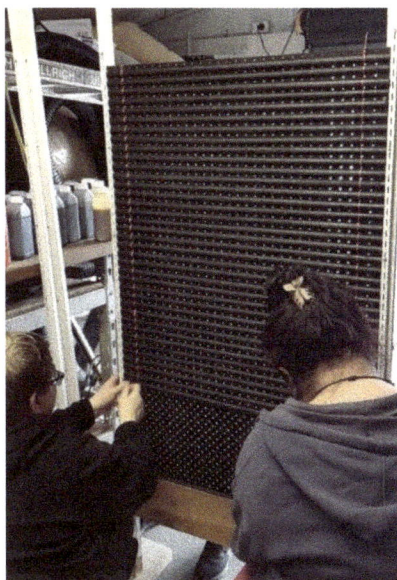

Figure 4.7. Setting up the tukutuku panel.

The second phase of the tukutuku creation unfolded during the Conference workshop. Participants were offered a rare, hands-on opportunity to contribute to the panel's construction under the guidance of Te Amokura Grigg, a skilled Māori weaver and fellow TA practitioner. Given the varying levels of familiarity with Māori cultural practices, participants were invited to opt in or out of the activity based on their comfort. This ensured respectful participation and preserved the integrity of both the cultural practice and the learning experience.

The final phase involved gifting the completed panel to representatives of the newly formed rōpū Māori (Māori group) within the TA community in Aotearoa New Zealand. This act of gifting symbolised recognition of Māori contributions to the field and embodied the values of kotahitanga and manaakitanga (reciprocity and care) (see p. 54, below).

Tukutuku as symbol of unity through diversity

The interactive weaving of the tukutuku provided a practical demonstration of unity through diversity. Participants working on opposite sides of the panel had to communicate their actions clearly in order to achieve a coherent pattern. This process served as an embodied metaphor for intercultural collaboration, reflecting how differing perspectives can contribute to shared meaning-making. The exercise highlighted that unity is not achieved through sameness but through the respectful integration of difference – a message highly relevant to culturally responsive therapeutic practice (Figure 4.8).

Figure 4.8. Front and back of the tukutuku panel.

Exploring cultural scripting in TA

The workshop also integrated theoretical insights from TA; specifically, the concept of cultural scripting. Berne (1961) suggests that understanding a person's cultural context is essential for meaningful script analysis. Following White and White's (1975) introduction of the concept, Shivanath and Hiremath (2003) further develop the idea of cultural scripting, which recognises that life scripts are not formed solely through individual experiences but are deeply influenced by cultural narratives and societal structures.

To illustrate these concepts, I shared aspects of my own cultural background. Born and raised in Aotearoa New Zealand, I understood my whakapapa (ancestry) included Scottish, Irish, Welsh, and French heritage. I later learnt this included Greenland Inuit, Nordic, Spanish, and North African heritage. I was raised within an extended family that included my whāngai grandfather, Te Mahi Tepae Remihana, and three Aunties, plus many cousins of Māori descent. Through these familial relationships, I developed a deep respect for mātauranga Māori, and learned values such as kotahitanga through lived experience. Simultaneously, I became aware of how dominant Pākehā culture shaped societal attitudes toward Māori, often perpetuating marginalisation and inequity.

Participants in the workshop were similarly invited to reflect on their own cultural influences, both familial and societal, and consider how these shape their practice. This introspective component aimed to increase cultural self-awareness, a foundational element in working ethically and effectively across cultural boundaries.

Participant reflections and insights

Participants who engaged in the weaving process expressed that it was a moving and meaningful experience. Many became engrossed in learning the pattern, adjusting to mistakes, and collaborating closely with others. These moments of shared activity fostered technical understanding, emotional connection, and reflective depth. Several participants noted how the act of co-creating something tangible reinforced their understanding of relational dynamics in psychotherapy. Others reflected on how cultural identity and healing are intrinsically linked – both for clients and therapists. There was strong recognition that healing is rarely an isolated process – it often unfolds within the context of whānau, hapū (sub-tribe), and community.

In closing reflections, participants articulated a desire to integrate cultural metaphors and creative processes into their own therapeutic practice. There was consensus that culturally responsive practice requires intentional engagement with one's own cultural scripting and the creation of therapeutic spaces that affirm clients' cultural identities. The use of Māori symbols such as tukutuku, pūrākau, whakapapa, tikanga (customs), and wairua (spirituality) were seen as particularly powerful in supporting clients' journeys toward self-definition, self-determination (tino rangatiratanga), and autonomy. Through collaborative creation and reflective dialogue, participants explored the intersections of personal and cultural identity, learned to hold multiple perspectives, and experienced the value of cultural metaphors in clinical settings. In doing so, they took steps toward embracing karanga rua – unity through diversity – as both a personal and professional ethic (Figure 4.9).

Figure 4.9. Tukutuku panel worked on by six Conference attendees.

Integrating mātauranga Māori into TA practice

Integrating mātauranga Māori with TA enhances culturally responsive therapy in Aotearoa New Zealand. Recognising the role of cultural scripting in shaping individual identity enables therapists to support clients, particularly Māori, in reclaiming and redefining their narratives, which have often been shaped by colonisation and systemic marginalisation. For Māori, cultural scripts are often intertwined with historical trauma (Tohiariki, 2024); therefore, therapeutic work that validates these narratives supports transformation towards autonomy and self-determination.

Tāne's ascension narrative offers a culturally grounded metaphor for positive script development, representing a movement from adversity toward light and knowledge. Cornell (1988) emphasises the potential of reframing experiences to create affirming life scripts. Engaging Māori clients with pūrākau like Tāne's can inspire new, culturally affirming self-concepts (Mikahere-Hall, 2013).

Therapist competence and ethical practice

Effective therapy is linked to the therapist's ability to form a culturally competent relationship (Norcross & Lambert, 2018). In Aotearoa New Zealand, ethical guidelines mandate therapists honour *Te Tiriti o Waitangi* and adopt practices that reflect Māori health models (Tudor et al., 2024). Concepts such as whakapapa, whānau, and wairua are integral to Māori wellbeing and can be incorporated meaningfully into practice to enhance effective outcomes for Māori (Mikahere-Hall, 2013; Tohiariki, 2024). In addition, models like te whare tapa whā (Durie, 1994), te wheke (Pere, 1991), and the meihana model (Pitama et al., 2007, 2017) provide culturally relevant frameworks to guide holistic assessment and engagement.

The pōwhiri poutama model

Paraire Huata's (Te Ngaru Learning Systems, 1997) pōwhiri poutama model presents a therapeutic process that mirrors Tāne's symbolic ascent and the poutama weaving pattern (Drury, 2007; Manning, 2014). It frames healing as a step-by-step journey toward emotional, spiritual, and relational balance, consistent with 'culturally safe trauma-informed care approaches that are cognisant of Māori experiences, as Māori' (Pihama et al., 2017, p. 25) (Figure 4.10).

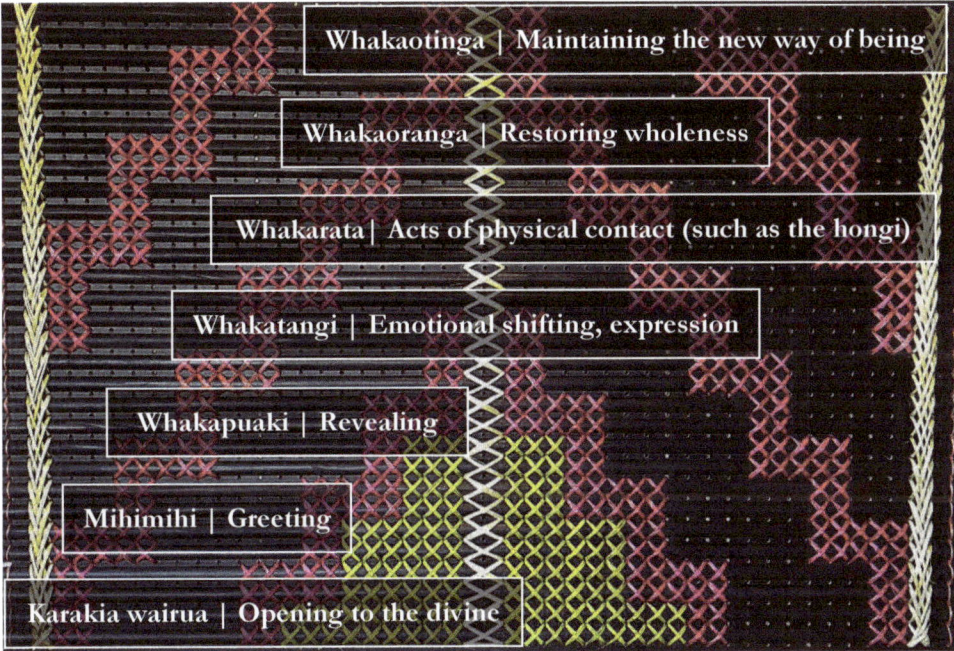

Whakaotinga | Maintaining the new way of being

Whakaoranga | Restoring wholeness

Whakarata | Acts of physical contact (such as the hongi)

Whakatangi | Emotional shifting, expression

Whakapuaki | Revealing

Mihimihi | Greeting

Karakia wairua | Opening to the divine

Figure 4.10. Based on Paraire Huata's Pōwhiri Poutama (Te Ngaru Learning Systems, 1997) programme outline.

From a TA perspective, this reflects script redefinition, anchored in Māori practices such as karakia (prayer), mihi (speech of greeting), and whakawhanaungatanga (process of establishing relationships), which foster familiarity and trust. When we meet people within a space that invites cultural values and ways of encountering each other, pray and name connections to land and people, we provide a context and environment that fosters greater engagement and safety for the client to trust the process. Either the therapist or client can open or close sessions with a prayer or karakia. Using words and concepts that hold cultural significance when meeting someone for the first time, for instance reciting your mihi, is an invitation for your client to do the same if they choose to. Demonstrating cultural respect by pronouncing Māori words correctly is a starting point. This model supports clients to explore their whakapapa and pūrākau within a secure therapeutic space. This can be done by referencing their whakapapa or connection to their land and people, and those narratives that they might be familiar with as guiding wisdoms of pūrākau can serve to deepen the therapeutic work. This could involve being familiar with specific narratives to introduce and complement the work you do, or introducing as tasks for clients to explore further as part of their own exploration outside of the therapy room, that might draw them closer to the wisdoms that can guide them for life. This process helps to restore cultural identity and relationships, and aligns with TA's autonomy goal, which results from increased awareness, spontaneity, and intimacy (Berne, 1961).

Relational and symbolic depth through TA

Hargaden and Sills (2002, 2022) describe three domains of transference that offer culturally responsive entry points: the archetypal, the developmental, and the cultural-social. Archetypal transference engages symbolic memory and aligns with Māori cosmology. Developmental transference surfaces early relational patterns, while cultural-social transference reflects systemic trauma shaped by breaches of *Te Tiriti o Waitangi*. Embedding mātauranga Māori into TA practice affirms Māori identity and enhances therapeutic outcomes. Culturally grounded models, narratives, and symbols offer healing pathways that are both relational and transformational. Upholding these practices reflects a commitment to ethical responsibility and decolonising therapy (Elkington et al., 2020), guiding clients toward mana motuhake –autonomy and self-defined wellbeing (Moorfield, 2011; Tohiariki, 2024).

When therapists enter an intercultural liminal space to engage with cultural difference, they can experience *integration of cultural difference* (Bennett, 1986). This involves a willingness to incorporate the values, beliefs, perspectives, and behaviours in authentic and appropriate ways. As a result, people's experience of self is expanded when they can move in and out of differing cultural worldviews, choosing the most appropriate behaviours within the appropriate cultural context (Bennett, 1986). Similarly, Tudor (2022) invites reflection in person-centred psychotherapy, that we, as Transactional Analysts in Aotearoa New Zealand, can heed; that is, to be open to change in how we practice where the ground is different.

Reflection and call to action: Weaving the wisdoms

Karangarua, the Conference theme, called on participants to reflect on their identities and embrace cultural diversity as a pathway toward unity within the self, professional practice, and wider community. A key message was the importance of cultivating curiosity – toward both our own cultural narratives and those of others – as a foundation for effective therapeutic engagement. By appreciating the richness of diverse backgrounds and exploring shared human experiences, therapists can create safe, affirming spaces for clients to examine their identities within relational contexts (Norcross & Lambert, 2018).

Incorporating mātauranga Māori and Indigenous wisdom offers valuable perspectives in therapeutic practice. Doing so strengthens therapeutic relationships and affirms the cultural identity of clients, particularly those from communities impacted by colonisation (Mikahere-Hall, 2013; Minikin, 2024). The symbolic weaving of tukutuku panels, alongside the poutama pattern and Tāne's ascension pūrākau, provide metaphors for healing, growth, and identity development. These traditional stories represent progression through challenges and toward enlightenment, mirroring the therapeutic journey of transformation and increased self-awareness and autonomy (Fleming, 2020; Rua et al., 2017).

Understanding one's own cultural scripting – the inherited beliefs and narratives that shape worldview and behaviour – is essential. As Shivanath and Hiremath (2003) assert, cultural scripting influences relational dynamics and therapeutic processes. When therapists reflect on their own scripts and how these may interact with those of Māori clients, they can provide more culturally attuned care. For Māori, engaging with traditional pūrākau, such as Tāne's ascent, enables the internalisation of positive, identity-affirming life plans. These stories, embedded within tukutuku as visual narratives, serve as healing resources that support autonomy and reconnection to whakapapa and wairua (Pihama et al., 2017).

It is difficult to portray the depth of the workshop experience for both the attendees or myself, except to say that I know (through subsequent correspondence and conversations) it has reverberated into people's personal and professional lives in a positive way. Engaging with tukutuku and purākau deepened my understanding and inspired my confidence to share these insights at the Conference. The collaborative, creative experience reinforced for me the power of culturally informed metaphors in therapy. These frameworks – rooted in mātauranga Māori and TA – offer tools for understanding the self in relation to others and honour the enduring relevance of

Indigenous knowledge systems, here in Aotearoa New Zealand, and for others in other lands. The depth of this type of learning can only occur within a genuine willingness to be curious and courageous about our own cultural origins and identity, being mindful of how we might encounter another. By being in relationship with another and their diverse culture and identity, in an open and respectful way, we can encounter each other authentically and navigate the process of unity through diversity in relationship – karanaga rua. As we acknowledge and affirm our complex and relational identities that are deeply rooted in our genealogy and lived experience, we can deconstruct and decolonise the culture-centred space between us (Figure 4.11).

Figure 4.11. The post-Conference tukutuku panel created in the workshop gifted to the Māori Rōpū of the Transactional Analysis Community in Aotearoa New Zealand (from left to right: Raewyn Knowles, Janet Matehe, and Te Amokura Griggs).

References

Te Aka Māori Dictionary. (n.d.). *Kotahitanga*. https://maoridictionary.co.nz/search?idiom=&phrase=&proverb=&loan=&histLoanWords=&keywords=kotahitanga

Te Ara. (2025). *Tukutuku panels and poutama patterns*. Te Ara – The Encyclopedia of New Zealand. https://teara.govt.nz/en/maori-weaving-and-tukutuku-te-raranga-me-te-whatu/page-3

Baskerville, V. (2022). A transcultural and intersectional ego state model of the self: The influence of transcultural and intersectional identity on self and other. *Transactional Analysis Journal, 52*(3), 228–243. https://doi.org/10.1080/03621537.2022.2076398

Bennett, M. J. (1986). A developmental approach to training for intercultural sensitivity. *International Journal of Intercultural Relations, 10*(2), 179–196. https://doi.org/10.1016/0147-1767(86)90005-2

Berne, E. (1961). *Transactional analysis in psychotherapy: A systematic individual and social psychiatry*. Grove Press. https://doi.org/10.1037/11495-000

Community Waikato. (2025). *Kotahitanga and Te Tiriti o Waitangi.*
https://www.communitywaikato.org.nz/blog/kotahitangaandtetiriti

Cornell, W. F. (1988). Life script theory: A critical review from a developmental perspective. *Transactional Analysis Journal, 18*(4), 270–282.
https://doi.org/10.1177/036215378801800402

Curtis, E., Jones, R., Tipene-Leach D., Walker, C., Loring, B., Paine, S., & Reid, P. (2019). Why cultural safety rather than cultural competency is required to achieve health equity: A literature review and recommended definition. *International Journal for Equity in Health, 18,* Article 174. https://doi.org/10.1186/s12939-019-1082-3

Drego, P. (1983). The cultural parent. *Transactional Analysis Journal, 13*(4), 224–227.
https://doi.org/10.1177/036215378301300404

Drury, N. (2007). A pōwhiri poutama approach to therapy. *New Zealand Journal of Counselling, 27*(1), 9–20. https://doi.org/10.24135/nzjc.v27i1.68

Durie, M. (1994). *Whaiora: Maori health development.* Oxford University Press.

Durie, M. (2007). Counselling Māori: Marae encounters as a basis for understanding and building relationships. *New Zealand Journal of Counselling, 27*(1), 1–8.
https://doi.org/10.24135/nzjc.v27i1.70

Elkington, B., Jackson, M., Kiddle, R., Ripeka-Mercier, O., Ross, M., Smeaton, J., & Thomas, A. (2020). *Imagining decolonisation.* Bridget Williams Books.

Fleming, A. H. (2018). Ngā Tāpiritanga: Secure attachments from a Māori perspective. *Ata: Journal of Psychotherapy Aotearoa New Zealand, 22*(1), 23–36.
https://doi.org/10.9791/ajpanz.2018.03

Fleming, A. H. (2020). Staying upright: Commentary on 'Standing at the Waharoa'. *Ata: Journal of Psychotherapy Aotearoa New Zealand, 24*(1), 79–80.
https://doi.org/10.9791/ajpanz.2020.07

Hargaden, H., & Sills, C. (2002). *Transactional analysis: A relational perspective.* Routledge.

Hargaden, H., & Sills, C. (2022). *Transactional analysis in contemporary psychotherapy.* Sage.

Kawharu, I. H. (1992a). Kotahitanga: Visions of unity. *Journal of the Polynesian Society, 101*(3), 221–240. https://www.jstor.org/stable/20706458

Kawharu, I. H. (1992b). *Waitangi: Māori and Pākehā perspectives of the Treaty of Waitangi.* Oxford University Press.

Keane, B. (2012). *Kotahitanga – unity movements.* Te Ara – The Encyclopedia of New Zealand. https://teara.govt.nz/en/kotahitanga-unity-movements

Köchler, H. (2012). Unity in diversity: The integrative approach to intercultural relations. *UN Chronicle, 49*(3), 7–10. https://www.un.org/en/chronicle/article/unity-diversitythe-integrative-approach-intercultural-relations

Mahuika, N. (2019). *Rethinking oral history and tradition: An Indigenous perspective.* Oxford University Press.

Manning, S. (2014). Paraire Huata (1946–2014): A personal appreciation. *Ata: Journal of Psychotherapy Aotearoa New Zealand, 18*(1), 81–86.
https://doi.org/10.9791/ajpanz.2014.07

Matike Mai Aotearoa. (2016). *He whakaaro here whakaumu mō Aotearoa: The report of Matike Mai Aotearoa – The independent working group on constitutional transformation.* https://nwo.org.nz/wp-content/uploads/2018/06/MatikeMaiAotearoa25Jan16.pdf

Mikahere-Hall, A. (2013). Ko Rangitoto, ko Waitemata: Cultural landmarks for the integration of a Māori indigenous psychotherapy in Aotearoa. *Ata Journal of Psychotherapy Aotearoa New Zealand, 17*(2), 139–157. https://doi.org/10.9791/ajpanz.2013.14

Minikin, K. S. (2024). *Radical-relational perspectives in transactional analysis psychotherapy – Oppression, alienation, reclamation.* Routledge.

Moorfield, J. C. (2011). *The Aka Māori dictionary.* https://maoridictionary.co.nz/maori-dictionary

Mutu, M. (2019). To honour the Treaty: The political management of Māori aspirations and relations in New Zealand. In J. Hayward (Ed.), *Treaty of Waitangi settlements* (pp. 230–252). Oxford University Press.

Te Ngaru Learning Systems. (1997). *Workbooks 1–5.*

Norcross, J. C., & Lambert, M. J. (2018). Psychotherapy relationships that work III. *Psychotherapy, 55*(4), 303–315. https://doi.org/10.1037/pst0000193

Paewai, P. (2024). *Treaty Principles Bill hīkoi from Far North to Parliament about Māori unity, organisers say.* RNZ. https://www.rnz.co.nz/news/te-manu-korihi/530951/treaty-principles-bill-hikoi-from-far-north-to-parliament-about-Māori-unity-organisers-say

Parekh, B. (2000). *Rethinking multiculturalism: Cultural diversity and political theory.* Harvard University Press.

Pere, R. (1991). *Te wheke: A celebration of infinite wisdom* (N. Nicholson, Illus.). Ao Ako Global Learning New Zealand.

Pihama, L., Smith, L. T., Evans-Campbell, T., Kohu-Morgan, H., Cameron, N., Mataki, T., Te Nana, R., Skipper, H., & Southey, K. (2017). Investigating Māori approaches to trauma-informed care. *Journal of Indidenous Wellbeing | Te Mauri – Pimatisiwin, 2*(3), Article 2. https://journalindigenouswellbeing.co.nz/media/2024/05/Investigating-Maori-approaches-to-trauma-informed-care.pdf

Pitama, S., Robertson, P., Cram, F., Gillies, M., Huria, T., & Dallas-Katoa, W. (2007). Meihana model: A clinical assessment framework. *New Zealand Journal of Psychology, 36*(3), 118–125. https://www.psychology.org.nz/journal-archive/Pitamaetal_NZJP36-3_pg118.pdf

Pitama, S. G., Bennett, S. T. M., Waitoki, W., Haitana, T. N., Valentine, H., Pahina, J., Taylor, J. E., Tassell Matamua, N., Rowe, L., Beckert, L., Palmer, S. C., Huria, T. M., Lacey, C. J., & McLachlan, A. (2017). A proposed Hauora Māori clinical guide for psychologists: Using the hui process and Meihana Model in clinical assessment and formulation. *New Zealand Journal of Psychology, 46*(3), 7–19. https://shorturl.at/NABrB

Psychotherapists Board of Aotearoa New Zealand. (2019). *Standards of ethical conduct.* https://pbanz.org.nz/common/Uploaded%20files/Standards/Psychotherapist%20Standards%20of%20Ethical%20Conduct.2022.pdf

Rua, M., Hodgetts, D., & Stolte, O. (2017). Māori men: An indigenous psychological perspective on the interconnected self. *New Zealand Journal of Psychology*, *46*(3), 55–63. https://www.psychology.org.nz/journal-archive/M%C4%81ori-men-private.pdf.pdf

Shivanath, S., & Hiremath, M. (2003). The psychodynamics of race and culture: An analysis of cultural scripting and ego state transference. In C. Sills & H. Hargaden (Eds.), *Key concepts in transactional analysis contemporary views - Ego states* (pp. 169–184). Worth Publishing.

Sills, C., & Hargaden, H. (Eds.). (2003). *Key concepts in transactional analysis contemporary views - Ego states*. Worth Publishing.

Steiner, C. (1971). *Games alcoholics play: The analysis of life scripts*. Grove Press.

Steiner, C. (1974). *Scripts people live: Transactional analysis of life scripts*. Grove Press.

Steiner, C., & Cassidy, W. (1969). Therapeutic contracts in group treatment. *Transactional Analysis Bulletin*, *8*(30), 29–31.

Taonui, R. (2012, September 22). *Ranginui – the sky – Ranginui as knowledge and life*. Te Ara – The Encyclopedia of New Zealand. https://teara.govt.nz/en/ranginui-the-sky/page-2

Tohiariki, B. (2024). Reindigenisation in the context of psychotherapy and counselling. *Te Tira: A Journal of Māori and Indigenous Leadership*, *2*(1), Article 1. https://doi.org/10.26021/15387

Tudor, K. (2022). Person-centred psychotherapy. *Ata: Journal of Psychotherapy Aotearoa New Zealand*, *26*(1), 11–37. https://doi.org/10.9791/ajpanz.2022.02

Tudor, K. (2025). *Transactional analysis proper – and improper: Selected and new papers*. Routledge.

Tudor, K., Gledhill, K., & Haenga-Collins, M. (2024). Whakaora, pae ora: Health principles and psychotherapy. *Ata: Journal of Psychotherapy Aotearoa New Zealand*, *27*(1), 135–162. https://doi.org/10.24135/ajpanz.2024.08

Waitangi Tribunal. (n.d.). *What is the Waitangi Tribunal?* https://www.waitangitribunal.govt.nz/en/about/about-the-waitangi-tribunal/about-the-waitangi-tribunal

White, J., & White, T. (1975). Cultural scripting. *Transactional Analysis Journal*, *5*(1), 12–23. https://doi.org/10.1177/036215377500500104

Paper 5

Karangarua – Being analytic and transactional, psychological and social, international and local

Keith Tudor

Abstract

Eric Berne founded transactional analysis (TA) in response to psychoanalysis, and referred to TA as a social psychiatry and, by implication, a social psychology, a perspective taken up by some early transactional analysts. Yet Berne himself focused his theory and practice primarily on transactions between therapist and patient in the clinic. Secondly, and similarly, and notwithstanding the radical psychiatry tradition in TA, and the presence and contributions of colleagues in the fields of education and organisations, transactional analysts in the fields of psychotherapy and counselling generally privilege the psychological over the social. Thirdly, as TA was founded in the Western – and Northern – intellectual tradition and, specifically, that of American ego psychology, this paper considers whether its theory and practice applies to and in other cultures and contexts. This paper considers various aspects of these three double relationships and the karanga or call between them, with regard not only to the evolution of TA theory, but also to the identity of the TA community both locally and internationally, and its functioning, with some reference to training, examination, and professional identity. While this paper has been developed from the keynote speech on which it is based, it retains some of the direct and relational style of the original presentation.

Tauparapara | Incantation/Beginning

Whakarongo ake au	I listen, where high up
Ki te tangi a te manu	A bird flies
E rere runga rawa e	Its cry rings out
Tui, tui, tui, tuia	'Sew, stitch, bind it together
Tuia i runga	From above
Tuia i raro	From below
Tuia i roto	From within
Tuia i waho	From outside
Tuia te here tangata	Sew and bind it together'
Kia rongo te pō	May there be peace at night
Kia rongo te ao	And peace by day.
Tui, tui, tui, tuia	Sew, stitch, bind it together.

Tuia te muka tangata	Intertwined with the cords of humankind
I takea mai nei i Hawaiki nui i Hawaiki roa,	Originating from the great homeland
I Hawaiki pāmaomao	From the far homeland
Oti rā me era atu anā Hawaiki	From the remote homeland
	And from all other ancestral lands
Ki te hono a wairua	Merging with the spirits there
Whakaputa ki te whaiao	Then coming into light
Ki te marama.	Out into the world of consciousness
Tihei mauri ora!	The living spirit is within us.
	(Tapiata, 1980)

Introduction

In her abstract for the keynote she would have delivered, Shirley Rivers notes that

> Traditional Māori society engaged seamlessly in the physical and the metaphysical realm of being. Both were natural environments to their wellbeing. Navigating these realms required knowledge of traditional Māori cultural constructs that guided engagements for Māori with each other and the wider environment. Understanding these constructs is fundamental for all practitioners working with Māori whānau. (Rivers, 2024)

She goes on to add that: 'The impact of colonisation for Māori has seen the fracturing from traditional engagement in these two realms culminating in serious consequences for their health and wellbeing.' (Rivers, 2024).

Taking inspiration from the idea of engaging in two realms, I present ideas about the realms of the transactional and the analytic, the social and the psychological, and the local and the international. With regard to each of these pairings, I emphasise one side, i.e., the transactional, the social, and the local, purely in the interests of developing my thesis, or, more accurately, my antithesis to the dominance in transactional analysis (TA) of the analytic, the psychological, and the international – and, in effect, the universal. I offer this antithesis as part of the process in promoting a synthesis that attempts to resolve the conflict between the thesis and antithesis, and, hopefully, help us to engage seamlessly in these different realms. Those interested in the philosophical origins of ideas, the triadic formulation of thesis–antithesis–synthesis derives from the work of Johann Gottlieb Fichte (1762–1814), the 18th century German philosopher, not Georg Hegel (to whom it is commonly attributed).

Finally, by way of introduction, in my tauparapara (incantation), I invoked the spirit of the tūī, one of the native birds of these islands, and the image of calling i runga (from above), i raro (from below), i roto (from inside), and i waho (from outside), prepositions of place or location to which I return throughout this paper.

Being analytic *and* transactional

There is an amusing video on YouTube which shows a group of actors and then Prince Charles (of the United Kingdom) each reciting the line from Shakespeare's Hamlet 'To be or not to be, that is the question', each emphasising a different word in the line, thus:

> To be or not to be, that *is* the question. (Paapa Essiedu)
> To be *or* not to be, that is the question. (Tim Minchin)
> To be or *not* to be, that is the question. (Benedict Cumberbatch)
> To be or not to *be*, that is the question. (Harriet Walter)
> To be or not to be, *that* is the question. (David Tennant)
> To be or not to be, that *is* the question. (Rory Kinnear)
> To be or not to be, that is *the* question. (Ian McKellen)
> To be or not *to* be, that is the question. (Judi Dench)
> To be or not to be, that is the *question*. (Prince Charles)
> (Animato, 2016)

Transactional analysts generally say and think we say the words 'transactional analysis' as if there were no emphasis, but may consciously or unconsciously be saying 'transactional *analysis*' with the emphasis on analysis, or '*transactional* analysis' with the emphasis on transactional. In the first part of this paper, I note and argue that, notwithstanding Berne's break from psychoanalysis, i.e., *psycho*analysis, TA (especially in its psychotherapy field of application) still emphasises and focuses more on the psychoanalytic and the psychodynamic, and less on the transactional. This is represented, for instance, in the work of Drye (1980), Moiso (1985), Novellino and Moiso (1990), Moiso and Novellino (2000), Novellino (2003, 2005), Little (2005), Cornell and Hargaden (2020), Landaiche (2020), Tangolo and Massi (2022), and others (for further references to which, see Tudor, 2025).

Writing about the social dynamics of games, Berne (1964/1968) states that:

> Theories of internal individual psychodynamics have so far not been able to solve satisfactorily the problems of human relationships. These are transactional situations which call for a theory of social dynamics that cannot be derived from consideration of individual motivations. (p. 59)

I say more about social dynamics in the second part of this paper. For now, I focus on the transactional and transactional situations.

So, what did Berne mean and intend by transactional analysis (with an even emphasis on the two words)? In *Principles of Group Treatment* (Berne, 1966) he writes:

> Transactional analysis is an actionist form of treatment, where psychoanalysis is to a much greater extent, a contemplative one. The transactional analyst says, 'Get better first, and we can analyse later.'…. Thus the transactional patient and his family benefit from the accomplishments that take place before the deeper analytic phase of his treatment, so that it is of relatively less consequence how long he remains in treatment after that. The psychoanalyst, on the other hand, may imply, 'After you have been analysed, you will get better.' (pp. 303–304)

This perspective is reflected in Berne's (1961, 1972/1975b) stages of cure, i.e., social control, symptomatic relief, transference cure, and script cure, and in his metaphor of the splinter in the toe (Berne, 1971). In their article, based on this metaphor, Wilson and Kalina (1978) summarise the apocryphal story as follows:

> a man got a splinter in his toe… [which] affected his whole physical and emotional well-being. One doctor he went to hedged, declared four to five years of treatment would be needed, and promised no cure. A second doctor discovered the splinter, removed it, the symptoms subsided, and the man was cured. (p. 201)

Commenting on the story, Berne (1971) declares: 'So that's the way to practice psychotherapy…. you find the splinter and you pull it out.' (p. 12)

With regard to the quotation about TA as an actionist form of treatment, this is a particularly interesting passage, not least as, in it, Berne is also acknowledging the significance of the benefit to the family of a client's individual therapy, a perspective which acknowledges the transactional impact of therapy outside and beyond the clinic.

Commenting on Berne's perspective, Shmukler (2001) argues that 'Berne's criticisms of classic psychoanalysis, which he answered by originating transactional analysis, are still answered in part by an ego psychology that stresses social and interactional factors, as does current transactional analysis theory.' (p. 95). In the sense that ego psychology focuses on adaptation and integration (see Tudor, 2025), I would agree with Shmukler's commentary; however, insofar as the development of ego psychology by Glover, Federn, Weiss, and Berne, as well as John and Helen Watkins, focuses on the intrapsychic dynamics of the ego and not so much on social and interactional factors, I disagree.

Given that, in 1958, Berne referred to this 'new and effective method of group therapy' (Berne, 1958/1977, p. 145), as transactional analysis (*transactional* analysis), I find it strange that some 12 years later, he's nailing ego states to his mast when he states that 'Parent, Adult, and Child ego states were first systematically studied by transactional analysis, and they're its foundation stones and its mark. Whatever deals with ego states is transactional analysis, and whatever overlooks them is not.' (Berne, 1970/1973, p. 223). I would – and do – say that 'to paraphrase but contra Berne... transactions were first systematically studied by transactional analysis, and they are its foundation stones and its mark. Whatever deals with the analysis of transactions is transactional analysis, and whatever overlooks them is not.' (Tudor, 2025, p. 116). Even Claude Steiner, who always referred to himself as a disciple of Eric Berne, and hardly if ever disagreed with him, when defining transactional analysis would say that it was – is – the analysis of transactions!

Of course, this emphasis is implied in the grammar of the term transactional analysis, as it is the adjective transactional that defines and distinguishes this form of analysis from other forms.

My interest in emphasising the transactional (and also in reclaiming the plurality of the relational approach in TA (see Hargaden et al., 2023; Sills & Tudor, 2025), and, thereby, evening up the call and dynamic between the analytic and the transactional, is driven by an interest not only in historical accuracy, theoretical integrity, philosophical congruence, and embracing diversity, but also in professional and organisational identity.

A significant number of colleagues drift away from TA, both after training, with the result that they don't take their CTA (certified transactional analyst) exam, and also after they qualify. Indeed, in this country, only 18 out of the 60 CTAs in Aotearoa New Zealand (that is 30%) attended the TA Conference in Whanganui-a-Tara | Wellington. While it was great to see those 18 colleagues at the Conference, at the same time, we (as a professional community and a national association [the Transactional Analysis Association of Aotearoa New Zealand]) need to understand why so many of our qualified colleagues weren't there, including 11 who live in Wellington, only a few kilometres from the Conference venue. Notwithstanding this, the good news, is that 13 out of 29 trainees in the country (45%) and nine out of 14 Māori TA colleagues (64%) attended the Conference.

There is also an issue with identity in that it appears that being a transactional analyst, especially, and, perhaps specifically, in the field of psychotherapy, isn't experienced as being good enough. I conducted some research on this some 25 years ago in the UK, when being 'integrative' was popular, and found that, following certification as a transactional analyst, on registering with the United Kingdom Council for Psychotherapy, 18% of CTAs in the field of psychotherapy registered as 'integrative' psychotherapists (Tudor, 1999). Undertaking similar research here, this time on therapists' websites, I found that 37 out of the 47 CTAs registered as psychotherapists in this country (i.e., 79%) do not state that they are transactional analysts, preferring the generic term 'psychotherapist' or 'registered psychotherapist' (which, in this country, is an oxymoron), or some other title and identity, including counsellor, nurse psychotherapist, and psychodynamic psychotherapist.

As a way of thinking about this from a transactional perspective, I offer a brief analysis based on Berne's six categories of the advantages of games, together with Bary and Hufford's (1997) addition of the physiological, using these to consider the importance and 'advantages' as well as the disadvantages of the transaction(s) involved in identifying as a transactional analyst:

1. The *biological advantage*, which, for Berne (1964/1968), is 'stated in tactile terms' (p. 56).
   In this context, I suggest that this is the physical sense of belonging to a community with a shared view of method and methodology, a physicality which is often manifested in the exchange of physical as well as psychological strokes or recognition when people meet and greet each other at TA events by shaking hands, hugging, and kissing – and, in our case, doing the hongi. Of course, if the tactility or sense of tactility in the community is negative, then this will be experienced as a biological disadvantage, and may be one reason why colleagues leave and/or stay away.

2. The *existential advantage*, which Berne (1964/1968) defines as 'a demonstration of the coherent structure which underlies all games' (p. 56) and, in this application, transactions.
   In this instance, I would see this as the coherent structure of the transactions in which we engage, for instance, in this Conference, from the welcome of the pōwhiri (welcome) to the poroporoaki (ending). Judging by the number of references to 'coherent' and 'coherence' in the international *Certification and Examinations Handbook* (International Transactional Analysis Association [ITAA] International Board of Certification [IBoC], 2022), it is clear that coherence is a core value of TA. Again, if the structure is incoherent, then that will be experienced as an existential

65

disadvantage – which is one reason I spend some of my intellectual time identifying and proposing solutions to the inconsistencies in TA theory (see Tudor, 2003, 2025).

3. The *internal psychological advantage*, which Berne (1964/1968) describes as the 'direct effect on the psychic economy (libido)' (p. 57).
   This is reflected in feeling good and excited about oneself and others as we transact. On the other hand, negative transactions, such as power plays, infantilisation, Rescues, lies, and so on, contribute to the internal psychological disadvantage(s) of these transactions.

4. The *external psychological advantage*, which Berne (1964/1968) describes as 'the avoidance of a feared situation' (p. 57).
   In this context, this represented in how people think and feel about how they identify themselves as a transactional analyst. I remember being quite shocked when, visiting Aotearoa New Zealand a couple of years before I emigrated here in 2009, a TA colleague advising me that, if I were to settle in Auckland, not to say that I was a transactional analyst. Interestingly enough, a couple of years after I had settled (in Auckland) and had presented lectures and papers, another (non-TA) colleague commented that he was struck by the fact that neither I nor Louise Embleton Tudor, my wife and colleague, apologised for not being Freudian! It's true; I didn't – and don't – apologise for not being Freudian. Equally, I don't apologise for being Bernian – and post-Bernian (see Lee, 2001). However, it is clear from the statistics I cited (above), that the majority (i.e., 79%) of CTAs in the field of psychotherapy and registered as psychotherapists in this country find greater external psychological advantages in identifying with something other than TA.

5. The *internal social advantage*, which, for Berne (1964/1968) 'is designated by the name of the game as it is played in the individual's intimate circle' (p. 57).
   I think about this as the internal aspect of the previous point which may be expressed as justifications for 'moving on', e.g., 'I'm more interested in other approaches now', 'TA is passé', etc.

6. The *external social advantage*, which 'is designated by the use made of the situation in outside social contacts' (Berne, 1964/1968, p. 57).
   In the context of this analysis, this is reflected in the ways people represent their identity both within and outside the TA community, and hence my interest in being clear about identity and coherence in TA, to whit, as part of the research for the book *Transactional Analysis Proper – and Improper* (Tudor, 2025), I identified some 23 'schools', branches, traditions, approaches, or sensibilities in TA. This could and

should be an external social advantage as, I would argue, those TA colleagues who are currently not identifying as transactional analysts could, I am sure, find something in contemporary TA with which to identify and represent outside TA.

7. The *physiological* advantage, the restrictive game version of which Bary and Hufford (1997) describe in terms of body armouring, the freedom from which is an openness and softening.

   This is reflected in the idea that, just as theory is and needs to be open and flexible (see Rogers, 1959; Tudor, 2018), and even pliable and certainly adaptable (Berne, 1972/1975b; Tudor, 2025), so, too, our transactions and TA itself can be welcoming, and as Stuthridge et al. (2012) put it some years ago, our tent(s) open to guests.

Considering that a part of the stated purpose of the written examination for certification as a transactional analyst is that the candidate 'works effectively and ethically as a theoretically based transactional analyst' (ITAA IBoC, 2022, Section 8.1.2), I suggest that the greater the alignment of these biological, existential, psychological, and social aspects and advantages, the more the candidate is likely to experience themselves as an integrated or integrating *transactional* analyst – or transactional analyst.

Being psychological *and* social

As a psychiatrist and a psychoanalyst in training, Berne was clearly at home in the psychological world; he was, however, more ambivalent about the social world (see Steiner, 2010; Tudor, 2020).

Despite the fact that Berne (1961/1975a) refers to TA as a social psychiatry, he defines this simply as denoting: 'the study of the psychiatric aspects of specific transactions or sets of transactions which take place between two or more particular individuals at a given time and place' (p. 12) and, as Steiner (2010) points out, Berne himself did not apply this to society at large.

In *Games People Play*, Berne (1964/1968) does consider social dynamics, which he refers to as a 'large field' (p. 51), and contrasts with individual psychodynamics, as referenced in the first part of this paper (p. xx, above).

In his earlier work on *The Structure and Dynamics of Organizations and Groups*, Berne (1963) refers to such dynamics as 'the science which treats of the forces acting on or within any social aggregation or between social aggregations.' (p. 318). Thus, as well as being interested in why two or more people are playing a game, we might also be interested in the forces in the field of that relationship (see Lewin, 1952) that drive, help, and enable, or restrain, discourage, and limit us from playing games. Similarly, Tudor and Summers (2014) reframe impasse theory in the context of field theory. Summerton (1993) sees social dynamics as concerned with intragroup and intergroup game analysis or 'the cultural matrices that support group games' (p. 102). Some years earlier, Summerton (1985) had developed the game pentagon, in which he identifies the game roles of stage manager, spectator, sniper, scapegoat, and saviour, and which, as far as I'm aware, is the only game theory in TA that explicitly references social dynamics (Summerton, 1992). (Summerton identified this role a couple of years before Clarkson's [1987] work on the Bystander role in which she adds to the original three roles of Karpman's [1968] drama triangle the role of 'Audience or Bystanders' [p. 84], though she does not acknowledge Summerton's work.) In any case, whenever and wherever two or more people are playing a game, there is a social matrix that supports that game, a perspective that immediately widens our field of game analysis.

Berne's ambivalence about the social world can be read and heard in the following:

- In 1966, he wrote: 'Existentially, the therapist should realize that he must have a heavy personal involvement with the human race if he is to keep his membership in it.' (Berne, 1966, p. 97).

- As a psychiatrist, he introduced the staff–patient staff conference which, he writes, 'first attacks the comfortable and well-established sociological roles of "therapist" and "patient" and substitutes a "bilateral contract"… Everyone is treated as a "person" with equal rights on his own merits' (p. 45). He continues: 'As a logical product of this "equality", categorization of patients has been abolished.' (p. 45; see also Rotondo, 2020). This suggests that transactional analysts could and should focus on *transactional* and *social ways* of understanding patients and their pathology and not rely on psychiatric diagnosis and manuals. In this, I consider Berne comes close to Rogers' (1951) view of diagnosis when he wrote: 'In a very meaningful and accurate sense, therapy *is* diagnosis, and this diagnosis is a process which goes on in the experience of the client, rather than the intellect of the clinician.' (p. 224).

- In 1969, in one of his last editorials in the *Transactional Analysis Bulletin*, Berne wrote that 'We are sufficiently well established to undertake one, or even two crusades, or rather the Editor feels that he can take it upon himself to do so' (Berne, 1969, p. 7). He went on to suggest crusades against infant mortality, war, and oppressive governments: what he summarised as 'the Four Horsemen' (of the Apocalypse), that is, war, pestilence, famine, and death. Whilst I wouldn't use the word crusade to describe such challenges, I agree with Berne's vision and exhortation that transactional analysts – and TA itself – could and should be impacting on the social world. In an interview with Bill Cornell, Eric Berne's son, Terry, expressed something similar: 'That brings to mind how TA can be applied to society and culture as a whole as opposed to just the individual… The way TA can be applied to broader societal and political patterns is of particular interest to me' (T. Berne & Cornell, 2004, p. 7).

However,

- In 1971, in an article published after his death, in the inaugural issue of the *Transactional Analysis Journal*, Berne appears to have retreated from the social, and contradicting the point he made five years earlier about seeing the patient (as he would call them) as part of a family by saying:

> Personally I'm a head mechanic – that's all I am. Like you come in with wheels wrong in your head, and I'll say, 'Okay we'll try and fix your head. What goes on outside your head belongs in a different department than I deal with, and I might be interested in dealing with it but I don't feel that that is my primary job.' And if you're going to do that then the first thing you have to learn is simple, pure psychotherapy. In other words: there's a patient sitting there in a chair and you're sitting there in a chair…. There's just two people – that's all there is. (Berne, 1971, pp. 12–13)

A number of TA colleagues have discussed Berne's limited view of social psychiatry, notably Baute (1979), Zalcman (1990), Moiso (1995), Barnes (2003), Massey (2007), and Steiner (2010). Some have also discussed the extent to which TA is a social *psychology*, i.e., a psychology that focuses on human behaviour in a relational and social context, namely, Price (1978), Massey (1996), and Tudor (2020), and a number of others have applied TA as a social psychology to all aspects of the social world, including: social issues (Boulton, 1976); social justice (Barnes, 1977; Campos, 2010); modern racism (Batts, 1982, 1983); cultural scripts (James, 1983); nuclear disarmament (Trautmann, 1984); power – Steiner (1981), Jacobs (1987, 1994), Althöfer and Tudor (2020), and Pandya (2024); nationalism (Jacobs, 1990); autocracy (Jacobs, 1991); social applications (Novey, 1996); gay and lesbian issues (Cornell & Simerly, 2004); critical whiteness (Naughton & Tudor, 2006; Tudor et al., 2022); war (Campos, 2014, 2015; Tudor, 2023); intrapsychic, interpersonal, and social conflict (Monin & Cornell, 2015); gender, sexuality, and identity (McLean & Cornell, 2017); social responsibility (Cornell & Monin, 2018); religion, faith, and spirituality (de Graaf & Monin, 2019); TA and politics (Tudor & Cornell, 2020); normativity, marginality, and deviance (Deaconu & Rowland,

2021); systemic oppression (Dhananjaya, 2022; Minikin, 2024; Minikin & Rowland, 2022; Shadbolt, 2024); intersectionality (Baskerville, 2022); and ecological TA (Barrow & Marshall, 2023).

Moreover, if we consider the organisation of TA, the International Transactional Analysis Association (ITAA) has had a Women's Caucus (see Levin, 1977); a Social Action Committee (see Levin & Fryer, 1980), and has a Committee for Social Engagement; has supported the network of Transactional Analysts for Social Responsibility (TASR) (see Campos, 2011), and Project TA101 (United States of America Transactional Analysis Association, 2023); has held and/or sponsored a number of conferences with social themes (for a summary of which, see Tudor, 2020); and, four years ago published a statement on anti-racism (ITAA, 2020). Of course, all this is consistent with the organisational values of the ITAA, especially integrity, inclusivity, community, and social justice (ITAA, 2025).

The colleagues who most represented the social and the political world in the early days of TA were the radical psychiatrists, whose work was a significant part of my initial engagement with TA. Indeed, radical psychiatry was recognised as a School of TA by Wilson and Kalina (1978), Woollams and Brown (1978), and Karpman (1981), though not by others who subsequently considered what constituted TA, i.e., Moiso and Novellino (2000), Lee (2001), Campos (2003), van Beekum (2006), Grégoire (2007), Novellino (2010), or Dijkman and Geuze (2021), for an analysis of which, see Tudor (2025).

Here, in the spirit of the Māori whakataukī (proverb), ka mua, ka muri, which represents the idea of walking backwards into the future, I present the three principles of radical psychiatry as outlined by Steiner in 1975 in order to emphasise the social or, to echo the call of the bird to stitch from outside into the psychological or intrapsychic world.

The first principle of radical psychiatry is:

> that in the absence of oppression, human beings will, due to their basic nature or soul, which is preservative of themselves and their species, live in harmony with nature and each other. Oppression is the coercion of human beings by force or threats of force and is the source of all human alienation. (Steiner, 1975, p. 11)

Elsewhere, Steiner (1974, 1981) identifies different forms of alienation – from love, mind, body and emotions, and work – the first three of which he relates to basic life scripts, i.e., loveless, mindless, and joyless, respectively. In 1988, Beth Roy, another radical psychiatrist and early eco psychologist (though not a transactional analyst), acknowledged a fifth form of alienation: that from the Earth. While it may be tempting to describe the alienation from work as a jobless script, this links work to employment, when there are many other unpaid forms of work; moreover, framing it as a script both suggests a certain blame of the person without a job, and discounts the social impact of the particular economic system in which the person is jobless, such as capitalism. Similarly, while it may be tempting to complete this taxonomy by referring to the person who is alienated from the Earth as landless, this again focuses on the person who has been alienated (the 'done to') rather than the person or people (the 'doer(s)') who were or are effecting the alienation, i.e., the raupatu or stealing or confiscation of land. In taking this perspective, I am informed by and reminded of Moana Jackson's (2009) critique of Western research and in particular the racist notion of warrior races and the warrior gene, and his citing of a young Mohawk researcher from North America who suggested that research into European people would no doubt discover a colonising gene!

The second principle of radical psychiatry is that: '*Alienation is the essence of all psychiatric conditions*…. Every psychiatric diagnosis except for those that are *clearly* organic in origin is a form of alienation.' (Steiner, 1975, p. 11). The clear implication of this principle is that we should eschew psychiatric diagnosis – or, more precisely, traditional Western psychiatric diagnosis based on an allopathic medical model of illness as represented by the American Psychiatric Association's (APA) *Diagnostic and Statistical Manual of Mental Disorders*, now in its fifth revised edition (APA, 2022) – in favour of a diagnosis or knowing (the English word diagnosis comes from the Greek word to recognise or to know) based on radical psychiatry (i.e., alienation), or forms of psychotherapy such as transactional analysis (for example, in terms of life scripts), person-centred psychology (in terms of conditionality, and isolation), neo-Reichian psychology (in terms of character structure), and so on. Within TA, we can consider this with regard to a number of, if not all our branches, traditions, approaches, or sensibilities. Some 45 years ago, drawing on Berne's (1971) metaphor of the splinter in the toe, Wilson and Kalina (1978) did this with regard to the aetiology of the symptoms and the problem of the splinter in five Schools of TA, i.e., Bernian (based on the work of Berne), Social Transaction (Karpman and Dusay), Radical Psychiatry (Steiner), Symbiosis/Passivity (Jacqui Schiff), and Redecision (Robert and Mary Goulding) (see Table 5.1).

Table 5.1. The splinter chart with regard to radical psychiatry (from Wilson & Kalina, 1978).

School	Radical Psychiatry
Models	Aetiology, diagnosis, and treatment: the social model
The splinter **What and how**	What: the Pig Parent (P₁) How: Harmful parental and societal programming (training) via injunctions and attributions: joylessness (body splits), lovelessness (scarcity of strokes), mindlessness (discounting and lies)
Symptoms/Problems **How they are described**	Within the context of the scripts: joyless (drug addiction, obesity, alcoholism) loveless (depression, psychosomatic illnesses) mindless (schizophrenia, thinking disorders)
Removing the splinter	Joyless – awareness of bodily sensations, permission(s) to feel and to use feelings as guides Loveless – awareness and permission(s) to go against injunctions and the (negative) stroke economy Mindless – accountability, awareness of discounts and power plays
The tools	• Organisation against social oppression • Contracts • Work transactions • Permission, protection, potency • Fun transactions • Group support • Permission classes • Bodywork: breathing, centring • Homework
The result	Decommission of the Pig Parent (P₁) Autonomy – in terms of • Co-operation • No scarcity of strokes • No power plays • Equal rights • No Rescues

On this basis, and enhanced by the development of theory within TA over the past 45 years, we could produce our own '*transactional* psychiatry' without relying on *Psychodynamic Psychiatry* (Gabbard, 2014), and a *transactional* diagnostic manual of different forms of alienation without reaching for the latest edition of the *Psychodynamic Diagnostic Manual* (Lingiardi & McWilliams, 2017). It's not that these books aren't useful. (I happen to think that they're very well researched, written, and presented.) It's simply that they don't reflect or represent our TA heritage or language; and that, by relying on them, we don't develop a *transactional* language for psychiatry or soul healing. Worse, uncritically accepting the medical model of psychiatry represents a social and institutional game ('Kick ourselves' or 'Own goal'), and another external social disadvantage to transactional analysis and transactional analysts.

The third principle of radical psychiatry is *'that all alienation is the result of oppression about which the oppressed has been mystified or deceived.'* (Steiner, 1975, p. 11). Steiner (1975) summarises this in two formulae:

$$Oppression + Deception = Alienation$$

and

$$Oppression + Awareness = Anger$$

Steiner defines deception as 'the mystification of the oppressed into believing that she is not oppressed or that there are good reasons for her oppression.' (p. 11). The view that alienation is the result of mystified oppression stems directly from Karl Marx, and, in the 1970s, found expression in the view that oppression is defined as prejudice plus power, which is why an analysis of oppression is based on an analysis of power, and hence the focus of Marxists, feminists, queer theorists, critical race theorists, and radical psychiatrists on power structures and dynamics in the external social world first. As Steiner (1975) puts it:

> A radical psychiatrist will take sides. He will advocate the side of those whom he is helping. The radical psychiatrist will not look for the wrongness within the person seeking psychiatric attention; rather, he will look for the way in which this person is being oppressed and how the person is going along with the oppression. The only problem that radical psychiatry looks for inside someone's head is how he empowers and enforces the lies of the oppressor and thereby enforces his own oppression. (p. 13)

These formulae went through a few variations, including the following, more familiar version:

$$Oppression = Alienation + Mystification + Isolation \text{ (Steiner, 1979)}$$

and its antithesis

$$Awareness + Contact = Action \rightarrow Liberation \text{ (Steiner, 1975)}$$

and

$$POWER\ IN\ THE\ WORLD = CONTACT + AWARENESS + ACTION$$
(Steiner, 2008/2020, p. 111; original emphasis)

73

Forged in the 1960s and '70s, radical psychiatry is more associated with those decades of social change and struggles, and, certainly in TA in the 1980s and '90s, it was rarely referenced, presented, or discussed. It has, nevertheless, remained a tradition outside TA – see Talbott (1974), Roy (2007), Foot (2014), Richert (2014, 2019), and Robcis (2021) – and, within TA has enjoyed something of a revival through my own work (Tudor, 2008, 2008/2017, 2010, 2011), and that of Minikin (2018), Dhananjaya (2022), Tudor et al. (2022), and Aldridge (2023). Most recently, Minikin has developed the interplay between radical psychiatry and psychodynamic relational TA in what she refers to as *Radical Relational Transactional Analysis* (Minikin, 2024). Of course, radical psychiatry is not confined to the psychotherapy field of application. Its theory and praxis was and can be applied to the social/political world (see The Rough Times Staff, 1973) and the challenges we currently face, not least as we stand or sit here in Te Whanganui-a-Tara | Wellington a few days after the massive hīkoi | demonstration in response to the proposal from the New Zealand Act Party to rip up *Te Tiriti o Waitangi*.

In this sense, an emphasis on the social and political world and its call brings some balance to the force(s) of and dynamics between this and the psychological world.

Being international *and* local

One of the things that first attracted me to TA was its internationalism. From early on in my training in the mid-1980s, I attended international conferences and loved the sense of being part of an international community, not least in seeing and sensing our cultural diversity.

There were and are, however, many challenges in being international, not least in how we understand and talk with each other, predominantly, by means of one dominant language, that is English, while maintaining our ethical principles of responsibility, protection, respect, commitment and fidelity in relationship, and empowerment (ITAA IBoC, 2022) with regard to clients, ourselves as practitioners, trainees, colleagues, and the human – and non-human – environment/community.

There are a number of problems with internationalism as it is currently framed and experienced of which, here, I briefly refer to four theses – universality, the hegemony of the centre, gestures of exclusion, and grand erasure. (Others include: the false neutrality of the dominant culture, and the espoused equality of all people, cultures, and nations.) In her book, *Southern Theory*, the title of which challenges the hegemony of the centre, Connell (2008) argues that, in order to counter these textual and political 'moves', we need, from a Southern – and, I would say, Eastern – perspective (see Tudor, 2015):

1) theories that are specific and contextual;
2) theories that are generated from and that reflect readings from the periphery, the edge, and the margins;
3) theories that are inclusive and specifically inclusive of ideas from the periphery; and
4) theories that present and represent experiences from the periphery and, therefore, that reclaim erased wisdom, knowledge, and experience.

Here I briefly introduce these theses and, framing these in the context of the tripartite analysis thesis–antithesis–synthesis (Table 5.2), give examples from the wider social/political world, from the psychological world; and from TA – and offer some antitheses, as well as some syntheses. (I acknowledge 'some' as the blank cells in Tables 5.3, 5.4, 5.5, and 5.6 both represent the fact that this is still work in progress, and invites the reader to think about and provide their own examples.)

Table 5.2. Four textual moves (Connell, 2008), their antitheses and syntheses.

Thesis	Antithesis	Synthesis
The claim of universality	Praxis that is specific and contextual	Pluralism based on local knowledge
Reading from the centre	Readings from the periphery	Biculturalism Multiculturalism
Gestures of exclusion	Praxis that is inclusive	Biculturalism Multiculturalism
Grand erasure	Praxis that reclaims erased wisdom and experience	Critical theory, e.g., Southern theory (Connell, 2008)

Universality

Universality refers to the notion that a (one) theory provides a complete understanding of everything, in this case, the field of human personality including behaviour, human relations, health and illness, healing and cure, and so on. Universalism refers to the view that a particular theory is applicable everywhere at any and every time. Both universality and universalism have been popular notions in Western philosophy and theology, and the subject of recent debates in the fields of linguistics, geography, and human rights, more so than in the field of psychology (see Table 5.3).

There is a number of theories and aspects of psychological theory which are based on universality, one example of which is the notion that there is a set number of personality disorders (APA, 2022) or personality adaptations (see Ware, 1983), for a critique of which see Tudor and Widdowson (2008), or drivers (Kahler with Capers, 1974), for a critique of which, see Tudor (2008). This kind of universal explanation is based on essentialism, i.e., that there are unchanging universal qualities, attributes or, in this instance, categories of personality, which pre-date existence; and on cultural neutrality, i.e., the (supposed) neutrality of theory across culture(s).

Table 5.3. The claim of universality and examples of its antithesis and synthesis.

	Thesis	Antithesis	Synthesis
	The claim of universality	*Praxis that is specific and contextual*	*Pluralism based on local knowledge*
Examples			
Social/political	Monotheistic religions	Pluralistic religions	
Psychological	Autonomy	Homonomy	Autonomy and homonomy in the context of heteronomy (Angyal, 1941)
	That there is a set number of personality disorders (APA, 2022)	That personality – and personality theory – is constructed	
In transactional analysis	That there is a set number of drivers (Kahler with Capers, 1974)	That there are more than five or a specific number of drivers – see M. Goulding (in Goulding & Goulding, 1979), Tudor (2008)	Pluralistic personality theory
	… and of personality adaptations (see Ware, 1983)	… and Tudor and Widdowson (2008)	

Reading from – and the hegemony of – the centre

This refers to the explicit claim or implicit assumption that ideas come from a centre from which they are applied outwards to the periphery. Connell (2008) refers to this as reading from the centre, e.g., sociology *in* Australia, a move or manoeuvre which presupposes that sociology or psychology has a centre and that that centre is 'neutral'. For example, when I was growing up in the 1950s and '60s in the Midlands of England, no-one talked about British culture as 'culture' referred to other cultures: those others over there (see Table 5.4). Personally, it was only as a result of living in Italy for two years in the mid-1980s where, notwithstanding my privilege as a white, middle-class, cis-gendered man, I was othered – and de-centred. Although some of those experiences were not easy, it was good experiential learning and, I would say, good for the soul or psyche.

One example of this reading from – and the hegemony of – the centre in transactional analysis is the universal promotion and application of autonomy both as an inherent quality and the goal of therapy and other activities, for a review of the historical origins of this in relation to the development of American ego psychology, see Tudor (2025). However, in TA, and in Western – and Northern – thinking generally, this is rarely balanced with its antonym, homonomy, meaning a sense of belonging (Angyal, 1941; see also Tudor & Worrall, 2006).

Table 5.4. Reading from the centre and examples of its antithesis and synthesis.

	Thesis	Antithesis	Synthesis
	Reading from the centre	*Readings from the periphery*	*Biculturalism Multiculturalism*
Examples			
Social/political	Culture is neutral	Cultural intentionality	Biculturalism Multiculturalism
Psychological	Culture is neutral	Cultural psychology (Shweder, 1990) Indigenous psychology	
In transactional analysis	Autonomy	Homonomy	Autonomy and homonomy in the context of heteronomy (Angyal, 1941)
	Professional associations are apolitical/neutral	Professional associations are inherently political	The political nature of professional associations is dependent on their context

Gestures of exclusion

In her work, Connell (2008) refers to 'gestures of exclusion' (p. 46) as the third of the four geopolitical assumptions of the Northernness of general theory, and one which is maintained (or gestured) through the exclusion of anything that is not Northern (or Western) and, therefore, metropole or mainstream (see Table 5.5).

Regarding the example of the *Tohunga Suppression Act 1907* (noted in Table 5.5), Woodard (2014) comments that, 'Although the Act was repealed in 1962, its oppressive ideology still continues' (p. 44), citing the example of the response to the presence of tohunga | Māori healers at a conference of the New Zealand Association of Psychotherapists (NZAP), held in 2013, on a marae. Despite the fact that 80% of conference delegates had availed themselves of some healing from the tohunga during the conference, 'some NZAP members at the Conference voiced concern that the presence of the tohunga was effectively an endorsement (by NZAP) of unregulated healing practice.' (p. 44).

Examples of this in TA include the fact that not enough time is allowed for the interpretation of non-English-speaking candidates in their oral exams which, therefore, disadvantages such candidates.

Table 5.5. Gestures of exclusion and examples of their antithesis and synthesis.

	Thesis	Antithesis	Synthesis
	Gestures of exclusion	*Praxis that is inclusive*	*Biculturalism Multiculturalism*
Examples			
Social/political	Māori models of healing by means of the *Tohunga Suppression Act 1907*...	... which was repealed – in 1962! The reclaiming of Māori models of health	Meta-theoretical work in progress, including the concept of awa whiria | braided rivers (Macfarlane et al., 2011**)**
Psychological	The exclusion of (what was then referred to as) homosexuals from training in psychoanalysis (see Schwartz, 1999)	Anti-oppressive practice, e.g., pink therapy (Davies & Neal, 1996)	Meta-theoretical work in progress
In transactional analysis	In the context of oral exams, that the ITAA gives a set allowance for translation (interpretation)	Work in progress (see Aonuma et al., 2026)...	... which, it is hoped, will contribute to changing the ITAA's policy re interpretation.
	Excluding or cancelling colleagues because of their views about the state registration of psychotherapists, their health choices in response to government mandated vaccinations, and/or their politics	Work in progress	Acceptance of difference, diversity, and pluralistic perspectives

Grand erasure

As Connell (2008) puts it:

> When... empirical knowledge derives wholly or mainly from the metropole, and where the theorist's concerns arise from the problems of metropolitan society, the effect is the erasure of the experience of the majority of human kind from the foundation of social thought. (p. 46)

Reflecting on the notion of terra nullius, meaning empty land (an example noted in Table 5.6), Connell (2008) comments: 'Terra nullius, the coloniser's dream, is a sinister presupposition for social science. It is invoked every time we try to theorise the formation of social institutions and systems from scratch, in a blank space.' (p. 47). She then adds: 'Whenever we see the words "building block" in a treatise of social theory, we should be asking who used to occupy the land.' (p. 47).

By definition, reclaiming erased wisdom and experience means listening to the voices of those who have been – or are still being – oppressed, and appreciating the reality and significance of both personal knowledge (Polanyi, 1962, 1969), and local knowledge(s) and theory – see van der Ploeg (1993), Wynne (1995), Totton (1999), and Yanow (2003). Interestingly, Totton (1999) applies van der Ploeg's ideas about local knowledge to the landscape of psychotherapy and specifically its professionalisation (see also Fay, 2013). This perspective is well-summarised by Connell (2008): 'Since the ground is different, the form of theorising is often different too' (p. xii). So, if we start from that premise, for instance, in this country, we would begin with mātauranga Māori (traditional knowledge) and work from there. For non-Māori, this requires having and knowing your tūrangawaewae (place to stand) and, therefore, having and knowing our positionality (for some of my own examples of which, see Tudor, 2021, in press), and, from that position, engaging respectfully (for an example of guidelines to which, see Tibble, 2015).

Table 5.6. Gestures of grand erasure and examples of their antithesis and synthesis.

	Thesis	Antithesis	Synthesis
	Grand erasure	*Praxis that reclaims erased wisdom and experience*	*Critical theory (e.g., Southern theory)*
Examples			
Social/political	The legal notion – and fiction – of 'terra nullius', a term applied by early settlers to Australia…	… which was overturned by the Australian High Court (in the Mabo judgement) – in 1992!	Local knowledges and theory
Psychological	The psychological impact of erasures such as land confiscation, exclusion from free association, the enforcement of binary ideas about gender, etc.	Social and psychological resistance to such erasures Civil, and psychological disobedience, for example, to scripting (see Steiner, 1974)	a) Moves to equality, i.e., treating people 'the same' b) An emphasis on equity (see Tudor in Tudor & Feltham, 2025) c) Taking sides (as per Steiner, 1975)
In transactional analysis	The treatment of Ukrainian colleagues by some Russian colleagues, and the general and specific lack of response to this from the TA community	Applying principles of autonomy and protection, and being an activist (see Tudor, 2025)	
	The lack of a response to the genocide in Gaza…	… with the exception of an article by Pool (2024)	

Conclusion

In *Principles of Group Treatment* Berne (1966) identifies three kinds of method or techniques: borrowed, opportunistic, and Indigenous. Borrowed methods are those derived from training, while opportunistic methods refer to those that the more experienced therapist tries and integrates, at which point Berne suggests that the group therapist may 'relinquish his clinical orientation in favour of a sociological or even metaphysical interest in the group as a whole' (p. 9). Interestingly, Berne defines Indigenous methods as those that make 'specific use of the inherent richness of the group situation' (p. 9); in other words, the methods – of group analysis and of transactional analysis – derive from the essence or ontology of the group. I think this gives us a basis for drawing on not only the inherent richness of the group but, more broadly, the inherent richness of the social situation such as living and working in bicultural nation, whose social contract rests on *He Whakaputanga* (The Declaration of the Independence of New Zealand) (in 1835) and *Te Tiriti o Waitangi* (The Treaty of Waitangi) (in 1840), which no term-limited politician with no understanding of equity can deny or erase – and the methods that derive from that contract.

In the tauparapara with which I began my speech, I referred to call of the bird, tui, tui, tuia to stitch from above, below, within, and outside. I hope that this paper stimulates the reader's thinking, feeling, sensing, disobedience, criticality, and argument to respond to the call and help find the synthesis from above, below, and outside as well as within to walk and talk seamlessly in the realms of transactional analysis, of social psychology, and of an international community working and talking across national states, while maintaining a deep respect for and grounding in local and Indigenous knowledge and practice.

Whakataukī

Hutia te rito o te harakeke	If you remove the heart of the flax bush
Kei whea te kōmako e kō?	From where will the Bellbird sing?
Kī mai ki ahau	If you say to me
'He aha te mea nui o te ao?'	'What is the most important thing in this world?'
Māku e kī atu	I will reply to you
'He tāngata, he tāngata, he tāngata, hī!'	'It is people, it is people, it is people!'

Tēnā koutou, tēnā koutou, tēnā koutou katoa. Thank you all.

References

Aldridge, B. (2023). Growing well: Providing secure attachment and reconnection to physis through eco-TA and farming. *Transactional Analysis Journal, 53*(1), 53–66. https://doi.org/10.1080/03621537.2022.2152560

Althöfer, G. L., & Tudor, K. (2020). On power. In K. Tudor (Ed.), *Claude Steiner, emotional activist: The life and work of Claude Michel Steiner* (pp. 155–171). Routledge.

Angyal, A. (1941). *Foundations for a science of personality.* Commonwealth Fund.

Animato, P. (2016). *To be or not to be...* [Video]. YouTube. https://www.youtube.com/watch?v=DFRoX1EV3zQ

Aonuma, M., Jacolin, K., Seki, M., & Tudor, K. (2026). You say translation, we say interpretation: Reflections on cross-cultural transactions in transactional analysis. In Barrow, G., Newton, T., & Tudor, K. (Eds.). *Transactional analysis education: Transformation from the periphery.* Karnac.

American Psychiatric Association. (2022). *Diagnostic and statistical manual of mental disorders* (5th ed., text rev.). https://doi.org/10.1176/appi.books.9780890425787

Barnes, G. (1977). Introduction. In G. Barnes (Ed.), *Transactional analysis after Eric Berne: Teachings and practices of three TA schools* (pp. 3–31). Harper's College Press.

Barnes, G. (2003). Introducing Graham Barnes. *Transactional Analysis Journal, 35*(4), 321–323. https://doi.org/10.1177/036215370503500405

Barrow, G., & Marshall, H. (2023). Revisiting ecological transactional analysis: Emerging perspectives. *Transactional Analysis Journal, 53*(1), 7–20. https://doi.org/10.1080/03621537.2023.2152528

Bary, B. B., & Hufford, F. M. (1997). The physiological factor: The 'seventh' advantage to games and its use in treatment planning. *Transactional Analysis Journal, 27*(1), 38–41. https://doi.org/10.1177/036215379702700109

Baskerville, V. (2022). A transcultural and intersectional ego state model of the self: The influence of transcultural and intersectional identity on self and other. *Transactional Analysis Journal, 52*(3), 228–243. https://doi.org/10.1080/03621537.2022.2076398

Batts, V. A. (1982). Modern racism: A TA perspective. *Transactional Analysis Journal, 12*(3), 207–209. https://doi.org/10.1177/036215378201200309

Batts, V. A. (1983). Knowing and changing the cultural script component of racism. *Transactional Analysis Journal, 13*(4), 255–257. https://doi.org/10.1177/036215378301300416

Baute, P. (1979). Intimacy and autonomy are not enough. (Is TA a middle-class tranquilizer?). *Transactional Analysis Journal, 9*(3), 170–173. https://doi.org/10.1177/036215377900900303

Berne, E. L. (1961). Cultural factors in group therapy. *International Mental Health Research Newsletter, 3*, 3–4.

Berne, E. (1963). *The structure and dynamics of organisations and groups.* Grove Press.

Berne, E. (1966). *Principles of group treatment.* Grove Press.

Berne, E. (1968). *Games people play: The psychology of human relationships.* Penguin. (Original work published 1964)

Berne, E. (1969). Editor's page. *Transactional Analysis Bulletin, 8*(29), 7–8.

Berne, E. (1971). Away from a theory of the impact of interpersonal interaction on non-verbal participation. *Transactional Analysis Journal, 1*(1), 6–13. https://10.1177/036215377100100103

Berne, E. (1973) *Sex in human loving.* Penguin. (Original work published 1970)

Berne, E. (1975a). *Transactional analysis in psychotherapy: A systematic individual and social psychiatry.* Souvenir Press. (Original work published 1961)

Berne, E. (1975b). *What do you say after you say hello? The psychology of human destiny*. Penguin. (Original work published 1972)

Berne, E. (1977). Transactional analysis: A new and effective method of group therapy. In P. McCormick (Ed.), *Intuition and ego states: The origins of transactional analysis* (pp. 145–158). Harper & Row. (Original work published 1958)

Berne, T., & Cornell, B. (2004). Remembering Eric Berne: A conversation with Terry Berne. *The Script, 34*(8), 6–7.

Boulton, M. (Ed.). (1976). Social issues [Special issue]. *Transactional Analysis Journal, 6*(1).

Campos, L. P. (2003). Care and maintenance of the tree of transactional analysis. *Transactional Analysis Journal, 33*(2), 115–125. https://doi.org/10.1177/036215370303300204

Campos, L. P. (2010). Redecision therapy and social justice. *Transactional Analysis Journal, 40*(2), 85–94. https://doi.org/10.1177/036215371004000202

Campos, L. P. (2011). Update on transactional analysts for social responsibility. *The Script, 41*(1), 5.

Campos, L. P. (2014). A transactional analytic view of war and peace. *Transactional Analysis Journal, 44*(1), 68–79. https://doi.org/10.1177/0362153714531722

Campos, L. P. (2015). Cultural scripting for forever wars. *Transactional Analysis Journal, 45*(4), 276–288. https://doi.org/10.1177/0362153715607242

Clarkson, P. (1987). The bystander role. *Transactional Analysis Journal, 17*(3), 82–87. https://doi.org/10.1177/036215378701700305

Connell, R. (2008). *Southern theory: The global dynamics of knowledge in social science*. Routledge.

Cornell, W. F., & Hargaden, H. (Eds.). (2020). *The evolution of a relational paradigm in transactional analysis: What's the relationship got to do with it?* Routledge.

Cornell, W., & Monin, S. (Eds.). (2018). Social responsibility in a vengeful world [Special issue]. *Transactional Analysis Journal, 48*(2).

Cornell, W., & Simerly, T. (Eds.). (2004). Gay and lesbian issues [Special issue]. *Transactional Analysis Journal, 34*(2).

Davies, D., & Neal, C. (Eds.). (1996). *Pink therapy: A guide for counsellors and therapists working with lesbian, gay and bisexual clients*. Open University Press.

de Graaf, A., & Monin, S. (2019). Letter from the coeditors. *Transactional Analysis Journal, 49*(2), 67–70. https://doi.org/10.1080/03621537.2019.1577333

Deaconu, D., & Rowland, H. (2021). Letter from the coeditors. *Transactional Analysis Journal, 51*(1), 1–4. https://doi.org/10.1080/03621537.2020.1853366

Dhananjaya, D. (2022). We are the oppressor and the oppressed: The interplay between intrapsychic, interpersonal, and societal intersectionality. *Transactional Analysis Journal, 52*(3), 244–258. https://doi.org/10.1080/03621537.2022.2082031

Dijkman, B., & Geuze, J. (Eds.). (2021). Schools in TA [Special issue]. *TA Magazine, 1* [English edition].

Drye, B. (1980). Psychoanalytic definitions of cure: Beyond contract completion. *Transactional Analysis Journal, 10*(2), 124–130. https://doi.org/10.1177/036215378001000210

Fay, J. (2013). The baby and the bathwater: An unreserved appreciation of Nick Totton's critique of the professionalisation of psychotherapy. *Psychotherapy & Politics International, 11*(1). https://ojs.aut.ac.nz/psychotherapy-politics-international/article/view/399

Foot, J. (2014). Franco Basaglia and the radical psychiatry movement in Italy, 1961–78. *Critical and Radical Social Work, 2*(2), 235–249. https://doi.org/10.1332/204986014X14002292074708

Gabbard, G. O. (2014). *Psychodynamic psychiatry in clinical practice* (5th ed.). American Psychiatric Publishing.

Goulding, M. M., & Goulding, R. (1979). *Changing lives through redecision therapy.* Grove Press.

Grégoire, J. (2007). *Les orientations récentes de l'analyse transactionnelle* [The recent orientations of transactional analysis]. Les Éditions d'Analyse Transactionnelle.

Hargaden, H., Sills, C., Summers, G., Tudor, K., with Lenner, N., & Wehrs, T. (2023). Relationale Zugänge zur Transaktionsanalyse [Relational approaches to transactional analysis]. *Zeitschrift für Transaktionsanalyse, 40*(3), 204–218.

International Transactional Analysis Association. (2020). *Anti-racism statement.* https://web.archive.org/web/20201205071712/https://www.itaaworld.org/sites/default/files/itaa-pdfs/gov-admin-docs/ITAA-Anti-Racism-Statement.pdf

International Transactional Analysis Association. (2025). *Our organisational values.* https://itaaworld.com/about-itaa/

International Transactional Analysis Association. International Board of Certification. (2022). *Certification and examinations handbook.* https://www.itaaworld.org/iboc-certification-examinations-handbook

Jackson, M. (2009). *Once were gardeners: On the scientific method and the 'warrior gene'* [Video]. YouTube. https://www.youtube.com/watch?v=HfAe3Zvgui4&t=314s

Jacobs, A. (1987). Autocratic power. *Transactional Analysis Journal, 17*(3), 59–71. https://doi.org/10.1177/036215378701700303

Jacobs, A. (1990). Nationalism. *Transactional Analysis Journal, 20*(4), 221–228. https://doi.org/10.1177/036215379002000403

Jacobs, A. (1991). Autocracy: Groups, organizations, nations, and players. *Transactional Analysis Journal, 21*(4), 199–206. https://doi.org/10.1177/036215379402400108

Jacobs, A. (1994). Theory as ideology: Reparenting and thought reform. *Transactional Analysis Journal, 24*(1), 39–55. https://doi.org/10.1177/036215379402400108

James, J. (Ed.). (1983). Cultural scripts [Special issue]. *Transactional Analysis Journal, 13*(4).

Kahler, T., with Capers, H. (1974). The miniscript. *Transactional Analysis Journal, 4*(1), 26–42. https://doi.org/10.1177/036215377400400110

Karpman, S. (1968). Fairy tales and script drama analysis. *Transactional Analysis Bulletin, 1–9,* 51–56.

Karpman, S. B. (1981). The politics of theory. *Transactional Analysis Journal, 11*(1), 68–76. https://doi.org/10.1177/036215378101100114

Landaiche, N. M., III. (2020). *Groups in transactional analysis, object relations, and family systems studying ourselves in collective life.* Routledge.

Lee, A. (2001). *Schools of change* [Handout]. Privately circulated manuscript.

Levin, P. (1977). Women's oppression. The women's journal [Special issue]. *Transactional Analysis Journal, 7*(1), 87–92. https://doi.org/10.1177/036215377700700121

Levin, P., & Fryer, R. (1980). Coming together: The evolution of women in ITAA. *The Script, 10*(9), 1–2.

Lewin, K. (1952). *Field theory in social science.* Harper & Row.

Lingiardi, V., & McWilliams, N. (2017). *Psychodynamic diagnostic manual* [PDM2]. Guilford.

Little, R. (2005). Integrating psychoanalytic understandings in the deconfusion of primitive Child ego states. *Transactional Analysis Journal, 35*(2), 132–146. https://doi.org/10.1177/036215370503500204

Macfarlane, A., Blampied, N., & Macfarlane, S. (2011). Blending the clinical and the cultural: A framework for conducting formal psychological assessment in bicultural settings. *New Zealand Journal of Psychology, 40*(2), 5–15. https://www.psychology.org.nz/journal-archive/NZJP-Macfarlane1.pdf

Massey, R. (1996). Transactional analysis as a social psychology. *Transactional Analysis Journal, 26*(1), 91–99. https://doi.org/10.1177/036215379602600114

Massey, R. F. (2007). Reexamining social psychiatry as a foundational framework for transactional analysis: Considering a social-psychological perspective. *Transactional Analysis Journal, 37*(1), 51–79. https://doi.org/10.1177/036215370703700109

McLean, B., & Cornell, W. (Eds.). (2017). Gender, sexuality, and identity [Special issue]. *Transactional Analysis Journal, 47*(4).

Minikin, K. (2018). Radical relational psychiatry: Toward a democracy of mind and people. *Transactional Analysis Journal, 48*(2), 111–125. https://doi.org/10.1080/03621537.2018.1429287

Minikin, K. (2024). *Radical-relational perspectives in transactional analysis psychotherapy: Oppression, alienation, reclamation.* Routledge.

Minikin, K., & Rowland, H. (2022). Letter from the coeditors: Systemic oppression: What part do we play? *Transactional Analysis Journal, 52*(3), 175–177. https://doi.org/10.1080/03621537.2022.2080263

Moiso, C. (1985). Ego states and transference. *Transactional Analysis Journal, 15*(3), 194–201. https://doi.org/10.1177/036215378501500302

Moiso, C. (1995). The commitments. *Transactional Analysis Journal, 25*(1), 75–76. https://doi.org/10.1177/036215379502500118

Moiso, C., & Novellino, M. (2000). An overview of the psychodynamic school of transactional analysis and its epistemological foundations. *Transactional Analysis Journal, 30*(3), 182–187. https://doi.org/10.1177/036215370003000302

Monin, S., & Cornell, W. (2015). Conflict: Intrapsychic, interpersonal, and societal [Special issue]. *Transactional Analysis Journal, 45*(5).

Naughton, M., & Tudor, K. (2006). Being white. *Transactional Analysis Journal, 36*(2), 159–171. https://doi.org/10.1177/036215370603600208

Novellino, M. (2003). Transactional psychoanalysis. *Transactional Analysis Journal, 33*(3), 223–230. https://doi.org/10.1177/036215370303300304

Novellino, M. (2005). Transactional psychoanalysis: Epistemological foundations. *Transactional Analysis Journal, 35*(2), 157–172. https://doi.org/10.1177/036215370503500206

Novellino, M. (2010). The demon and sloppiness: From Berne to transactional psychoanalysis. *Transactional Analysis Journal, 40*(3–4), 288–294. https://doi.org/10.1177/036215371004000313

Novellino, M., & Moiso, C. (1990). The psychodynamic approach to transactional analysis. *Transactional Analysis Journal, 20*(3), 187–192. https://doi.org/10.1177/036215379002000308

Novey, T. (Ed.). (1996). Integrative psychotherapy [Special Issue]. *Transactional Analysis Journal, 26*(4).

Pandya, A. (2024). System imago: A new perspective on leadership and power. *Transactional Analysis Journal, 54*(3), 216–230. https://doi.org/10.1080/03621537.2024.2359287

Polanyi, M. (1962). *Personal knowledge: Towards a post-critical philosophy.* University of Chicago.

Polanyi, M. (1969). *Knowing and being* (M. Green, Ed.). University of Chicago Press.

Pool, J. (2024). Thoughts about Gaza. Letter to the editor. *The Script, 54*(7), 3–4.

Price, D. A. (1978). Social-psychological roots of transactional analysis: Exchange as symbolic interaction. *Transactional Analysis Journal, 8*(3), 212–215. https://doi.org/10.1177/036215377800800306

Richert, L. (2014). 'Therapy means political change, not peanut butter': American radical psychiatry, 1968–1975. *Social History of Medicine, 27*(1), 104–121. https://doi.org/10.1093/shm/hkt072

Richert, L. (2019). *Break on through: Radical psychiatry and the American counterculture.* The MIT Press.

Rivers, S. (2024). *Karangarua: Unity through diversity in relationship.* https://www.taaanz.nz/post/karangarua-unity-th

Robcis, C. (2021) *Disalienation: Politics, philosophy, and radical psychiatry in postwar France.* The University of Chicago Press.

Rogers, C. R. (1951). *Client-centered therapy.* Constable.

Rogers, C. R. (1959). A theory of therapy, personality and interpersonal relationships, as developed in the client-centred framework. In S. Koch (Ed.), *Psychology: A study of science, Vol. 3: Formulation of the person and the social context* (pp. 184–256). McGraw-Hill.

Rotondo, A. (2020). Rethinking contracts: The heart of Eric Berne's transactional analysis. *Transactional Analysis Journal, 50*(3), 236–250. https://doi.org/10.1080/03621537.2020.1771032

The Rough Times Staff. (1973). *Rough times* [J. Agel, Producer]. Ballantine Books.

Roy, B. (2007). Radical psychiatry: An approach to personal and political change. In E. Aldarondo (Ed.), *Advancing social justice through clinical practice* (pp. 65–90). Lawrence Erlbaum Associates Publishers.

Schwartz, J. (1999). *Cassandra's daughter: A history of psychoanalysis*. Routledge.

Shadbolt, C. (2004). Homophobia and gay affirmative transactional analysis. *Transactional Analysis Journal, 34*(2), 113–125. https://doi.org/10.1177/036215370403400204

Shmukler, D. (2001). Reflections on transactional analysis in the context of contemporary relational approaches. *Transactional Analysis Journal, 31*(2), 94–102. https://doi.org/10.1177/036215370103100204

Shweder, R. A. (1990). Cultural psychology—What is it? In J. W. Stigler, R. A. Shweder, & G. Herdt (Eds.), *Cultural psychology* (pp. 27–66). Cambridge University Press.

Sills, C., & Tudor, K. (2025, April 25th). *Relational transactional analyses, plural* [Workshop]. Auckland, Aotearoa New Zealand.

Steiner, C. (1974). *Scripts people live: Transactional analysis of life scripts*. Grove Press.

Steiner, C. (1975). Radical psychiatry: Principles. In C. Steiner (Ed.), *Readings in radical psychiatry* (pp. 9–16). Grove Press.

Steiner, C. M. (1979). The pig Parent. *Transactional Analysis Journal, 9*(1), 26–37. https://doi.org/10.1177/036215377900900106

Steiner, C. M. (1981). *The other side of power*. Grove Press.

Steiner, C. M. (2010). Eric Berne's politics: 'The great pyramid'. *Transactional Analysis Journal, 40*(3–4), 212–216. https://doi.org/10.1177/036215371004000306

Steiner, C. (2020). Confessions of a psychomechanic: Excerpts on radical psychiatry. In K. Tudor (Ed.), *Claude Steiner, emotional activist: The life and work of Claude Michel Steiner* (pp. 105–115). Routledge. (Original work privately circulated 2008)

Stuthridge, J., Moeke-Maxwell, T., Orange, D., Woodard, W., & Younger, J. (2012). On open tents, beaches and cultural divides: A panel discussion. *Ata: Journal of Psychotherapy Aotearoa New Zealand, 16*(2), 179-200. https://doi.org/10.9791/ajpanz.2012.18

Summerton, O. (1985). The game pentagon. *Tasi Darshan, 5*(4), 39–51.

Summerton, O. (1992). Game analysis in two planes. *Transactional Analysis Journal, 22*(4), 210–215. https://doi.org/10.1177/036215379202200403

Summerton, O. (1993). Games in organizations. *Transactional Analysis Journal, 23*(2), 87–103. https://doi.org/10.1177/036215379302300206

Talbott, J. A. (1974). Radical psychiatry: An examination of the issues. *The American Journal of Psychiatry, 131*(2), 121–128. https://doi.org/10.1176/ajp.131.2.121

Tangolo, A. E., & Massi, A. (2022). *Group therapy in transactional analysis: Theory through practice*. Routledge.

Tapiata, J. (1980). *Whakarongo ake au*. New Zealand Folk Song.
https://folksong.org.nz/tui_tuia/

Tibble, A. (2015). *The five 'wai's for Māori engagement*. https://www.linkedin.com/pulse/5-wais-m%C4%81ori-engagement-atawhai-tibble/

Tohunga Suppression Act 1907.
https://www.nzlii.org/nz/legis/hist_act/tsa19077ev1907n13353/

Totton, N. (1999). The baby and the bathwater: 'Professionalisation' in psychotherapy and counseling. *British Journal of Guidance and Counselling, 27*(3), 313–324.

Trautmann, R. (Ed.). (1984). Nuclear disarmament [Special issue]. *Transactional Analysis Journal, 14*(4).

Tudor, K. (1999). 'I'm OK, You're OK – and They're OK': Therapeutic relationships in transactional analysis. In C. Feltham (Ed.), *Understanding the counselling relationship* (pp. 90–119). Sage.

Tudor, K. (2003). The neopsyche: The integrating adult ego state. In C. Sills & H. Hargaden (Eds.), *Ego states* (pp. 201–231). Worth Publishing.

Tudor, K. (2008, December 8th). *L'analisi transazionale o è radicale o non è analisi transazionale* [Transactional analysis is radical or it is not transactional analysis] [Keynote speech]. Annual Conference of IAT/AIAT, Torino, Italy.

Tudor, K. (2010). Transactional analysis: A little liberal, a little conservative, and a little radical. *The Psychotherapist, 46*, 17–20.

Tudor, K. (2011). There ain't no license that protects: Bowen theory and the regulation of psychotherapy. *Transactional Analysis Journal, 41*(2), 154–161.
https://doi.org/10.1177/036215371104100212

Tudor, K. (2015). 疎外,異なる立場の専門家、精神科医 精神病理学への批判的かつ異文化的視点 [Alienation, aliens, and alienists: A critical and cross-cultural perspective on psychopathology] [Keynote speech]. Association of Japanese Clinical Psychology, Yokohama, Japan.
http://www.ajcp.info/archive/33/000jikko0/data/20140825a_02.pdf

Tudor, K. (2017). Transactional analysis is radical or it is not transactional analysis (2008). In K. Tudor *Conscience and critic: The selected works of Keith Tudor* (pp. 125–139). Routledge. (Original work published 2008)

Tudor, K. (2018). *Psychotherapy: A critical examination*. PCCS Books.

Tudor, K. (2020). Transactional analysis and politics: A critical review. Transactional analysis and politics [Special issue]. *Psychotherapy and Politics International, 18*(3), Article e1555. http://dx.doi.org/10.1002/ppi.1555

Tudor, K. (2021). He tangata Tiriti tatou. In *20/20 vision, 2020* (pp. 1–9). Tuwhera Open Access Books. https://ojs.aut.ac.nz/tuwhera_open_monographs/catalog/book/6

Tudor, K. (2023). War: A transactional group analysis. *Transactional Analysis Journal, 53*(4), 306–322. https://doi.org/10.1080/03621537.2023.2251837

Tudor, K. (2025). *Transactional analysis proper – and improper: Selected and new papers*. Routledge.

Tudor, K, (in press). Crouch, touch, pause, and engage: Positioning the researcher in cross-cultural research. In K. Tudor & J. Wyatt (Eds.), *Qualitative research approaches for psychotherapy: Further reflexivity, methodology, and criticality*. Routledge.

Tudor, K., & Cornell, W. (Eds.). (2020). Transactional analysis and politics [Special issue]. *Psychotherapy and Politics International, 18*(3).

Tudor, K., & Feltham, C. (2025). Competing ideologies in and about psychotherapy. *Psychotherapy and Politics International, 23*(1), 1–19. https://doi.org/10.24135/ppi.v23i1.05

Tudor, K., Green, E., & Brett, E. (2022). Critical whiteness: A transactional analysis of a systemic oppression. *Transactional Analysis Journal, 52*(3), 193–208. https://doi.org/10.1080/03621537.2022.2076394

Tudor, K., & Summers, G. (2014). *Co-creative transactional analysis: Papers, dialogues, responses, and developments*. Karnac Books.

Tudor, K., & Widdowson, M. (2008). From client process to therapeutic relating: A critique of the process model and personality adaptations. *Transactional Analysis Journal, 38*(3), 218–232. https://doi.org/10.1177/036215370803800304

Tudor, K., & Worrall, M. (2006). *Person-centred therapy: A clinical philosophy*. Routledge.

United States of America Transactional Analysis Association. (2023). *Project TA 101: Personal tools for social transformation*. https://www.usataa.org/circles-of-interest/social-justice-circle/project-ta-101 /

van Beekum, S. (2006). The relational consultant. *Transactional Analysis Journal, 36*(4), 318–329. https://doi.org/10.1177/036215370603600406

van der Ploeg, J. D. (1993). Potatoes and knowledge. In M. Hobart (Ed.), *An anthropological critique of development: The growth of ignorance* (pp. 209–227). Routledge.

Ware, P. (1983). Personality adaptations: Doors to therapy. *Transactional Analysis Journal, 13*(1), 11–19. https://doi.org/10.1177/036215378301300104

Wilson, J., & Kalina, I. (1978). The splinter chart. *Transactional Analysis Journal, 8*(3), 200–205. https://doi.org/10.1177/036215377800800303

Woodard, W. (2014). Politics, psychotherapy, and the 1907 Tohunga Suppression Act. *Psychotherapy & Politics International, 12*(1). https://ojs.aut.ac.nz/psychotherapy-politics-international/article/view/429

Woollams, S., & Brown, M. (1978). *Transactional analysis*. Huron Valley Institute Press.

Wynne, B. (1995). May the sheep safely graze? A reflexive view of the expert-lay knowledge divide. In S. Lash, B. Szerszynski, & B. Wynne (Eds.), *Risk, environment and modernity: Towards a new ecology* (pp. 44–83). Sage Publications.

Yanow, D. (2003). Accessing local knowledge. In M. A. Hajer & H. Wagenaar (Eds.), *Deliberative policy analysis: Understanding governance in the network society* (pp. 228–246). Cambridge University Press.

Zalcman, M. (1990). Game analysis and racket analysis: Overview, critique, and future developments. *Transactional Analysis Journal, 20*(1), 4–19. https://doi.org/10.1177/036215379002000102

Karangarua: Unity through diversity in relationship – A personal story

Bev Gibbons

Abstract

In this paper the author tells the story of her personal experience of the international TA Conference in Aotearoa New Zealand, and of the karangarua that she was part of and contributed to. It reflects on the author's experience of being welcomed and of stepping into that welcome and all that it brought to her.

The author relates how this experience brought questions relating to her history as a North Yorkshire born British citizen and what that, and she, might represent in terms of the British colonial past. She reflects on the deep intrapsychic and interpersonal process emerging from her experience of being different; on questions arising for her given the cultural mantle her past lay over her; and how she was met and stood in a dual relationship between her own culture and the Māori culture and people.

The international TA Conference 2024 was the first live TA conference to be held in Aotearoa New Zealand for 15 years and was the reason I and my husband decided to take a 4-week holiday to the North Island. I was excited!

The Conference theme was Karangarua – Unity Through Diversity in Relationship; this title in te reo Māori (the Māori language) acknowledges the significance of the karanga or exchange of calls that forms part of the pōwhiri, a Māori welcoming ceremony, and also refers to people related through two different lines, and those standing in a double relationship (TAAANZ, 2024). This spirit wove through our 3 days together via the open-hearted sharing and showing by our Māori colleagues of Māori cultural practice and wisdom. I invite you into my experience, which includes in-the-moment snapshots and also reflections gathered since my time at the Conference. There was so much learning for me, and my frame of reference was blown open many times, in this truly humbling, disturbing, deeply contactful, warm, and goodwill-imbued experience.

My dear friend and colleague Bèrit and I headed out for the Conference on a bright sunny and breezy November day, walking down into the centre of Wellington from our Airbnb perched at the top of the city. As it happened, we had arrived in Wellington a day after a 30,000 strong protest march to the nation's houses of parliament in the city. The Hīkoi mō te Tiriti (Māori for 'March for the Treaty') were hīkoi protests in New Zealand against the *Treaty Principles Bill*, proposed by the ACT Party, that occurred from the 10th of November to the 19th of November 2024. The bill would redefine the principles of the *Treaty of Waitangi* and change the Māori rights protected in it (Watson, 2024).

British colonisation of Aotearoa New Zealand began in 1840 with the signing of the *Tiriti o Waitangi*, known in English as the *Treaty of Waitangi*. This treaty signed between the British crown and Māori leaders was a contract setting out a partnership agreement in which the crown would respect, uphold, and protect the rights of the Māori people to enable peaceful living alongside pākehā – white British settlers (Orange, n.d.). The exact meaning and interpretation of this historic document in Māori differed from the English meaning, and, reportedly has long been the subject of debate. In more recent times this difference in understanding of the meaning of the Tiriti has been the cause of political struggle with Māori people feeling that the key goal of true partnership and power-sharing was not being upheld.

With this potent energy swirling around us, we wound our way through wide streets of Wellington, past many tempting shops and finally finding Taranaki Wharf and the Te Raukura building, which houses Whare Tāpere, an events and entertainment space which hosted the Conference. Te Raukura is of special significance to descendants from Taranaki iwi of Te Atiawa, Taranaki, Ngāti Ruanui, Ngāti Tama, and Ngāti Mutunga. I include this connection here as a mark of respect, of which there will be more later. The building is under the protection of Rongo, the god of Peace, and 'it is in this atmosphere, under a cloak of peace, that people interact with one another and with the spirits of their ancestors.' (Te Raukura, n.d., p. 1).

I immediately noticed that most, if not all, the staff in the building were Māori, which brought me a sense of warmth and wanting to meet, particularly helped by the friendly energy I felt. I also noticed a sense of anxiety that I might 'get something wrong' and do something unknowingly disrespectful, look stupid, and show my ignorance, becoming the patronising or entitled white person, or pākehā in the Māori language. The tingle of a fearful sense that I somehow wouldn't be able to belong fizzed in me… this was uncomfortable, a shift in power dynamic that jolted me to think about this tiny experience of being different. I decided, right then and there, that I would hold particularly open, observant space in myself and ask at every opportunity, no matter how clunky or awkward I felt.

We Conference delegates all gathered on the wharf side in front of Te Raukura around the magnificent statue of the explorer Kupe, his wife, and their companion, showing them as they get their first sight of Aotearoa. Kupe, an important ancestor to the Māori people is credited with being the first Polynesian to discover the islands of Aotearoa New Zealand over a thousand years ago. The building we met in includes architectural design elements to symbolically represent a ceremonial waka (canoe) linked to Kupe and the voyaging traditions of the Pacific peoples who arrived at Aotearoa in tribal canoes.

The pōwhiri then began. This is a significant and sacred ceremony in Māori culture, serving as a formal process of welcoming visitors and allowing hosts and guests to establish mutual respect and understanding. The pōwhiri begins with the karanga, the first of the eight steps of the process, which is the call to visitors to welcome them to the marae – a communal and sacred space – and is performed by women (Metawhenua, 2025). We responded to the call by quietly entering the building and taking our seats. The pōwhiri process continued with speeches, responses, and singing together. The pōwhiri concluded with food and drinks for all to share, and time and space for the final step – whakawhanaungatanga (building relationships).

I walked around the open, airy space trying delicious food, noticing snatches of animated conversations, laughter, friendship… welcome. I enjoyed the experience of belonging via the shared connection of TA alongside my awareness of and interest in the differences between me and my colleagues from Aotearoa New Zealand and all over the world. As I threaded through people, I held in my hand a stone I had brought with me from my home, in North Yorkshire in the UK. The idea had come to me, when preparing for the trip to Aotearoa New Zealand to take with me a piece of my land to give to someone I met there. The stone had also lived in my therapy room for several years, part of a bowl of natural treasures that I used with people in creative work together. I had no idea who I would pass this stone onto; it was someone I hadn't yet encountered. My sense was that I would intuitively know when I met them. It felt strange and mysterious to have had a sense of waiting to meet this person, whom I hadn't met so far after three weeks in Aotearoa New Zealand carrying the stone around with me.

This small piece of my homeland began to take on more significance for me as I witnessed and learned about the Māori pepeha. The traditional Māori introduction, the pepeha, is an identity statement in which the person who is introducing themselves first honours the features of the land of their birth – mountain and water, then the ancestral areas – town or city, then community, tribe, family, and finally self and one's own name.

The pepeha is about connection and belonging, and I found it very profound each time I heard and witnessed someone introducing themselves this way. It struck me as an offering of one's deep roots and history in which to contextualise and anchor in the places and people from which you come as you go towards others, and all that they have come from, and bring with them. The pepeha invited me to deeply account for my lands and landscapes, my ancestral places and tribes; the context and system first, the 'we' that I came from honoured and introduced before I step forward with my name. A Māori colleague invited me and others to introduce ourselves in the ritual of the pepeha, and it was powerful! My Yorkshire cultural conditioning of not making myself overly important, or 'being a clever clogs' was challenged as I took the space to share all that came before me, all that is in me and made me. To share all of that gave me a sense of pride and also exposure. I pushed through it, like pushing through a prickly hedge to find the reward of new land to be explored on the other side, feeling the intimacy of being much more known than in any introduction of myself I had ever done.

As I write this, I remember the feel of that stone from my homeland in my hands on that first day at the Conference, warm and comforting in my palm, reminding me of the sea, the beach, the views, my grandparents, and my North Yorkshire roots. The stone came from a beach in Whitby, a town on the coast, and the town where Captain James Cook – who was born at nearby Great Ayton – served his apprenticeship as a seaman, and where the ship Endeavour was built. The Endeavour was the ship from which Cook, its captain, first sighted Aotearoa in September 1769 (Gibson, 2022).

Like me, Cook was born and raised in North Yorkshire in England. In an article about Cook his Yorkshire soul and being is reflected on: 'One cannot underplay that Yorkshire makes for tough, hardy people with adventurous spirits' (Gibson, 2022, para. 30). This resonates deeply with me. We are tough, plain-speaking, warm-hearted folk who don't back down from a challenge. My land, my community, my places, and my kin have strong connection to Cook, the man whose mapping of the land of Aotearoa paved the way for its colonisation. This realisation thumped into me as I walked, being part of the whakawhanaungatanga and finding connections. Was Cook a hero or a villain? He was an explorer who mapped Aotearoa New Zealand and brought its existence to the awareness of the British crown and government who went on to colonise it. I wonder what story he would have told, what his narrative and 'spin' would have been, and the stories and narratives of the Māori people at that time.

On the second day of the Conference I needed some printing doing for a workshop I was running on the subject of intuition. I was directed to the bar to find someone who would be able to help. As I waited, a young Māori staff member was cheerfully stocking the bar and said into the space, with a huge smile, 'Feeling proud to be Māori today'. Our eyes met and held for a moment. I smiled back. I felt that fierce, joyful pride, I really did, and it made my arms break out in goosebumps. It plugged me into a recent learning gathered in my research for an article I've just finished writing, about the nature of intuition. My research took me on a voyage around different belief systems and cultural frames of reference, including Māori. Māori beliefs recognise that dynamic energies and essences flow between humans that pass on, travel to, and traverse through to other people. In this belief system a person's spirit energy is called hau, described as 'a person's spiritual essence, [which] can intertwine and mesh with another's hau in a reciprocal exchange of life-energies' (Dell, 2021, p. 4). This exchange is described through the term rongo, meaning 'to know or get to know through, not only hearing but also by touching, feeling, seeing, intuition or any other means' (Smith, 2000, cited in Dell, 2021, p. 4).

When I read this, something was mirrored back to me; I felt met in the words of the author and her culture that believe in the twine-ment of spiritual flow between people as part of their interactions, the 'reciprocal exchange of life-energies' – what a beautiful phrase. In the article I'd wondered if we might think of 'rongo' as the human capacity of intuition that connects with and 'tastes' the other's 'hau', activating the potential for connection of the two or more full bodyminds – i.e., the intricately entwined single complex systems that integrates mind, brain, and embodiment.

Reflecting later I realised that Rongo was also the name of the Māori god of peace, the protector of the Conference building.

The first workshop I attended was a touching and deeply interesting and contactful experience that unfolded the presenter's personal story alongside her sharing of the Māori art of tukutuku. This is a form of weaving that requires great collaboration to create beautiful decorative wall panels, using, traditionally, long strands, called whenu, in Māori, of haraeke, or flax, to use the English word, to create panels within a frame of strong poles made from raupō (bullrush in English).

These panels are then woven together. The work is done by people working in pairs from either side of the tukutuku frame. There was a large frame set up in the workshop space and we participants were invited to contribute to the weaving. I stepped forward, pushing myself out of my comfort zone and into the wide wastes beyond, to take my place at the frame, in front of the rows of participants.

Here again I felt clunky and exposed, the one who didn't have the cultural script for this. Then I looked through the criss-cross of leaves and grasses already woven across the tall and wooden frame and could see glimpses of Māori wāhine – women – some of whom had led us in the pōwhiri, on the other side of it. I was encouraged, welcomed, and patiently guided by a Māori woman with kind and beautiful brown eyes. We looked at each other through the frame, not able to see much of each other and completely new to each other and got to work together with no further ceremony. We immediately had close contact with each other's hands and fingers as we worked together from each side of the frame to push the stems and strands back and forth in the traditional way.

Reflecting later, the idea of 'rongo' came to mind – a co-created process of feeling into each other, with an exchange of our 'hau', our life-energies, as we stood close together, touching hands and with the tukutuku frame between us. My bodymind memory is of her eyes; the feel of the grasses; the tall, wide frame between us; concentrating and being guided kindly; lots of laughter. Wāhine/women coming together as we have since the dawn of time – is this a form of karangarua/double relationship? I felt the sense of sisterhood I very often get when I'm part of a group of women who come together to complete a task. The tendency of women to share a process of collaboration rather than competition goes across cultures, classes, social structures – when we allow it. The Māori pepeha ritual had opened something in me. As I stood fumblingly collaborating with my sister-in-weaving my mind went to the Yorkshire Dales villages of my ancestors, and the women who would have worked together on farms, on the land, and in textile mills.

When I stepped away from the tukutuku frame to invite someone else to take my place I looked around the frame to see the woman who had worked with me and taught me. She had such a warm, kind face, the lower part of which was decorated with a traditional moko (tattoo) kauae (chin). My new friend introduced herself as Te Amokura and she later told me that moko kauae is only used for moko worn on chin or jaw of wāhine, and that men (tāne) wear mataora on their faces (any part of their face). Tā moko is worn on any other part of the body depicting ancestral stories and events. Kauae (women) and mataora (men) depicts whakapapa (genealogy; who a person descends from) as well as their position and role in their family. Mataora and kauae are reservedly for those of Māori descent only.

Reading further for this piece I learned that the moko kauae is a birthright of a Māori wahine, through which she can 'assert her identity, femininity, whakapapa and the mana of her iwi (tribe)' (Content Catnip, 2021, para. 7). It was traditionally reserved 'for Māori women with mana (high status and power) and older women of experience and

95

achievement. Although in a contemporary view, this can be seen as the birthright of all Māori wahine regardless of their age, experience or achievements in life' (para. 2).

How fantastic is this! And, also culturally challenging to my British frame of reference, in which tattoos on the face had long been considered controversial, unfavourable, and often not something tattooists would agree to undertake. Only in more recent years, when tattooing has experienced a wonderful renaissance – in the UK anyway – and tattoo artistry has evolved into something truly amazing to behold, has facial and head tattooing begun to appear much more, although still not mainstream.

Tattoos were my second point of connection with Te Amokura. I'd had a full arm tattoo of a coiling dragon done on my right arm whilst staying in Whitianga two weeks earlier, acting very much against my deeply ingrained scripting, received from my parents and grandparents and wider Yorkshire communities, which said that tattoos on women signified low morals and on men violence, criminality, seamanship, or gang membership. Breaking out of the bindings of this oppressive and alienating script has been life-changing for me. For so long I felt the shame of being 'too much, too dogged, too intense, too weird' – until, after a series of domino moments, I took the permission to be fully me. My dragon tattoo is my soul symbol of my yang, my fire-spirit, my power, my force. Not so far away from the symbolic meaning of the moko kauae.

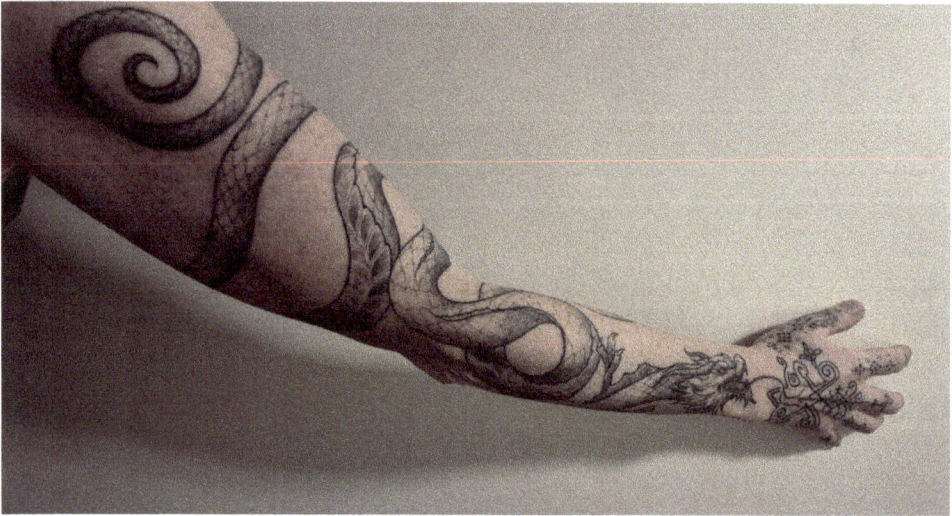

Figure 6.1. My dragon tattoo. (Photo by author)

With my Whitby stone warm and solid in my pocket I went into co-presenting a workshop with Bèrit. I was feeling a mixture of emotions: exposure, vulnerability, nervousness, and uncertainty, and with the shadow of the potential for shame hovering alongside excitement, curiosity, and a bubbling sense of the joyful energy of the Conference.

We were quite blown away by the number of people who joined us, and we had a wonderful experience with a rich cultural diversity of participants both from Aotearoa New Zealand and far beyond. As was the ritual of the Conference we were formally presented with greenstone pendants as a thank you at the end of the workshop. The person presenting the pendants to Bèrit and me was Te Amokura. As everyone was leaving the room, Te Amokura came to us and asked if she could do a ritual with us to bless the greenstone. We stood with our arms wrapped around each other as she spoke some words. She explained that the stone, also known as pounamu, is sacred to Māori people, and that it absorbs negative energy and needs to be cleansed regularly by rain or sea water. I learned from another Māori colleague that gifting pounamu is a deeply meaningful tradition within Māori culture, often used to show respect, love, and that the traditional way to receive the stone is to be given it as a gift.

As we three walked out of the workshop space to join the throng of people enjoying refreshments, I knew I had found the person who my Whitby stone belonged with. I put my hand on Te Amokura's arm and said, 'I have something for you too'.

My writing down of my Conference story relates my personal experience of karangarua that I was part of and contributed to. It reflects on my experience of being welcomed and of stepping into that welcome and all that it brought to me. I stood in dual relationship with, in particular, a new culture, the Māori culture. In this duality I brought my history and what that might represent in terms of the British colonial past, and also as me, myself – Bev – with a keen sense of how I might seem to others, how I would find a way to bring myself into relationship with a different culture. I was also challenged – within myself and by the invitations that came to me – to revisit my relationship with my roots, my heritage, my mountain, my rivers and seas, and my ancestors. I also stood in dual relationship with Te Amokura. We are two women who had points of deep contact and found surprising similarities between us. At the same time, we live on lands at opposite ends of the earth with vastly different tribal and national histories. This is a story of transformative learning and cross-cultural connection, of what emerged through the exchange of calls.

Acknowledgement

My thanks to Te Amokura Griggs for her kind guidance on the Māori cultural references in this paper.

References

Content Catnip. (2021, April 9). *Mana wahine: The female moko in Māori culture.* https://contentcatnip.com/2021/04/09/mana-wahine-the-female-moko-in-maori-culture/

Dell, K. (2021). Rongomātau – 'Sensing the knowing': An indigenous methodology utilising sensed knowledge from the researcher. *International Journal of Qualitative Methods, 20.* https://doi.org/10.1177/16094069211062411

Gibson, D. (2022). *James Cook's Whitby years, 1746–1755.* Captain Cook Society. https://www.captaincooksociety.com/cooks-voyages/early-voyages/whitby-voyages/james-cook-s-whitby-years-1746-1755

Metawhenua. (2025). *Māramatanga: 8 steps in a basic pōwhiri process.* https://metawhenua.com/blog/maramatanga-8-steps-in-a-basic-pwhiri-process

Orange, C. (n.d.). *Te Tiriti o Waitangi – the Treaty of Waitangi.* Te Ara The Encyclopedia of New Zealand. https://teara.govt.nz/en/te-tiriti-o-waitangi-the-treaty-of-waitangi/print

Te Raukura. (n.d.). *History.* https://www.taaanz.nz/_files/ugd/a38528_e82cee3c1377491ca9a1890385162987.pdf

Transactional Analysis Association of Aotearoa New Zealand. (2024). *2024 international conference. Wellington, Aotearoa New Zealand, 21st–23rd November.* https://www.taaanz.nz/2024-international-conference

Watson, K. (2024, November 19). *Thousands flock to NZ capital in huge Māori protests.* BBC News. https://www.bbc.com/news/articles/cdd0qr9mv9mo

Paper 7

Exploring we-ness across cultures: Our we-ness and your we-ness

Mariko Seki and Masumi Aonuma

Abstract

Two Japanese participants, trusting in the Transactional Analysis (TA) community in New Zealand, conducted a workshop on the above theme with the aim of mutual growth. This paper describes their workshop. This paper explores our path of co-creation – from the decision to attend and present at the New Zealand Conference to the experiences that broadened our perspectives, clarified our objectives, and helped us learn to express ourselves in the language of TA. We hope that presenting this journey in chronological order offers the most meaningful way to convey how we, as both Japanese and TA members, connected with the Conference theme, *karangarua*.

This paper presents our original insights into the central principle of co-creative transactional analysis, 'we-ness', based on three important concepts that have greatly shaped the history of transactional analysis: 'group culture', derived from Berne's (1963) ego state model; Drego's (2006) concept of the 'Cultural Parent'; and the 'integrating Adult' concept of co-creative transactional analysis (Summers & Tudor, 2000; Tudor, 2003). Building on these foundations, the authors presented concrete examples to discuss 'we-ness' as a collectivist value in Japanese culture. These everyday specific examples engaged workshop participants and encouraged reflection on their own cultural frames of reference. In their presentations, the authors asserted their own views; that, based on mutual respect, transforming cultural scripts requires attentiveness to relational needs and critical awareness. The authors then presented the expression '自他共栄' (jita kyōei) as a Japanese manifestation of 'we-ness' to the audience. The workshop became a space for mutual learning, and the sense of dissonance we had felt regarding differences in 'we-ness' prior to the presentation significantly transformed into a sense of connection. This demonstrated how TA holds promise for co-creating an international 'we-ness' that transcends cultural differences.

Background: Meeting friends from across the sea

In early spring 2024, we received information about a conference from the Transactional Analysis Association of Aotearoa New Zealand (TAAANZ). The theme of the Conference, '*Karangarua*: Unity through Diversity in Relationship', was accompanied by the following explanation:

The themes of the Conference invite us to experience, think about, and discuss how we do this – meeting, greeting, and seating – in a way that is respectful of both hosts and guests, while also acknowledging difference and diversity. (TAAANZ, 2024, para. 3)

These few lines seemed to have been written especially for us, living in Japan, some 8,830 kilometres away from New Zealand as the crow flies. We trusted these words and decided to participate in the Conference with hope in our hearts. However, at the same time, we were faced with a mountain of concerns.

At first, we had to struggle with the application process. The primary language in Japan is Japanese, and although basic English is provided as part of compulsory schooling, there are few opportunities to use English in everyday life. As a result, many Japanese people find it difficult to communicate in English when participating in international activities.

We were no exception, and we felt uneasy about the application process in English. However, strangely enough, by working together to complete this difficult task, our motivation to participate in the Conference grew. It felt like two Japanese people in a small rowboat, desperately trying to cross the wide ocean (Figure 7.1).

Figure 7.1. The authors attempting to cross the vast ocean. (Created by Masumi Aonuma)

The next hurdle was arranging interpreters. Given the duration of the event, we needed at least two interpreters. Fortunately, we were able to secure two excellent local interpreters through a contact we made at the NZ workshop the previous year. Thanks to the excellent interpretation provided by these experienced interpreters, along with their thoughtful support that extended beyond the scope of their formal duties, we were able to fulfil our mission of participating in the Conference and leading the workshop. We would like to take this opportunity to express our gratitude once again.

With interpreters secured, we felt confident that we could overcome the language barrier – and with that momentum, we boldly signed up to run a workshop. Dr Keith Tudor's encouragement gave us an extra push along the way for our motivation.

That year, we were learning about co-creative TA directly from its co-founder, Dr Keith Tudor. Through an eight-month course, we became familiar with the approach of co-creative TA. Among the many interesting ideas we explored, we felt that the concept of 'we-ness' was the most appealing and resonated with us the most – so we decided to make it the focus of our workshop. We were able to understand we-ness naturally, even with an English interpretation, and it felt surprisingly familiar. On one hand, it was very enjoyable process for the two of us to reconfirm this shared understanding. On the other hand, the more we discussed it, the more the feeling of the 'we-ness discomfort' became apparent when interacting with people from other countries at international TA conferences and workshops, in which there seemed to be an emphasis on the negative aspect of the life position, 'I'm not OK, You're OK'. We could have simply dismissed it as a difference in frames of reference, but that made us more eager to explore this sense of discomfort and clarify what might be contributing to it. We wanted to discuss we-ness with the participants who would be attending the workshop. That is how we arrived at the theme of our workshop.

The day of the workshop

It was a rough start. We got the venue wrong, and the laptop we brought didn't work with the projector. But even then, there were people in the audience who tried to help us. Some people were interested in our topic, and some were participants we had met at the International Board of Certification (IBOC) exam two days earlier. Thanks to their support, the session was a success. This scene also made us feel like we are never alone.

Content

In our presentation, we first wanted to convey that the meaning embodied in the word 'we-ness' is already embedded in the historical background and national character of

Japan, and is one aspect of Japanese identity. We felt that Drego's (1983) concept was appropriate for explaining this idea, and so we incorporated it into our presentation. Drego developed Eric Berne's idea that 'the TA method of understanding personality through the ego states of parents, adults, and children can be applied to the study of cultural characteristics' (Berne, 1963, p. 110) and introduced the concept of the Cultural Parent. This concept suggests that the study of a culture's 'personality' can be used as an effective tool for cultural and social transformation.

Berne developed the concept of group culture based on his model of individual personality. As Drego (1983) puts it:

> When a group forms a social network or community, its members share Parental values, Adult procedures, and Child emotions, which Berne (Berne, 1963) respectively termed *Etiquette*, *Technicalities*, and *Character*. This tripartite classification aligns closely with many anthropological perspectives on culture. (p. 224)

Drego (1983) continues:

> In summary, the *etiquette* – that is, the Parent-type content of a culture – refers to the transmitted designs for thinking, behaving, and valuing within a particular society. The *technicalities*, or Adult-type content, consist of the actual organization of the material and social life of a specific human group. The *character*, or Child-type content, includes socially programmed ways of feeling, handling biological needs, and emotional expression – particularly in the forms of compliance and rebellion. Any object, event, or pattern in a culture can be understood within the framework of this threefold system. (pp. 224–225; our emphasis)

We challenged ourselves to use this concept to examine the national character of the Japanese people.

Summary of the presentation

Togetherness and sharing form the basis of our Japanese 'we-ness'

The main point we aimed to convey in our presentation was that the concept of 'we-ness' is already deeply embedded in Japan's historical background and national character and represents an important aspect of Japanese identity. We incorporated Drego's (1983) concept, cited above, into our presentation as we considered it provided a useful framework for explaining this idea.

In Japan, people at the national, regional, and local levels place great importance on 'being together', and both adults and children share a sense of existing together within the community. They are together, they struggle together, and they live together. On one hand, this shared mindset drives people to ask themselves what they can do to contribute to that togetherness. On the other hand, this way of thinking can lead individuals to become absorbed into the group – to the point of 'dissolving' their individuality for the sake of the collective group.

Explanations based on everyday scenes from life in Japan often elicited surprise and emotion from participants. At the same time, many expressed confusion or difficulty in understanding, saying things such as, 'That would never happen in my country'.

Examples

Here are three examples that illustrate these points.

1. When children are young, parents and children sleep together in the same room on *futons* (mattresses) laid out side by side. This resembles the Chinese character for '川' (river). The Japanese kanji for river depicts its flow by drawing three vertical lines, with the middle line being shorter. Using this character as a metaphor, parents and children sleeping together is expressed as 'Kawanojide neru' (sleeping in the shape of the river). That is, by sleeping surrounded by their parents, children form their attachment to them. This is an important custom for strengthening the bond between parents and children, as mothers in particular want to feel connected to their children, even while they sleep.

   The participants were surprised and asked, 'Until what age do children sleep with their parents?' We answered, 'In many families, children sleep in the same room as their parents until around the middle of elementary school. This is partly due to housing situations, but it is also to provide a sense of psychological security'.

2. Ekiden (駅伝/road relay) is a special team sport that stirs the soul of the Japanese people.

   This is a competition where multiple runners cover long distances in a relay format, competing for speed. The tasuki (襷/a team-coloured sash) used in the event plays an especially important role. When one runner passes the tasuki to the next, they are filled with a profound sense of relief. Above all, what matters most is passing it on to their teammates. As a result, the members and the order in which they run are often decided by the coach on the morning of the event. It is not uncommon for an athlete who looked promising the day before to be moved to a reserve runner just a few hours before the race. Those who do not make the cut do not express their disappointment outwardly; instead, they keep it to themselves and take pride in supporting the runners who have been selected. The individual desire to run is set aside for the sake of favouring the team's success.

The participants at the workshop were amazed by the photos shown on the screen and were curious about the real tasuki we had brought with us.

3. Throughout their lives, community clean-up activities are considered 'natural behaviour' for Japanese people. When we were children, we brought our own dust cloths to school and cleaned our classrooms every day. It was natural for everyone to work together to keep things clean. When we explained this custom, people who had visited Japan praised the cleanliness of Japanese tourist attractions. At the same time, what stood out most was the sense of self-sacrifice, accompanied by surprise and fear. The Great East Japan Earthquake, which struck on the 11th of March 2011, also highlighted the Japanese national character of people patiently queuing in an orderly manner at petrol stations and supermarkets even during the chaos following the earthquake, but the discussion also touched on the drawbacks of this trait in emergency situations.

The example of an elementary school where all students were unable to evacuate in time due to delayed evacuation instructions from leaders, who were overly focused on collective action, can only be described as a tragedy. Everyone who was in the workshop felt as though they were with us, sharing our sorrow.

These three examples are consistent with Drego's core concepts discussed earlier and clearly reflect cultural characteristics distinctive of the Japanese people.

The Cultural Parent ego state exists in both social groups and individuals (Drego, 1983) and it proved effective in conveying to participants that the elements embedded in these Cultural Parent ego states can exert either positive or negative influences on a given situation. This also reminded us, once again, as Drego (2006) pointed out, that there are many positive options within these states: 'The freedom and responsibility of that choice lies with us.' (p. 94). Indeed, the power to choose future-oriented options lies within us as learners of TA.

'We-ness' derived from 'Cultural Parent' and 'integrating Adult'

There were two reasons why we decided to make 'we-ness' the theme of our workshop. Firstly, it felt very familiar and resonated with us from the start. Secondly, we wanted to clarify what exactly causes the sense of discomfort that sometimes arises when the behaviours and judgements we consider natural in Japan clash with those of people from other parts of the world. The answer to this question can be found here. The elements embedded in our cultural parental ego states can have both positive and negative influences in certain situations. The modesty and obedience that we Japanese consider virtues can sometimes manifest as uncritical obedience, leading to tragedy. In other words, in cultural scripts, our actions, words, and attitudes are a mix of what is appropriate for the situation and what is not, existing in an unclassified state. And we, as Drego puts it, have the ability to select what is appropriate for the situation and act accordingly. The force that grants us this ability to choose is the integrating Adult. This is characterised by several key elements: autonomy, relational needs, consciousness, reflective awareness, critical consciousness, maturity, motivation, and imagination (Tudor & Summers, 2014). Among these, we identified relational needs and critical consciousness as particularly significant, and in the context of Japanese culture, expanding these two dimensions is essential. The reason for this is that I think it's important to positively change the aspect of Japanese national character that tends to be swayed by unofficial norms without critical thinking or awareness, and without necessary consideration. To do this, we need to be critical and make conscious choices, and to choose and achieve this ourselves, we need to rethink the nature of our relational needs.

Furthermore, within the context of our identity, the previous example effectively captures Tudor's insight that 'the individual can only be understood in the context of society, the group or groups, and the other, and that "I" comes from and comes after "we".' (Tudor, 2016, p. 164) This led us to the idea that the Japanese 'Cultural Parent' can be integrated into the integrating Adult when it is activated by relational needs and critical consciousness, which then leads to the Japanese 'we-ness' based on 'I am OK, You are OK, We are OK'.

We developed a diagram (see Figure 7.2) illustrating the integrating Adult that characterises the expansion of these two dimensions, which we incorporated into the latter half of our presentation.

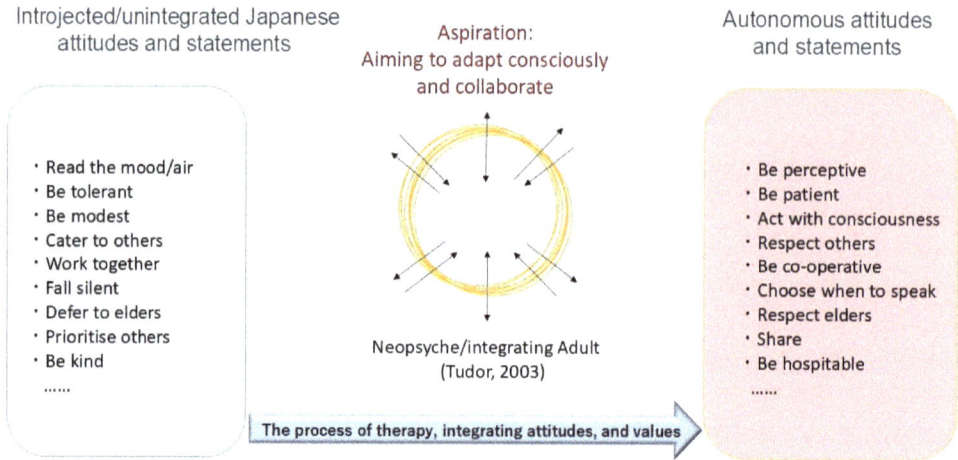

Figure 7.2. Behavioural change of Japanese people by integrating Adult. Explanatory material by authors.

Finally, we sought to articulate our ideal concept of Japanese we-ness through Japanese terms that resonate with its cultural meaning.

We summarised this Japanese concept of we-ness as **自他共栄** (jita-kyoei), which can be translated as mutual prosperity, referring to the creation of a world where people respect and appreciate each other, build mutual trust, support one another, and strive to grow together through mutual encouragement and cooperation (see Figure 7.3).

自他共栄(jita-kyoei)
means respecting and being grateful to the other person, developing a spirit of mutual trust and helping each other, and working together to create a world that is prosperous not only for ourselves but also for others.

Figure 7.3. Excerpt from our workshop document expressing the Japanese notion of 'we-ness'.

Comments from participants

Participants shared a wealth of information with us, and we were able to engage in a rich exchange of ideas.

• Participant A (who has been to Japan before):
"In the morning, I saw the children going to school in an orderly line and in groups. Is it the same on the way back?"

The workshop presenter's response:
"Yes. This is why parents and senior members of the community form "safety patrol" groups and support the children's independence on a rotating basis. This local norm has been practised throughout Japan for decades."

• Participant B:
"In my country, too, it is important that 'there is the land, there is the community, and there I am'. I feel this is very similar to the Japanese."

• Participant C:
"I heard at the conference that 'tall poppies are cut down', something similar in my country."

The workshop presenter's response:

"In Japan, there is a saying: 'The nail that sticks out gets hammered down'." (This is a good example of the Japanese counter injunctions to always be modest.)

We listened intently to what each person had to say. By the end of this enriching session, we felt a sense of joy and relief, as though we had achieved our initial mission of 'learning together with the participants'. It was a time when no one was in the role of teacher; rather, everyone was learning from each other. Then someone said, 'Just like this theme, we have all connected with each other beyond our cultural differences'.

As expected, each participant's sense of 'we-ness' varied, but we were able to discover many similarities. The discomfort we initially felt had changed into a comfortable feeling of acceptance of each other's differences. By showing mutual respect, taking an interest in each other, and engaging in open-minded discussions, we were able to accept each other's differences. We were able to reaffirm that this is what TA is all about.

We would also like to mention here that some participants expressed an interest in hearing our thoughts on the ego state of the Child. It goes without saying that the comments from participants who were interested by our short presentation – given by 'two Japanese who crossed the ocean in a small rowboat' (as shown in Figure 7.1) – encouraged us and sparked hope for further progress on this topic.

Summary

Taking inspiration from the theme of the New Zealand Conference, *Karangarua*, we focused on the differences between our sense of 'we-ness' and that of our colleagues who participated in our workshop.

We realised that it was indeed possible to get to know each other well, even within a limited amount of time. We felt this was due to the precision and relevance accuracy of both Berne's and Drego's Transactional Analysis concepts.

By recognising these differences, we were also able to develop mutual empathy and respect. These kinds of strokes are difficult to achieve in an online setting, which highlights the importance of direct human interaction.

Finally, we would like to express our sincere gratitude to the Transactional Analysis Association of Aotearoa New Zealand for allowing us to participate. We would also like to extend our heartful thanks to everyone who took an interest in our ideas and participated in our workshop. Thanks to everyone's active participation, mutual respect, and wonderful exchange of opinions, we were able to engage in fruitful mutual learning.

After returning to Japan, we shared our experiences of this enriching experience with our friends in the learning community who had been waiting for us. We would be delighted if our participation in this Conference and our workshop experience could serve as a 'bridge' connecting our TA colleagues in New Zealand and Japan.

We would also like to thank you for reading this paper. What does 'we-ness' mean to you, in your country? Please let us know. And when we meet someday, let's talk about it together (Figure 7.3).

♡Please let us know about your 'we-ness'.

Figure 7.3. Worksheet distributed during the workshop.

References

Berne, E. (1963). *The structure and dynamics of organizations and groups*. Grove Press.
Drego, P. (1983). The cultural parent. *Transactional Analysis Journal, 13*(4), 224–227. https://doi.org/10.1177/036215378301300404

Drego, P. (2006). Freedom and responsibility: Social empowerment and the altruistic model of ego states. *Transactional Analysis Journal, 36*(2), 90–104. https://doi.org/10.1177/036215370603600203

Summers, G., & Tudor, K. (2000). Cocreative transactional analysis. *Transactional Analysis Journal, 30*(1), 23–40. https://doi.org/10.1177/036215370003000104

Transactional Analysis Association of Aotearoa New Zealand. (2024). *2024 International Conference. Wellington, Aotearoa New Zealand. 21st–23rd November.* https://www.taaanz.nz/2024-international-conference

Tudor, K. (2003). The neopsyche: The integrating adult ego state. In C. Sills & H. Hargaden (Eds.), *Ego states: Key concepts in transactional analysis: Contemporary views* (pp. 201–231). Worth Publishing.

Tudor, K. (2016). 'We are': The fundamental life position. *Transactional Analysis Journal, 46*(2), 164–176. https://doi.org/10.1177/0362153716637064

Tudor, K., & Summers, G. (2014). *Co-creative transactional analysis: Papers, responses, dialogues, and developments.* Routledge.

Paper 8

Creativity reimagined: Expanding our capacity for diversity

Mandy Lacy

Abstract

This paper explores the intrinsic relationship between creativity and diversity, proposing that they are not separate phenomena but dynamically interconnected forces that enrich individual and collective growth. Drawing from neuroscience, psychology, and transactional analysis (TA), it reimagines creativity as a universal human capacity rather than a rare talent. Through concepts such as Berne's 'secret garden' metaphor, physis, ego states, and script theory, creativity is framed as both a living force and an everyday act of self-expression. The discussion highlights how early scripts and injunctions can limit creative potential and how reconnecting with the Free Child and integrating Adult can restore spontaneity, curiosity, and flow. A practical seven-step framework from the 'Ignite Your Creativity' workshop is introduced, offering reflective and experiential practices to nurture creative reawakening. Ultimately, this paper invites readers to embrace creativity as a pathway to inclusion, resilience, and authenticity – an expression of human diversity in its most life-affirming form.

Introduction

Creativity and diversity are not only compatible, they are fundamentally interconnected and mutually enriching. Creative expression thrives on diversity, drawing from a broad spectrum of perspectives, experiences, and cultural influences. Likewise, diversity is amplified through creativity, which offers the tools to explore, honour, and integrate difference in inclusive and transformative ways. In this paper, creativity is understood to inherently include diversity; the two are inseparable, forming a dynamic synergy that nurtures resilience, innovation, and human growth, individually and collectively.

When we embrace creativity, we expand our capacity for diverse thinking and expression which, in turn, nurtures greater empathy, inclusion, and tolerance for difference in others. This paper explores creativity through a multidimensional lens, weaving together insights from creativity research, literature, neuroscience, psychology, and transactional analysis (TA). It offers a powerful reframing: creativity is not a rare talent or gift, rather it is a fundamental human capacity and a birthright.

111

Drawing on concepts such as the *secret garden* metaphor, *physis*, ego states, and script theory, creativity is explored as a living force and an everyday expression of self. A practical seven-step framework is included from the *Ignite Your Creativity* workshop presented at the 2024 international TA Conference. These steps are designed to help you reawaken your creative energy and live more expressively, intuitively, and fully. Whether creativity feels near or far, this article invites you to rediscover the essential role it plays in your life, and to embrace its deep connection to the richness and wellbeing of human diversity.

What is creativity?

Gilbert (2015) describes creativity as 'the relationship between a human being and the mysteries of inspiration' (p. 1). I would take this a step further adding that acts of creativity are also acts of self-expression. Creativity can take grand, inspiring forms like painting a masterpiece or launching an innovative company and it can also be present in the everyday. Life itself demands diversity, ingenuity, adaptation, and invention. In this broader sense, everyone possesses creative potential.

A quote often attributed to Helena Bonham Carter (n.d.) beautifully captures this expansive view:

> I think everything in life is art. What you do. How you dress. The way you love someone and how you talk. Your smile and your personality. What you believe in, and all your dreams. The way you drink your tea. How you decorate your home. Or party. Your grocery list. The food you make. How your writing looks. And the way you feel. Life is art. (para. 1)

Creativity doesn't need to be on the global stage to be meaningful. Ruth Richards, Dennis Kinney, and colleagues at Harvard Medical School (Richards et al., 1988) champion this view through their work on everyday creativity, defining it as expressions of originality and meaning in daily life, whether through errands, hobbies, or problem-solving at work. Their research concluded that the first step in becoming more creative is simply believing you can be.

Richards (2007) suggests that creativity blossoms when our lifestyles support it and when we are inspired, connected with others, learning new things, along with being curious about the world around us. She encourages us to seek out novelty, step outside our comfort zones, and stay connected to creative stimuli: books, social media, conversations, and art. In doing so, we nourish our creative selves.

More broadly, creativity is often defined as the capacity to generate or recognise ideas, alternatives, diversity, or possibilities that are useful in solving problems, communicating, or entertaining. It allows for lateral thinking and imaginative exploration beyond traditional boundaries. In the course of my research, I experienced firsthand how creativity powerfully enhanced both my diversity of thinking and academic writing skills (Lacy, 2022).

Recent research by Tabor et al. (2023) highlights creativity not just as a cognitive skill but as an intervention for wellness that supports life skill-building, emotional regulation, learning, and even spiritual healing. Creativity is also a driving force behind human progress. As we continue to evolve as societies, it is often creative thought that enables transformation, connection, and new solutions.

Glaveanu et al. (2020) mark a shift toward understanding creativity as multidimensional, occurring not in isolation but through interaction within our social and material worlds, whereas Sawyer and Henriksen (2024) expand this into two key perspectives:

- The individualist view, which sees creativity as residing within individuals who think or behave creatively.
- The socio-cultural view, which focuses on creativity as a collaborative process that emerges through shared cultural systems and social interactions.

This dual perspective is echoed by Morrison (2015) and many others who view creativity and artistic expression as essential to the healing and flourishing of communities and civilisations. For millennia, Indigenous and ancient cultures have harnessed creativity in the form of dance, music, storytelling, and visual art as a means of spiritual and communal healing (Archibald & Dewar, 2010).

In times of hardship, it is often the artist, whether writer, painter, dancer, or everyday creative, who offers vision, voice, and hope. Toni Morrison (2015) captured this beautifully in response to a period of social and political unrest:

> This is precisely the time when artists go to work.
> There is no time for despair, no place for self-pity,
> No need for silence, no room for fear.
> We speak, we write, we do language.
> That is how civilisations heal. (para. 14)

The neuroscience of creativity

Neuroscience has made significant strides in understanding the benefits of creativity, revealing how artistic expression impacts the brain in profound ways. Early work by Zeki (1998) found that experiencing beauty whether visual or musical activates the decision-making areas of the brain. Importantly, creating art stimulates the brain differently than simply viewing it, engaging a wider network of cognitive functions.

Cognitive neuroscience research supports this distinction. Bolwerk et al. (2014) demonstrate that producing visual art enhances effective brain connectivity and interaction, suggesting that creative expression actively improves cognitive integration. This aligns with core tenets of art therapy, which proposes that any form of creative expression can facilitate emotional healing and mental wellbeing. Neuroscientific research now helps explain this therapeutic effect, particularly in relation to how the brain processes traumatic memories, stress, and emotional regulation during art-making.

A 2017 study by Drexel University's College of Nursing and Health Professions further supports these findings. By monitoring serotonin levels and blood flow in the prefrontal cortex of both artists and non-artists, researchers found a significant increase in neural activity across both groups. This suggests that both engaging with and observing art stimulates the brain, encouraging the formation of new neural pathways. Similarly, Mendick (2011) reports that simply viewing artwork perceived as beautiful can lead to a 10% increase in cerebral blood flow, offering a physiological basis for the emotional uplift people often feel around art.

Jacolbe (2019), whose research focuses on neuroaesthetics, the study of the brain's response to creative experiences found that creativity, whether through making or viewing, significantly improves mental health and emotional regulation. Echoing this, Magsamen and Ross (2023) argue that aesthetic experiences are vital to our wellbeing, demonstrating that just 45 minutes of creative engagement can meaningfully reduce levels of the stress hormone cortisol regardless of artistic skill level.

In both rehabilitation medicine and neuroscience, growing evidence suggests that creative activity influences brain wave patterns, emotional states, and nervous system functioning. As Christianne Strang (2020), neuroscientist and past president of the American Art Therapy Association, explains: 'Creativity in and of itself is important for remaining healthy, remaining connected to yourself and connected to the world' (para. 4).

In summary, neuroscience is purporting that visual and artistic expression activates the brain's reward pathways, resulting in positive emotional states and enhanced cognitive performance. Art-making supports problem-solving, emotional processing, and overall wellbeing. Research now likens creative engagement to exercise for the brain, offering cognitive benefits similar to the way physical activity benefits the body.

Misconceptions about creativity

First let's cover the common misconception that creativity cannot be cultivated. That it is a mysterious gift possessed only by a fortunate few, those born with an innate ability and confidence to be 'good' at creative pursuits. This belief is not only incorrect but arguably one of the most prevalent self-limiting assumptions and barriers to creative expression. Rubin (2023) challenges this misconception directly:

> Those who do not engage in the traditional arts might be wary of calling themselves artists. They might perceive creativity as something extraordinary or beyond their capabilities. A calling for the special few who are born with these gifts. Fortunately, this is not the case. Creativity is not a rare ability. It is not difficult to access. Creativity is a fundamental aspect of being human. It's our birthright. And it's for all of us. (p. 1)

Lehrer (2012) similarly works to dismantle the myth of the muse, the chosen few, or the idea of 'creative types'. He asserts that creativity is not a singular gift, rather that it is a set of learnable cognitive processes which can be nurtured and refined in the following ways:

- embracing periods of stuckness or 'the rut' as part of the process,
- adopting a childlike perspective,
- daydreaming productively, and
- thinking from an outsider's viewpoint.

These accessible strategies suggest that creativity is not elusive, rather that it is something we all have the capacity to tap into if we want to shift our mindset. Rubin (2023), a prolific and reflective music producer, further describes creativity not as an elite talent but as a way of being. He states: 'Attuned choice by attuned choice, your entire life is a form of expression. You exist as a creative being in a creative universe. A singular work of art.' (p. 3).

This view aligns powerfully with TA concepts, particularly the idea that our Free Child ego state holds within it the capacity for spontaneity, joy, and creativity. It also echoes Berne's (1972) belief that we each have a 'secret garden' of aspirations waiting to be expressed. Recognising that creativity is not exclusive or unattainable, that it is intrinsic and universal, can be a first step toward exploring our creative selves.

Exploring the secret garden

Berne's secret garden metaphor offers a compelling way to understand why we may hide, avoid, or feel reticent about exploring our creativity. Metaphorically, the secret garden represents our inner self, a space we may or may not be aware of, and one we are often reluctant to share with others. Berne (1972) introduces this metaphor by stating:

> All men and all women have their secret gardens, whose gates they guard against the profane invasion of the vulgar crowd. These are visual pictures of what they would do if they could do as they pleased. The lucky ones find the right time, place, and person, and get to do it, while the rest must wander wistfully outside their own walls. (p. 130)

According to Deaconu (2016), 'in this context, Berne viewed internal life in terms of aspirations that could be thwarted by a hostile environment. To prevent that from happening, various script mechanisms are put in place as the individual develops' (p. 299). Deaconu wasn't the first to make this connection. Nuttall (2003) posits Berne's belief that the purpose of script analysis is to free people 'so that they can open the garden of their aspirations to the world' (p. 231).

When viewed through the lens of creativity, Berne's metaphor is particularly illuminating. The gates of the secret garden can be seen as symbolic of psychological defences, i.e., scripts, injunctions, ego-state dynamics, and games that serve to protect the vulnerable self from fears of judgment, rejection, or inadequacy when creative expression is brought into the open.

'These are visual pictures of what they would do if they could do as they pleased.' (Berne, 1972, p. 130). This part of the metaphor speaks to the hidden dreams and aspirations and the image of the Free Child running with wild abandon, revelling in the joy of freedom, creativity, love, and laughter. As Nuttall (2003) emphasises, the goal of script analysis is to enable the Child to declare, 'this is what I want to do, and I would rather do it my own way' (p. 231).

116

'The lucky ones find the right time, place, and person…' (Berne, 1975, p. 130). This reflects the common misconception as mentioned earlier, that only a select few are born with the talent, confidence, or permission to live creatively as a belief rooted in early injunctions and limiting beliefs. Novak (2016) further develops the metaphor, describing the garden as the space where 'certain known and unknown parts of the self (script) are housed' (p. 290). Also noted was that 'garden work not only addresses the conscious visual pictures and conscious decisions but also the unconscious processes, dissociation, and resistances to revealing, exploring or living particular parts of the self' (p. 290). This is where constructs like injunctions (Goulding & Goulding, 1976) and script protocols (Cornell & Landaiche, 2008) can provide deeper insight into how these aspects remain hidden. Cornell (2010) expands on the metaphor, writing:

> The secret gardens to which Berne so longingly and passionately referred are filled with delicate, precious, but precarious hopes that seek a life structure that can finally bring them to fruition and realisation. It is not an easy path; it is marked by the dialectic tensions of accompaniment and aloneness. (p. 251)

Later, Cornell (2017) suggests that had Berne lived longer, his next book 'might have been one about "watering" those secret gardens so they would not become parched' (p. 3).

Creativity reticence

In thinking about gardens that become parched (Cornell, 2017), it is our script that often keeps the creativity drought in place by manifesting as resistance, avoidance, or fear when it comes to creativity. As Rubin (2023) reflects: 'With each story we tell ourselves, we negate possibility. Reality is diminished. Rooms of the self are walled off. Truth collapses to fit a fictional organising principle we have adopted' (p. 404).

Such stories include internalised script messages like 'I'm not creative', 'I can't draw, sing or paint', which, when reinforced over time, can become self-fulfilling prophecies. A lack of positive strokes or an excess of negative ones regarding our creative expression can significantly affect self-esteem, diminishing the confidence needed for experimentation, play, and risk-taking inherent to the creative process.

These beliefs are often formed in childhood, especially through negative experiences, and can shape the Child ego state's view of self and others. If, for instance, a person was repeatedly dismissed or criticised when expressing creativity, the internalised message might be: 'It's not safe to be expressive'. Berne (1972) describes this process as the development of an unconscious life path, created in childhood, reinforced by caregivers, and later validated by selective life experiences that affirm the script.

This aligns with Freud's (1920) concept of repetition compulsion which is the tendency to unconsciously seek out familiar but potentially damaging patterns. Within TA, this might look like repeatedly avoiding creative opportunities or self-sabotaging through perfectionism or procrastination, in order to maintain script consistency. As Cornell (1988) notes, Berne's conceptualisation of script development reflects a profound focus on self-limiting adaptation, with little emphasis on its self-enhancing counterpart.

These early messages such as 'Don't be different', 'Don't succeed', or 'You're not good enough' can become internalised injunctions that later express through ego-state conflicts. For instance:

- A Critical Parent may harshly judge new ideas ('That's silly' or 'That won't work'), blocking innovation.
- An Adapted Child may fear criticism or rejection, inhibiting expression or refusing to take creative risks.
- The Free Child, the source of spontaneity and play, may be suppressed, hidden behind the garden gates.

Inadequate integration between ego states can create internal tension. A healthy integrating Adult, as described by Tudor (2003), is needed to mediate between these voices – to allow space for curiosity, reflection, and informed action. However, if the Adult becomes overly aligned with rationalisations and responsibilities (e.g., 'I don't have time for this', 'Creativity is not practical'), creative pursuits may be dismissed as indulgent or unnecessary. This mindset can further be reinforced by drivers, e.g., Be Perfect, Try Hard, Please Others, games 'I'm Too Busy', or 'Until' scripts 'I'll be creative once the real work is done'; all of which limit spontaneity and defer creative fulfilment. In such cases, avoidance transactions such as changing the subject, making jokes, or dismissing creativity as frivolous help maintain the belief that creativity is unimportant or irrelevant.

These dynamics can also manifest in the form of creativity blocks, even for those who identify as creative. Over-identification with the Critical Parent may lead to inner perfectionism, while a compliant Adapted Child might suppress unconventional or bold ideas out of fear of stepping outside norms.

Ultimately, as Novak (2016) and Cornell (2010) highlight, the secret garden is filled with delicate and often hidden hopes. When the gate is kept shut by these psychological mechanisms, energy is consumed not in creation, but in maintaining defence. As TA theory reminds us, true creative engagement requires access to the Free Child, support from the Nurturing Parent, and an integrating Adult capable of challenging limiting beliefs and facilitating permission to play.

Reconnecting and integrating creativity

Stewart and Joines (1987) outline the Free Child ego state as having spontaneity, joy, and creativity, with the Adapted Child ego state having conforming and rebellious responses to parental expectations. Accordingly, it is the Free Child that is the source of our spontaneity, creativity, and intuition and contains the capacity for delight, humour, and genuine emotional responses.

Generally, it has been considered that the ego states are a steady state, whereas Tudor (2025) posits that rather than the ego states being viewed in this way that they are a fluid process. Further, that by focusing on an integrating Adult process as opposed to re-Child work is a 'co-creative process of neo psychic functioning which describes a person who is, at best, in a process of fluidity or in flow' (Tudor, 2025, p. 159).

When presenting the concept of the integrating Adult, Tudor (2003) argues that the Adult ego state should not be viewed as entirely autonomous or separate from the Parent and Child. Rather, it plays a central role in integrating the influences and experiences of all ego states, supporting greater psychological flexibility and a more authentic therapeutic presence. Building on this, when considering the organisational implications of the integrating Adult in relation to the values of curiosity, creativity, and compassion, Tudor and Summers (2014) suggest that the first two, curiosity and creativity, are essential for fostering an appreciation of uncertainty and for risk-taking, both of which are seen as necessary for growth and vitality.

However, as Berne (1972) notes, it is important for individuals to understand their Child ego state, not only because 'it is going to be with [them] all [their] life' (p. 12), but also because it represents 'the most valuable part of [their] personality' (p. 12). In this light, facilitating a process for individuals to reconnect with and explore their creativity involves actively engaging the Free Child ego state. Stewart and Joines (1987) emphasise that the Free Child is the source of creativity and energy, and thus plays a vital role in learning experiences. They assert that this aspect of the personality must be actively included in any developmental process that fosters growth and self-expression.

Physis

Discussing how we explore our creativity wouldn't be complete without bringing in the TA concept of physis. Koopmans (2020) begins by stating that 'physis is the most sparkling concept in transactional analysis' (p. 81) – precisely because, just when we think we understand it, it slips away again. One of the ways Koopmans makes sense of physis is through the work of John and Muriel James (1991), who expanded their ideas on the 'inner core' by introducing the concept of 'urges'. They described these as a hunger for more meaning and likened physis to 'the urge of plants towards sun and water; there is always an irresistible urge within us for growth' (p. 9).

Berne (1972) illustrates physis with an upward-pointing arrow through the ego states, symbolising aspiration and developmental drive. Later, Kolb (1984) and Napper and Newton (2000) use spirals to visualise learning and personal growth. Koopmans adapted Napper and Newton's horizontal spiral into a multi-dimensional model that moves in all directions as we learn and grow called the physis lemniscate. The same is true of creativity. Exploring self-expression, problem-solving, or innovation through various mediums or situations is rarely tidy or predictable. Creativity is often chaotic, nonlinear, and wonderfully unorganised.

Physis is growth. Just as plants reach toward the light, so too does physis move us toward our fullest expression. The physis of creativity is a living energy dynamic, shifting and illuminating our desire to understand and express ourselves more deeply. Through exploring and experimenting with our creativity, we allow ourselves to become lifelong adventurers expressing our inner selves openly through a continuous, transformative learning journey.

Steps to creativity

You can't use up creativity, the more you use, the more you have.

(Maya Angelou)

This section outlines the core principles shared in the creativity workshop I presented at the 2024 international TA Conference. The workshop emerged from years of personal reflection, practice-based facilitation, and co-creative dialogue with others. It offers seven gentle yet powerful steps to help reawaken your creative energy, some of which can be applied immediately, while others invite ongoing exploration.

Participants often arrive somewhere along a continuum from curiosity tinged with uncertainty, to creative self-doubt, or the quiet ache of feeling creatively lost. Yet beneath these experiences is a shared truth: a sense that creativity still lives within. This workshop honours that inner knowing and is designed to support participants as they:

- Explore how and where creativity self-limiting beliefs were formed,
- Reframe outdated narratives through redecision and positive reinforcement, and
- Give themselves permission to rediscover and express their creative self.

The foundations of the workshop are grounded in a co-creative approach, where the therapeutic relationship is seen as a collaborative process, and that change and meaning are co-created through mutual influence and dialogue (Summers & Tudor, 2000). It is also a process of observing self and others, practicing, doing, and refining (Lacy, 2012). Drawing on Robinson's (2020) co-creative learning contract, the agreement is built on permission to explore, shared responsibility, learning in the here-and-now, openness to past influences, and mutual respect. Transactional Analysis concepts such as ego states, scripts, transactions, injunctions, strokes, rackets, and/or drivers are introduced and integrated depending on participants' familiarity and readiness.

The following framework forms the basis of the workshop and includes individual and group activities, reflective exercises, and shared dialogue. Participants are encouraged to begin a creativity journal, starting with insights gathered during the workshop. These seven steps are not linear instructions – they are flexible gateways. Each offers an invitation to begin, return to, or deepen your relationship with creativity.

1. **Begin without needing to already be 'creative'**
   Start by making commitments to your creative self. Include promises that you will not compare yourself with others, and that you will be open to falling in love with a creativity journey that has no timeframe or set destination.

2. **Be inspired by others**
   Curate your world with what lights you up and brings you joy. Follow creatives, artists, musicians, writers, dancers, gardeners – anyone who sparks your curiosity and stirs your imagination. Fill your digital world with inspiration so there's always something creative, interesting, and beautiful to view.

3. Trust your inner self

Your intuition and your inner knowing are the compass guiding your creativity. Intuition is the heart of creativity. Set aside the voice of the inner critic and cultivate supportive inner messages that encourage, affirm, and guide you gently forward.

4. Focus on the process not the end result

Creativity lives in the making and messiness – the exploring, testing, experimenting, and learning. Release the need for validation, polished outcomes, or perfection from yourself or anyone else. Creativity is growth, not performance.

5. Seek out creative opportunities

Explore new mediums and unfamiliar spaces. Some paths may not feel right, and others will call you home. Keep following the threads of joy, curiosity, and self-expression until something clicks. Follow the sparks.

6. Create a dedicated creativity space

Claim or make a space where your creativity can live. No matter how simple, keep it accessible and yours only. Whether it's a corner of a room or a folder on your desktop, having a ready space saves time setting up and packing away, and it signals to your creative self: 'You are welcome here'.

7. Invite lightness and laughter

Laughter softens self-judgement and brings warmth to the creative process. When you laugh with yourself, from a place of compassion rather than criticism, you invite healing, ease, and joy. It reminds us not to take ourselves too seriously and to stay connected to the joy of being creative.

These steps are not rules, they are reminders. Creativity flourishes through permission not pressure. Permission to begin. To be curious. To fail. To try again. And most of all, to show up and be your whole creative self –without apology.

Conclusion

Ultimately creativity opens the door to diverse ways of thinking and being and in doing so, cultivates greater tolerance, empathy, and respect for the richness of human difference. Creativity becomes both a personal and collective act of bridging perspectives.

In seeking to understand creativity through the lenses of neuroscience, psychology, and transactional analysis, this article has explored common misconceptions and shown how creativity supports wellbeing, fosters growth, and challenges the scripts and myths that keep us distant from our creative selves. Drawing on Berne's metaphor of the 'secret garden', creativity is reimagined as an inner sanctuary that is rich with possibility, often buried beneath conditioning, but always alive, diverse, and waiting.

Creativity is physis in motion and a vital force for growth, healing, and transformation. It is not a luxury or a rare gift reserved for a talented few. Rather, it is a universal, life-affirming capacity that lives within us all, regardless of background, diversity, or experience. It's how we make meaning, connect with others, and shape our place in the world.

Creative self-expression is deeply personal. Some find it in solitude; others, in collaboration. Its forms and expression are as diverse as we are. Transactional Analysis offers powerful tools to uncover and release the internal blocks that hold creativity hostage, such as scripts, injunctions, ego states, and outdated narratives. Through the Free Child, the integrating Adult, and co-creative learning, we can reclaim creativity not as a pastime, more as a way of being.

The creative journey is not linear; it loops, pauses, and surprises. It moves in spirals of exploration, insight, play, reflection, and reinvention. The seven-step framework shared here is not a prescription, rather a map as a gentle invitation to begin. Whether you're reconnecting with creativity after a long pause or discovering it anew, these steps invite you to trust your inner voice, play without apology, and release the need for perfection. When we create, we reconnect with the part of ourselves that is spontaneous, curious, and joyfully expressive. We water the garden of our inner world, cultivating space for resilience, growth, and authenticity.

> Creativity is a universal human capacity and birthright that is woven into our biology, psychology, and relationships. It is not a rare talent, but an innate potential that lives within us all. When we create, we express our uniqueness, deepen our connections, and contribute to a more vibrant, diverse, and inclusive world. Embracing creativity not only enhances cognitive and experiential diversity, but also fosters greater openness and tolerance toward difference more broadly. To embrace creativity is to honour both our individuality and collectiveness through the rich diversity of human expression. Whether through words, movement, image, or play, the creative act becomes a pathway to authenticity, renewal, and collective healing. As Gilbert (2015) suggests: 'A

creative life is an amplified life. It's a bigger life, a happier life, an expanded life, and a hell of a lot more interesting life.' (p. 1).

References

Angelou, M. (n.d.). *Maya Angelou – Quotes*. Goodreads. https://www.goodreads.com/quotes/153929-you-can-t-use-up-creativity-the-more-you-use-the

Archibald, L., & Dewar, J. (2010). Creative arts, culture, and healing: Building an evidence base. *Pimatisiwin: A Journal of Aboriginal and Indigenous Community Health, 8*(3), 1–25. https://journalindigenouswellbeing.co.nz/media/2018/12/1_Archibald.pdf

Berne, E. (1972). *What do you say after you say hello? The psychology of human destiny*. Grove Press.

Bolwerk, A., Mack-Andrick, J., Lang, F. R., Dörfler, A., & Maihöfner, C. (2014). How art changes your brain: Differential effects of visual art production and cognitive art evaluation on functional brain connectivity. *PloS ONE, 9*(7), Article e101035. https://doi.org/10.1371/journal.pone.0101035

Bonham Carter, H. (n.d.). *Helena Bonham Carter – Quotes*. Goodreads. https://www.goodreads.com/author/quotes/370877.Helena_Bonham_Carter

Cornell, W. F. (1988). Life script theory: A critical review from a developmental perspective. *Transactional Analysis Journal, 18*(4), 270–282. https://doi.org/10.1177/036215378801800402

Cornell, W. F. (2010). Aspiration or adaptation? An unresolved tension in Eric Berne's basic beliefs. *Transactional Analysis Journal, 40*(3–4), 243–253. https://doi.org/10.1177/036215371004000309

Cornell, W. F. (2017). Letter from the coeditor. *Transactional Analysis Journal, 47*(1), 3–5. https://doi.org/10.1177/0362153716681291

Cornell, W. F., & Landaiche, N. M., III. (2008). Nonconscious processes and self-development: Key concepts from Eric Berne and Christopher Bollas. *Transactional Analysis Journal, 38*(3), 200–217. https://doi.org/10.1177/036215370803800303

Deaconu, D. (2016). A life yet to be found: On the necessity and fragility of self-inquiry. *Transactional Analysis Journal, 46*(4), 299–310. https://doi.org/10.1177/0362153716661722

Drexel University. (2017, June 13). *Making art activates brain's reward pathway*. ScienceDaily. www.sciencedaily.com/releases/2017/06/170613120531.htm

Freud, S. (1920). *Beyond the pleasure principle* (J. Strachey, Trans.). The International Psycho-Analytical Press.

Gilbert, E. (2015). *Big magic: Creative living beyond fear*. Riverhead Books.

Glaveanu, V. P., Hanchett Hanson, M., Baer, J., Barbot, B., Clapp, E. P., Corazza, G. E., Hennessey, B., Kaufman, J. C., Lebuda, I., Lubart, T., Montuori, A., Ness, I. J.,

Plucker, J., Reiter-Palmon, R., Sierra, Z., Simonton, D. K., Neves-Pereira, M. S., & Sternberg, R. J. (2020). Advancing creativity theory and research: A socio-cultural manifesto. *The Journal of Creative Behavior*, *54*(3), 741–745. https://doi.org/10.1002/jocb.395

Goulding, R. L., & Goulding, M. M. (1976). Injunctions, decisions, and redecisions. *Transactional Analysis Journal*, *6*(1), 41–48. https://doi.org/10.1177/036215377600600110

Jacolbe, J. (2019, June 28). *Art is good for your brain*. JSTOR Daily. https://daily.jstor.org/art-is-good-for-your-brain/

James, M., & James, J. (1991). *Passion for life: Psychology and the human spirit*. Dutton.

Kolb, D. (1984). *Experiential learning*. Prentice Hall.

Koopmans, L. (2020). A fruitless attempt to cultivate physis. *Transactional Analysis Journal*, *50*(1), 81–92. https://doi.org/10.1080/03621537.2019.1690247

Lacy, M. (2012). Learning transactional analysis through cognitive apprenticeship. *Transactional Analysis Journal*, *42*(4), 265–276. https://doi.org/10.1177/036215371204200405

Lacy, M. (2022). *Creative oxygen for the writing soul: A writing journey where creativity provided the energy and way forward*. Lulu Publishing USA.

Lehrer, J. (2012). *Imagine: How creativity works*. Houghton Mifflin Harcourt.

Magsamen, S., & Ross, I. (2023). *Your brain on art: How the arts transform us*. Random House.

Mendick, R. (2011). *Brain scans reveal the power of art*. The Telegraph. https://www.telegraph.co.uk/culture/art/art-news/8500012/Brain-scans-reveal-the-power-of-art.html

Morrison, T. (2015). *No place for self-pity, no room for fear*. The Nation. https://www.thenation.com/article/archive/no-place-self-pity-no-room-fear/

Napper, R., & Newton, T. (2000). *Tactics*. TA Resources.

Novak, E. T. (2016). When transgressing standard therapeutic frames leads to progressive change, not ethical violations: Secret garden work. *Transactional Analysis Journal*, *46*(4), 288–298. https://doi.org/10.1177/0362153716662267

Nuttall, J. (2003). Script Analysis and Change in the Rosarium Philosophorum. *Transactional Analysis Journal*, *33*(3), 231–245. https://doi.org/10.1177/036215370303300305

Richards, R. (2007). Everyday creativity: Our hidden potential. In R. Richards (Ed.), *Everyday creativity and new views of human nature: Psychological, social, and spiritual perspectives* (pp. 25–53). American Psychological Association. https://doi.org/10.1037/11595-001

Richards, R., Kinney, D. K., Benet, M., & Merzel, A. P. (1988). Assessing everyday creativity: Characteristics of the Lifetime Creativity Scales and validation with three large samples. *Journal of Personality and Social Psychology*, *54*(3), 476–485. https://doi.org/10.1037/0022-3514.54.3.476

Robinson, P. (2020). Cocreative transformational learning as a way to break out of script. *Transactional Analysis Journal, 50*(1), 41–55. https://doi.org/10.1080/03621537.2019.1690237

Rubin, R. (2023). *The creative act: A way of being.* Penguin.

Sawyer, R. K., & Henriksen, D. (2024). *Explaining creativity: The science of human innovation.* Oxford University Press.

Stewart, I., & Joines, V. (1987). *TA today: A new introduction to transactional analysis.* Lifespace Publishing.

Strang, C. (2020). *How the brain is affected by art.* American Congress of Rehabilitation Medicine. https://acrm.org/rehabilitation-medicine/how-the-brain-is-affected-by-art/

Summers, G., & Tudor, K. (2000). Cocreative transactional analysis. *Transactional Analysis Journal, 30*(1), 23–40. https://doi.org/10.1177/036215370003000104

Summers, G., & Tudor, K. (2014). *Transactional analysis: A relational perspective.* Sage Publications.

Tabor, S. M., Van Bavel, M., Fellner, K. D., Schwartz, K. D., Black, T., Black Water, C., Crop Eared Wolf, S., Day Chief, P., Krugar, D., Monroe, L., & Pepion, J. (2023). Healing, empowering, engaging, learning, and decolonizing through culture: Living wellness, resilience, and resurgence in the classroom through creative arts. *Canadian Journal of School Psychology, 38*(1), 86–104. https://doi.org/10.1177/08295735221147322

Tudor, K. (2003). The adult is not integrative: A critique of the theory of ego states. *Transactional Analysis Journal, 33*(3), 215–222. https://doi.org/10.1177/036215370303300307

Tudor, K. (2025). *Transactional analysis proper—and improper: Selected and new papers.* Routledge.

Tudor, K., & Summers, G. (2014). *Co-creative transactional analysis: Papers, responses, dialogues, and developments.* Karnac Books.

Zeki, S. (1998). Art and the brain. *Daedalus: Journal of American Academy of Arts & Sciences: The Brain, 127*(2), 71–103. https://www.amacad.org/publication/daedalus-art-and-brain

Creating an inspiring adult learning environment: Perspectives for educators

Rhae Hooper

Abstract

This paper examines how educators can create inspiring adult learning environments by integrating transactional analysis (TA) with adult learning theory and group facilitation. Drawing on more than 30 years of professional experience, it highlights the facilitator's role as designer, relational leader, and catalyst for reflection and transformation. Grounded in the work of Berne, Knowles, Kolb, and Tuckman, and informed by research from Yalom, Lieberman, Miles, and Gage, it synthesises psychological and andragogic insights into a practical framework. Key models include Functional Fluency, developmental cycles, and Clarke's planning wheel. Centred on *Karangarua – unity through diversity*, the paper advocates culturally responsive, psychologically safe, and collaborative approaches that support learner autonomy and promote transformational learning.

1. Introduction

In this introduction, I provide some background to my interest in inspiring adult learning environments. In the second part of this paper, I describe theories, principles of, and research in adult learning, TA, and Functional Fluency. In the third part of the paper, I consider what the research tells us about learning. In the fourth part of the paper, I discuss conditions for learning, including group leadership, group stages, and group imagoes, and managing the physical space. In the fifth part of the paper, I turn my attention to cycles of development and learner steps. In the sixth part of the paper, I discuss designing and facilitating learning, and follow this with a last part which comprises notes on practical techniques for educators.

This work aligns with the spirit of karangarua – unity through diversity as it represents a principle of inclusivity across cultures within educational settings promoting equity. It is a call to acknowledge the worlds of equity and inclusivity; the worlds of te Ao Māori and a Western educational system. The workshop from which this paper has been developed considers the diversity of learners broadly and comprehensively substantiated by research evidence of the needs of adult learners and the philosophy of TA. In this sense, karangarua may be viewed as a value that epitomises values recognised by the International Transactional Analysis Association (ITAA) and was the theme of the Conference in New Zealand.

TA has four recognised fields of application: psychotherapy, counselling, organisational, and educational. While my primary focus lies within the educational application, the observations and practices shared in this paper are designed to support professionals across all four fields, especially when they are involved in adult education. Whether in therapeutic sessions, group counselling, or organisational coaching, fostering adult learning with respect, reflection, and psychological safety enhances the impact of that learning.

1.1 Background

I recently attended three seminars involving health and wellbeing. Listening, taking notes (although we were told not to as 'everything is in the handouts'), I was again reminded of the incredible difference the facilitator can make to the learning experience.

I began this particular journey towards becoming a better facilitator over 30 years ago. I came from a technical and marketing background in which content was the hero. However, I realised that I needed to integrate the wisdom of those researchers and academics before me in order to deliver the best possible training and workshops, as they needed to be easier, less pressured, and time consuming for me, and, most importantly, to afford the audience the optimum opportunity to learn. In 2016, I contributed to a publication *Educational Transactional Analysis* (Barrow & Newton, 2016) specifically focusing on training in organisations with TA (Hooper, 2016). My research and experience in adult education is not restricted to training in organisations; it is totally applicable to any training with adult audiences – TA training groups, art workshops, health and wellbeing seminars, first aid training, indeed, any situation in which adults are the learners.

Creating an inspiring adult learning environment requires more than delivering content. It involves fostering connection, facilitating time to process, and guiding transformation. In adult education, learners arrive not as blank slates but as individuals rich with experience. This paper explores how the framework of TA, when woven with adult learning theory and informed by group dynamics research, can support educators to build learning environments that are purposeful, relational, and inspiring.

Drawing from foundational thinkers such as Eric Berne, Malcolm Knowles, David Kolb, Bruce Tuckman, and researchers such as Irvin Yalom, Morton Lieberman, and

Matthew Miles, and Nathaniel Gage, this paper brings together psychological insight, leadership research, and andragogical strategy. At the heart of the approach are the TA beliefs in the learner's potential: that people are OK; that everyone can think for themselves, and that people can change – and that autonomy can be supported through respectful, responsive teaching.

My intention in this paper is to blend theory and practice. As in the workshop facilitated at the international TA Conference in Wellington, 'Karangarua – Unity through Diversity in Relationship', this paper introduces key models and research findings, and then explores how these can be practically applied in educational settings. Whether you are leading a workshop, coaching in organisations, or facilitating professional development, the ideas shared here are intended to support you to consider, design, and lead with greater confidence and connection and create an inspiring adult learning environment.

2. Grounding the work in theory

2.1 Adult learning: A foundation of respect and autonomy
Adult learners differ dramatically from children not just in age, but in expectations, motivations, and life experience. Although, many times, some of these 'grown ups' bring with them their childhood memories of what learning is all about and need a little education as to how it is different in their older stage of life. Malcolm Knowles' (1980) theory of andragogy, generally seen as the cornerstone of adult learning, offers six key principles that remain deeply relevant for educators:

1. **Personal involvement**: Adults want to be active participants.
2. **Experience**: Adults bring their life's experience to any new learning.
3. **Open to learning**: Adult learners are curious and open to learning new skills when content is relevant to their goals.
4. **Problem-solving**: Practical, real-world challenges engage adult learners more than abstract theory.
5. **Internal motivation**: Adults prefer to learn what they need, when they need it.
6. **Thirst for knowledge**: Adults are keen to know the how, why, and what (Figure 9.1.

At the core of Knowles' philosophy is the educator's respect for the learner's autonomy. Of course, those of us with TA training understand and embrace this philosophy. This approach shifts the educator's role from 'expert', which over 35 years ago I thought I had to be, to facilitator – someone who guides, listens, and co-creates learning experiences.

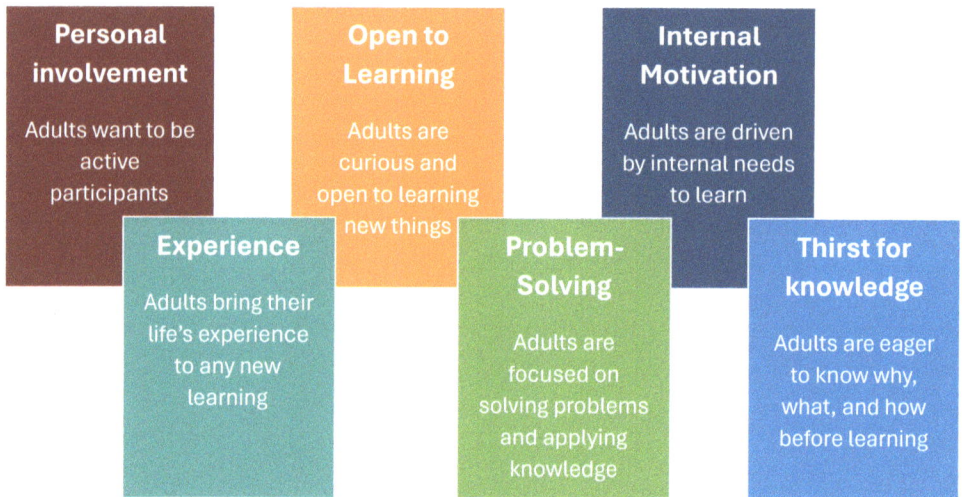

Figure 9.1. Principles of effective adult learning – A contemporary interpretation (inspired by the work of Knowles, 1980).

David Kolb adds further depth to this understanding with his experiential learning model (Figure 9.2). He suggests that learning is a cycle of **concrete experience**, **reflective observation**, **abstract conceptualisation**, and **active experimentation**. This cycle emphasises that knowledge is built through doing and reflecting, not just receiving information. It is the combination of these two models that assist the educator with the design and execution of the training programme. It also allows the educator to have the courage to spend more time in the reflective stage than the actual experience stage. Adult learners thrive in environments where they are seen, heard, and respected.

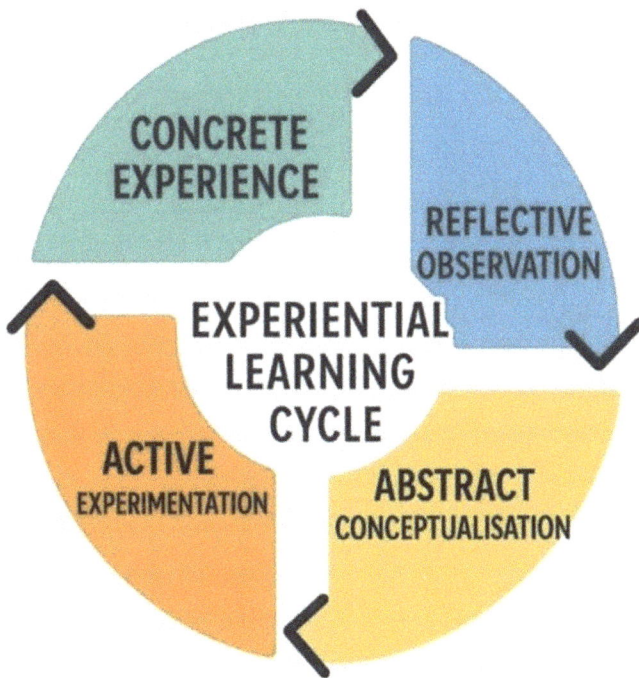

Figure 9.2. The continuing cycle of experiential learning (inspired by the work of Kolb, 1984).

2.2 Transactional analysis: A psychology of growth and change

TA offers a psychological lens through which we can understand interpersonal dynamics in the learning environment. Originally developed as a theory of psychotherapy, it is widely applied in education, leadership, and group facilitation.

At its core, there are three foundational assumptions:

- **People are OK**: Every person has value, dignity, and the capacity for growth.
- **Everyone can think**: Learners can engage in rational thinking and decision-making.
- **People decide their own destiny, and these decisions can be changed**: Change is possible, and autonomy is within reach.

When we merge these basics with the principles of adult learning, we see that learning is not something 'done' to someone but something they 'do' for themselves with support. This principle is supported by the work of Tudor & Summers (2014) around the principle of shared responsibility – 'co-creative transactional analysis supports the practical manifestation of interdependence, co-operation and mutuality' (p. 4). Those same therapeutic principles apply in androgogy.

Educators can benefit from recognising when they are operating from the positive aspects of nurturing and/or controlling Parent states, an objective and here-and-now Adult state, and/or the positive spontaneous and/or adaptive Child states. Learners do the same.

Awareness of the traditional functional model of these ego states can assist in the transforming the learning space. It allows educators and facilitators to engage from a position of integrating Adult. Boundaries are clear, dialogue is respectful, and each person's contribution is valued. Stewart and Joines (1987/2012) point out that a number of scholars have argued that, because the functional model of ego states does not sufficiently encompass the dimensions of thinking and feeling, it may be more appropriate to refrain from using the term '*ego states*' in discussions of functional analysis. To that end, they refer to a 'Five Behaviours Model' made up of five rectangles, further developed by Susannah Temple as being an alternative way to 'tell the whole story'.

Connecting with more practical tools like Susannah Temple's (2004) Functional Fluency model and how it can help educators respond to group dynamics, emotions, and emerging needs, is more beneficial to creating and delivering inspiring adult learning environments.

2.3 Functional fluency: The fab five
Susannah Temple's (2004) **Functional Fluency** model gives educators a clear, behavioural map for how to lead well. Building on Berne's 'embryonic integrated Adult' (1961/1975, p. 194), Temple identifies five '**positive modes**' that promote effective interaction:

1. **Guiding and directing** – Providing clarity, structure, and boundaries.
2. **Looking after people** – Offering warmth, support, and encouragement.
3. **Doing my own thing** – Encouraging spontaneity, creativity, and playfulness.
4. **Relating to others** – Showing responsiveness and cooperation.
5. **Accounting** – Engaging with clarity, logic, and present-moment awareness (Figure 9.3).

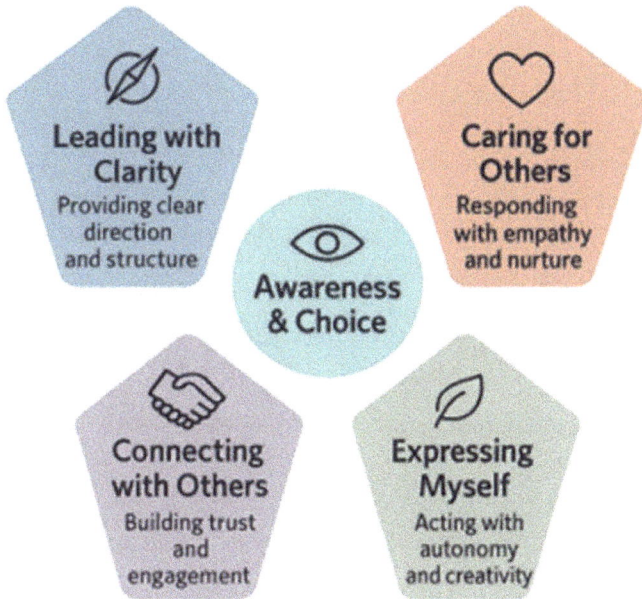

Figure 9.3. Five elements of Functional Fluency (inspired by Temple, 2002).

These modes are dynamic. The key is **intentional fluency**: moving between them with purpose and awareness based on her original construction of the of the functional fluency map of nine behaviours. The five positive modes are Positive Control, Positive Care, Accounting, Positive Socialized Self, and Positive Natural Self.

A practical takeaway from Functional Fluency is to check in with yourself:

- Am I being too directive?
- Could I offer more warmth?
- Am I letting playfulness into the space?
- Am I modelling calm, Adult thinking?

By cultivating these behaviours in ourselves, we make it more likely that learners will do the same. Later, we'll see how these ideas are made visible in practice through ground rules, developmental cycles, group stages, and behavioural models.

3. What the research tells us: Insights from psychotherapy and education

What makes a learning experience impactful? What role does the facilitator play in shaping the outcomes for participants? These questions were central to the results of both psychotherapy researchers and an educational theorist in the 20th century. While they approached the question from different fields, their findings converge in ways that offer valuable insights for us as educators today.

3.1 Yalom, Lieberman, and Miles: The human factor in group change

Irvin Yalom, Morton Lieberman, and Matthew Miles (1973) conducted a landmark study on encounter groups – intensive small-group sessions designed to foster personal growth. Their research aimed to examine two key questions:

Could personality and behaviour really change in these settings?

Which modality of group psychotherapy was the most effective?

Surprisingly, their findings, published in *Encounter Groups: First Facts* (Yalom et al., 1973) reveal four essential characteristics of the effectiveness of the group leader are strongly associated with positive outcomes:

- **Meaning attribution** – Leaders possess strong capabilities in explaining, clarifying, interpreting, and providing a cognitive framework or narrative for change. They didn't simply let things unfold; they actively translated feelings and events to ideas, and helped learners interpret what was happening.
- **Caring** – Participants responded to facilitators who showed support, warmth, encouragement, and genuine concern. The emotional climate mattered as much as the content.
- **Executive function** – Effective leaders possessed strength in setting limits, rules, norms, and goals through managing time, pacing, stopping, interceding, and suggesting procedures.
- **Emotional stimulation** – Good facilitators could be challenging and confronting, actively modelling personal risk taking and self-disclosure.

These elements, particularly meaning attribution and caring, form the backbone of effective adult education, just as they do in therapeutic groups. They remind us that learning is not only cognitive; it is also relational and emotional.

3.2 Gage and the science of teaching

From a totally different direction, educational psychologist Nathaniel Gage seeks to understand what made teachers effective in adult learning settings. In his 1972 work, *Teacher Effectiveness and Teacher Education*, Gage explores the behavioural characteristics of instructors who were most successful in enriching learning.

Four qualities emerge from his research that align closely with the findings from psychotherapy research:

- **Indirectness** – Instead of prescribing or lecturing, effective teachers prompted discovery and were willing to refrain from sharing everything they know, even when it would be 'good for them'. They asked questions, created space for exploration, and trusted learners to find meaning for themselves.
- **Warmth** –This was about establishing warm relationships – teachers who were approachable, empathetic, and respectful.
- **Cognitive organisation** – The ability to hold clear behavioural objectives in mind and divide learning into orderly steps, offering appropriate data in response to questions and clearly conveying what they know and don't know.
- **Enthusiasm** – Passion is contagious. Learners responded to instructors who were genuinely excited by the subject matter. The most effective leaders have an innate enthusiasm for people and the subject matter.

Quite independently, on different research topics, these findings suggest that the educator is central – not just what they teach, but how they show up. The learning environment is profoundly shaped by tone, presence, and relationship. As a result, I have devised a form for educators to use to assess where they believe their developmental stage is in relation to their current leadership skills (modified for this publication). This is intended to assist in identifying areas for improvement and can also be used to facilitate feedback to the trainer by the learners (Figure 9.4).

Your Group Leadership Qualities

Rate your leadership qualities by circling a number for each of these qualities.
Keep this scale and rate yourself again at the end of this course.

Gage's (1972) study found that Warmth, Indirectness, Cognitive Organisation and Enthusiasm were the qualities found in the effective leaders in adult groups. Yalom et al.'s (1973) study indicated that Meaning Attribution, Caring, Emotional Stimulation and Executive Functioning were the qualities of effective group leaders with the most effective leaders rating high on Caring and Meaning Attribute and moderate on Emotional Stimulation and Executive Function.

Caring
10   5   0
Supportive, Praises, Shows concern   Critical, unsupportive

Meaning attribution
10   5   0
Explains, Relates learning to   Is not OK, Does not relate learning
life experience   life experience

Emotional stimulation
10   5   0
Challenges, Confronts, Self-discloses   Uninvolved, Closed, Unsupportive

Executive function
10   5   0
Sets limits, manages time, Suggests   Is not directive, Doesn't take leadership
procedures   role in time of crisis

Warmth
10   5   0
Warm, Open, Friendly   Cold, Closed

Indirectness
10   5   0
Helpful in allowing people to discover   Eager to tell all you know
for themselves

Enthusiasm
10   5   0
Positive about subject and people,   Flat, Passive, Cynical
Expressive

Cognitive organisation
10   5   0
Clear about goals, Well-organised,   Disorganised, Rambling, Unable
Willing to say "I don't know"   to complete things

Figure 9.4. Group leadership qualities form.

4. Creating conditions for learning

The space in which we learn ideally needs to be one where people can feel safe to be seen, to interact, to stretch themselves. Whether in a workplace, a training room, or a community setting, the educator's role is to shape this space intentionally. Drawing from TA, group theory, and adult learning principles, this section explores how to establish the foundation for real learning to occur. We can often be restricted in the space. It might be a board room for example, with a big table in the middle. It could be an enormous room for a small group of people. Whichever it is, the following two group stage theories will inform the educator as to why preparing the space assists with learners moving as quickly as is comfortable into their best learning mode and how physically dealing with the arrangement may facilitate a more optimum setting.

4.1 Group stages and the imago

It's very useful to understand group dynamics. While they are very different models, I have found that being aware of both Tuckman's (1965) and Berne's (1966) group models helps understand that there are two processes going on. Tuckman's model indicates the development of the group and Berne's, the development of the individual's intrapsychic imago. Both are important for the leader to take into consideration when preparing the room/space, any pre-group work or contact, the meeting and greeting of learners, and the initial exercises (see Table 9.1).

Drawing on Bruce Tuckman's (1965) group development model – **forming, storming, norming, performing**, and **adjourning** – we can anticipate the emotional rhythms of a group.

Each stage has its challenges:

- **Forming** – anxiety and politeness, often upon arrival.
- **Storming** – conflict or resistance, when ground rules are being established and during various stages of the training.
- **Norming** – developing trust and structure once they feel part of the process.
- **Performing** – productive learning and creativity.
- **Adjourning** – closure, debriefing, and processing. Tuckman also called this phase Mourning.

An additional lens is also added through the concept of the Berne's (1966) group imago. These internalised images each learner carries about what groups are like, based on early experiences, come into the learning space.

Each of these imagoes have their challenges:

- **Provisional** – when members are asking who are all these people? do I know anyone? where's this trainer from?
- **Adapted** – when group members begin to alter their internalised images towards a more realistic picture.
- **Operative** – when members have begun the work, decided where they fit in the pecking order, understood the stance of the leader and others and the learning.
- **Adjusted** – when members are finally ready to move into the real work of the training.
- **Clarified** – when members have gained what they sought.

Table 9.1. A comparison of Berne's and Tuckman's group theories.

Berne	Tuckman	Participant	Facilitator
Provisional Imago	Forming	Participants may be nervous and reserved – past experience of a group leader	Provides: Structure Safety Clear guidelines Mutually decided ground rules
Adapted Imago	Storming	Expectations versus reality Disagreements surface	Holds firm boundaries Encourages respect Normalises differences
Operative Imago	Norming	Confidence and trust builds Co-operation and creativity	Strokes growth Acknowledges collaboration Creates environment for peer support
Secondarily Adjusted Imago	Performing	Effective collaboration and co-creativity Authenticity	Challenge Encourage difference of ideas
Clarified Imago	Adjourning	Preparation for closure Integration of the day's learning	Structure and support a closing exercise Reflection and review

As educators, we can't control the imago and each member will not be in synchronisation with each other, but we can create an environment that offers a new, more empowering experience of group life.

4.2 Managing the physical space

The physical space can be managed consciously as well. It is helpful to have space where people can easily move around. This is useful for demonstration exercises, small groups to break out, and generally encourage freedom for action. A rich learning experience includes all opportunities for interaction (Section 6.2).

Dependent on numbers, an optimum space setting (for a group of up to 12–14) is to have a room where the delegates are able to sit comfortably in a circle with the facilitator as part of the circle. If it is a small group in a large room, then taking just one section of the room for the whole group and allowing the rest of the space to be used for breakout work with smaller groups as needed is useful.

In a training room with a big table in the middle (boardroom table) or desks, it is ideal if there are small rooms or spaces where smaller groups can go for breakout work. Weather permitting, this can be done outside. It is useful to keep the 'head' of the table free so as not to set up a power position. The facilitator can work off to the side.

Whatever the training facilities and conditions are, it is useful to be creative in finding places where delegates can move and interact.

5. Cycles of development and learner steps

Adult learners arrive with their life's experiences, their identity and, of course, their imago. It's worth acknowledging the various frustrations that many will experience as they adjust to change and learning something new.

5.1 Cycles of development

Pam Levin's (1988) work on cycles of development and the further contributions by Napper and Newton (2000) and Hay (1996) outline predictable stages of human development. These stages – *Being, Doing, Thinking, Identity, Skilful & Structure, Integration,* and *Recycling* exemplify the cyclical nature of adult learning and change.

This is a simplified view of how these stages can show up in a learning setting:

- **Being** – Learners need to feel safe, accepted, and grounded. Here we build rapport and establish presence. Pre-course work and contact, warmth and welcoming from the educator assist this stage.

- **Doing** – Learners take action, often before fully understanding. Energy is high; structure is essential. Clear, firm directions with the process such as having the Agenda visible; discussion of the Ground Rules; clear instructions when directing activities are vital.
- **Thinking** – Reflection kicks in. Learners seek to make sense of their experience and connect it to prior knowledge. Allow time after an exercise or activity.
- **Identity** – New skills or insights begin to influence self-concept.
- **Skilful & Structure** – Competence grows through repetition and feedback.
- **Integration** – The learning becomes internalised. It's no longer 'something I do', it's part of who I am.

This developmental model helps us shift from a one-size-fits-all delivery model to a more responsive facilitation style; one where we are interactive, observant, and flexible in the process. It reminds us that some learners need affirmation before challenge, or time to think before acting. It's useful to use pairs, trios, or small groups for exercises to ensure everyone is involved and included. Learners can resist or withdraw if pushed beyond their comfort zone too early.

5.2 Learner steps: A developmental lens
Jean Illsley Clarke and Connie Dawson (1998) adapt these developmental ideas for adult group work, particularly in parenting and educational contexts. Clarke emphasises that learning is not linear; people cycle through stages as they encounter new challenges, build skills, or return to areas of uncertainty.

In practice, this might mean:

- Offering time for 'Being' after an intense task through processing, journaling, or quiet conversation.
- Designing activities that are creative for 'Doing', structured for 'Skilful'.
- Recognising when resistance or disengagement may show that a learner is being 'pushed past' their developmental readiness.

Educators become guides, not just content deliverers. The diagram below (Figure 9.5) is one that can be on a flip chart on a wall as a guide, reminder, and permission to learners. Quite often, they are already very skilled in various aspects of their lives and expect that they will easily learn and to be frustrated when it is not the case.

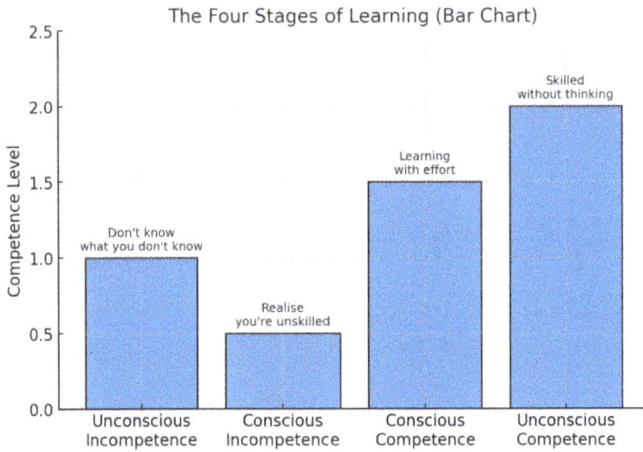

Figure 9.5. The four stages of learning (adapted from Burch, n.d.): A specific profile.[2]

6. Designing and facilitating learning

A powerful learning environment is not only about *what* is taught, but *how* it's planned, delivered, and thought about. As we have discovered through the groundwork theories and research already discussed, designing for adult learners means recognising that learning is as much about relationship as it is about content.

6.1 The planning wheel: A framework for educators

Jean Illsley Clarke's (1984) **Planning Wheel** offers a six-step process that supports thoughtful, responsive educational design. It's not just about delivering content; it's about creating transformational experiences that engage the head, heart, and hands.

The six steps are:

1. **Identify outcomes** – What do we want learners to *know*, *do*, or *feel* differently after this experience?
2. **Assess needs** – What do the learners bring? What are their existing capabilities, fears, hopes?
3. **Design experiences** – Activities are chosen to match learner needs and stages.
4. **Facilitate learning** – The educator attends to timing, pacing, tone, and engagement using both planned and emergent moments.

---

[2] This model was developed by De Phillips et al. (1960).

5. **Evaluate learning** – Assessment includes observation, feedback, and behavioural signs of learning.
6. **Integrate and follow up** – The final step reinforces learning over time, connecting new insights to daily work/life.

Educators can use this model to design whole programs, or even review a single session asking, 'Did I consider all the elements of the wheel?'

6.2 Engaging the whole learner: Sensory and cognitive styles

As we discovered earlier, adults learn best by having concrete experience and then reflecting; however, they differ in how they take in information, engage with ideas, and express understanding. A rich learning environment appeals to multiple senses, offering **visual, auditory, kinaesthetic,** and **interpersonal** opportunities for interaction.

The form below has been inspired by the work of Jean Illsley Clarke (1984) which also provides assistance the educator when designing the training programme (Figure 9.6).

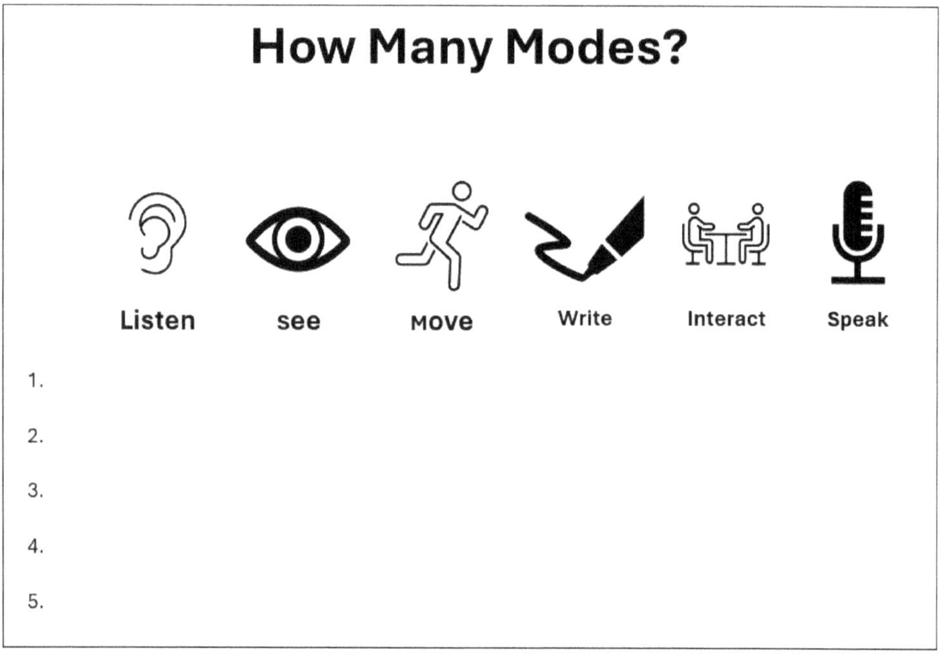

Figure 9.6. The number of modes/senses when designing training (inspired by the work of Clarke, 1984).

One way to explore this is through the opening activity you use. For example:

- Invite learners to **listen** to a short audio.
- Ask them to **see** and interpret a visual diagram.
- Prompt them to **speak** about what stands out.
- Get them to **write** a thought or intention.
- Encourage them to **interact** in pairs or small groups.

7. Practical techniques for educators

Theory provides the framework, but training really comes to life when we are authentic and organic in structuring the discussions, handling discomfort, responding to questions, and interacting with the learners. This section offers a collection of practical techniques drawn from transactional analysis, adult learning theory, and experiential practice.

7.1 Ground rules: Setting the frame

Ground rules are more than housekeeping. They are boundary markers that signal psychological safety and clarify expectations. When co-created with learners at the start of a session, ground rules establish a contract for mutual respect and personal responsibility as indicated in Section 2.1.

Examples might include:

- Confidentiality
- Respect for self and others' contributions
- Permission to 'pass' in activities or discussions
- Everyone participates
- Having fun
- Having mobile phones off or on silent

This practice sets the tone by modelling the functional ego state behaviours of Adult, Nurturing Parent, Controlling Parent (Section 2.2), and sets the frame for behaviours you hope to see.

7.2 Behavioural anchors: Leading with intention

Drawing on Susannah Temple's (2002) **Functional Fluency** model, facilitators can intentionally move between five effective behaviour modes as described in Section 2.3, depending on what the group needs.

- Use **Firm mode (Controlling Parent+)** when you need to create clarity: 'We'll take five minutes for this activity, and then come back together.'
- Shift into **Friendly mode (Nurturing Parent+)** to support participation: 'Take your time. There's no fixed way to approach this.'
- Activate **Free mode (Free Child+)** to energise the group: 'Let's play with some ideas before we land on a final version.'
- Engage **Flexible mode (Adapted Child+)** to model cooperation: 'I hear you – let's see if that works.'
- Stay in **Focused mode (Adult)** to remain steady in uncertainty: 'Let's pause here and discuss that for a moment.'

These behavioural anchors allow facilitators to remain responsive and grounded, adjusting not just the activity, but *how* they show up in the room.

7.3 Meaning attribution: Connecting experience to insight

As found in Yalom, Lieberman, and Miles' research (1973; Section 3.1), **meaning attribution** was shown to be a key group leader's attribute.

Educators can:

- Name the purpose of an activity before and after it occurs.
- Connect experiences to theory: 'That's an example of the non-negotiable elements in managing this situation.'
- Invite learners to describe their own takeaways: 'What meaning are you making from this?'

Meaning attribution transforms exercises from 'busywork' into powerful moments of understanding and change. It's important to allow for ample time for absorption and feedback after an exercise.

7.4 Indirectness: Supporting autonomy

Nathaniel Gage's (1972) concept of **indirectness** (Section 3.2) encourages educators to resist the urge to over-explain or rescue. Adult learners benefit most when they are given the space to explore, contemplate, and discover meaning for themselves.

In practice, this might look like:

- Asking open-ended questions: 'What's your interpretation of that?'

- Giving time to sit with discomfort or silence.
- Offering invitations instead of directives: 'You might want to spend time thinking about this overnight.'

This approach respects the learner's autonomy and ability.

7.5 Warmth and care building a supportive environment

Learners respond not just to the material, but to the *tone* and *emotion* in the space.

To create an environment of caring and warmth:

- If it's possible, make contact with the training attendees before the event – email or text.
- Greet each learner individually at the start.
- Use learners' names, and remember personal details when appropriate.
- Respond to vulnerability with positive strokes and empathy: 'Thank you for sharing that, it's important.'
- Celebrate effort, not just success: 'That was a brave contribution.'

Warmth does not mean being permissive or passive. It is active, intentional, and protective.

7.6 Strokes and permission empowering engagement

Berne (1964) describes certain hungers experienced by all of us. One of them is the need to be recognised. This can come in the form of a smile, a nod, a frown, a compliment, or an insult – commonly referred to as strokes – verbal or non-verbal, positive or negative. In the learning space, positive strokes such as 'I liked how you explained that' helps build connection and motivation.

Educators can:

- Stroke effort as well as insight 'That's a great start.'
- Offer permission: 'It's okay not to know yet.'
- Model empowerment: 'You already have many of the answers, you just haven't uncovered them all.'

Have fun wherever it can be incorporated.

8. Bringing it together

Creating an inspiring adult learning environment is not about following a set script, it's far more organic. It's about developing the capacity to respond, relate, and reflect in real time. By blending **transactional analysis**, **adult learning theory**, and **research-informed facilitation**, educators can create the atmosphere where adults feel comfortable enough to take risks, supported enough to explore change, and heard/seen enough to feel valued and to stay engaged.

We have explored how concepts such as ego states, functional fluency, developmental cycles, and group dynamics give us powerful tools to not just understand learning but to lead it with skill and compassion. It has also shown that the role of the educator or facilitator goes beyond instruction. You are:

- A designer and guide through cycles of doing, experimenting, and reflection (Kolb, 1984) (see Section 2.1 above).
- A collaborator in mutual contract and discovery (Tudor & Summers, 2014) (Section 2.2).
- A leader of emotional tone and psychological safety (Gage, 1972; Yalom et al., 1973) (Sections 3.1 and 3.2).
- A flexible responder to developmental needs (Clarke, 1984; Clarke & Dawson, 1998; Levin, 1988; Napper & Newton, 2000) (Sections 5.1, 5.2 and 6).

At its best, adult education can be transformational. This paper is informed by karangarua – unity through diversity in relationship as the theme of the 2024 international TA Conference. The principle acknowledges the value of inclusivity across cultures and supports equity within educational settings. Drawing on adult learning theory and the philosophy of TA and its applications, this paper positions the educator as a catalyst in which that transformation unfolds. The tools, theories, frameworks, and practices examined here aim to strengthen educator responsiveness, flexibility, and relational presence supporting learners across differences in culture, learning styles, developmental stages, and group dynamics. In doing so, educators are positioned to foster learning environments that are equitable and inspirational.

8.1 Reflective questions for practice
To end, here are some questions to help you integrate this material into your own educational setting:

- Which of the Functional Fluency modes do I naturally use? Which might I develop further?
- How do I establish psychological safety and a clear contract at the beginning of a session?
- When do I offer too much information or direction? Could more indirectness empower learners?
- How do I support learners who are at different stages of development or readiness?
- What's one small change I could make in delivering my next training session to bring more warmth, care, or meaning into my learning environment?

References

Barrow, G., & Newton, T. (Eds.). (2016). *Educational transactional analysis: An international guide to theory and practice*. Routledge.

Berne, E. (1975). *Transactional analysis in psychotherapy: A systematic individual and social psychiatry*. Grove Press. (Original work published 1961)

Berne, E. (1964). *Games people play: The psychology of human relationships*. Grove Press.

Berne, E. (1966). *Principles of group treatment*. Oxford University Press.

Burch, N. (n.d.). *The four stages for learning any new skill*. Gordon Training International.

Clarke, J. I. (1984). *Who, me lead a group?* Parenting Press.

Clarke, J. I., & Dawson, C. (1998). *Growing up again: Parenting ourselves, parenting our children* (2nd ed.). Hazelden.

Clarkson, P. (1991). Group imago and the stages of group development. *Transactional Analysis Journal, 21*(1), 39–47. https://doi.org/10.1177/036215379102100106

De Phillips, F. A., Berliner, W. M., & Cribbin, J. J. (1960). *Management of training programs*. Richard D. Irwin.

Gage, N. L. (1972). *Teacher effectiveness and teacher education: The search for a scientific basis*. Pacific Books.

Hay, J. (1996). *Transactional analysis for trainers*. Sherwood Publishing.

Hooper, R. (2016). Training in organisations with TA. In G. Barrow & T. Newton (Eds.), *Educational transactional analysis: An international guide to theory and practice* (pp. 216–226). Routledge.

Knowles, M. S. (1980). *The modern practice of adult education: From pedagogy to andragogy* (2nd ed.). Cambridge Books.

Kolb, D. A. (1984). *Experiential learning: Experience as the source of learning and development*. Prentice Hall.

Levin, P. (1988). *Becoming the way we are: The universal stages of growth*. Transactional Publications.

Napper, R., & Newton, T. (2000). *Tactics: Transactional analysis concepts for all trainers, teachers and tutors plus insight into collaborative learning strategies*. TA Resources.

Stewart, I., & Joines, V. (2012). *TA today: A new introduction to transactional analysis*. Lifespace Publishing. (Original work published 1987)

Temple, S. (2002). Celebrating functional fluency and its contribution to transactional analysis theory. *Transactional Analysis Journal, 45*(1), 10–22. https://doi.org/10.1177/0362153714568803

Temple, S. (2004). Functional fluency for educational leadership. In C. Day & J. Sachs (Eds.), *International handbook on the continuing professional development of teachers* (pp. 257–282). Open University Press.

Tuckman, B. W. (1965). Developmental sequence in small groups. *Psychological Bulletin, 63*(6), 384–399. https://doi.org/10.1037/h0022100

Tudor, K., & Summers, G. (2014). *Co-creative Transactional Analysis: Papers, responses, dialogues, and developments*. Karnac.

Yalom, I. D., Lieberman, M. A., & Miles, M. B. (1973). *Encounter groups: First facts*. Basic Books.

Paper 10

Working with bad men: TA approaches to the discursively constructed criminal self

Seán Manning, Dave Nicholls, and Elizabeth Day

Abstract

This paper is based on experience working with criminal men, a population of whom it is said, with some justification, that 'nothing works' (Newbold, 2008, p. 385). Yet over and over, we see people change, and we wonder what makes this happen. The conclusions presented here are based on over three decades of group and individual psychotherapy in prison, in a therapeutic community, and in a community-based Stopping Violence programme.

In this paper I reference the writings of Michel Foucault, Judith Butler, and Nikolas Rose, with certain transactional analysis concepts. The developing thesis uses the notion of two voices exploring the origin of things, but not in the individual. Everything we do, feel, and think arises out of relations of power and resistance. This applies to the deployment of ideas, the structure of institutions, to customs, to ways of understanding that control, produce, and distribute knowledge in a society. This apparatus that allows and inhibits ways of thinking, feeling, and doing things is known as discourse and *dispositif* (Foucault, 1978).

If discourse is identified with language (M. G. Kelly, 2020), then when we enter into dialogue, we can 'exercise upon language, with every word... a sort of constant interior pressure which makes it shift imperceptibly upon itself at any given moment in time' (Foucault, 1966/1989, p. 403). History is all around us, in everything we do, feel, think, and say, given form by language. This thesis suggests that dialogue, in other words the interaction of two voices, shifts discourse, imperceptibly changing our phenomenology and the world we live in. While we cannot escape power, that is to say, our autonomy is an illusion, we can produce change, though unpredictably and almost certainly not by contracting for it, a popular strategy in transactional analysis psychotherapy and counselling (Manning, 1995, 1997; Manning et al., 2024; Manning & Nicholls, 2020; Manning et al., 2025).

Introductory remarks

This paper contains reflections on psychotherapy with men who have considerable experience of imprisonment, a population concerning whom it is said, with some justification, that 'nothing works' (Newbold, 2008, p. 385). The conclusions presented here are based on over three decades of group and individual psychotherapy with men who have histories of serious criminal offending, working in prison as a visiting psychotherapist, in a therapeutic community treatment facility that specialises in treating parolees under orders from a court or Parole Board, and in a community-based Stopping Violence programme to which men and women are referred by the criminal and family courts and by themselves.

The conclusions presented here are derived from working with men. The consequences of the imprisonment of women are unlikely to be the same. However, it may be that the perspective of this chapter, particularly the theory of subjectification derived from Foucault (2002, 2010), Foucault et al. (1988), Rose (1998, 1999), and Butler (1990, 1993) and applied to psychotherapy, has some value for work in a wider field.

The impetus for this work has been guided by a simple, practical observation, gained from facilitating groups in a therapeutic community and in a community-based Stopping Violence programme. It is this: if we can get a group of men together for a couple of hours or more each week, if we can guide the conversation towards talking about the experience of living and being in relationship, and if we can keep doing that for a year or more; then the lives of those men and those around them will reliably change for the better (Manning et al., 2017). They will abandon violence as a way of being in the world and in their families, they will reduce or cease their use of intoxicating substances, and if they engaged in other criminal offending, they will stop. They will sometimes become mentors, continuing to attend the meetings, becoming a resource for the other men attending and being paid for doing so. Of course, these conclusions are unreferenced, and largely unresearched. We suspect that the 2017 report in the primary author's name is a rare exception, as research on similar programmes has been hard to find. Nevertheless, these ideas are widely held among experienced clinicians working in the field, hence this paper and other papers in the same body of work (Manning, 1995, 1997; Manning et al., 2024; Manning & Nicholls, 2020; Manning et al., 2025).

In this paper we introduce some ideas concerning what is known as *discourse* (Foucault, 1981), *dispositif* (Foucault, 1978), and Judith Butler's *performativity* (Butler, 1990) to explain some observations made in the course of my work. There is then an attempt to work with certain transactional analysis concepts, introducing a critique based on *discourse* and *dispositif* but hopefully without undermining TA theory.

Discourse

It is difficult, and perhaps impossible to any high degree of detail, to examine or describe discourse as it affects us in the present, since we are likely to be conducting such an analysis from a perspective, and within a system of truth, determined, or at least influenced by the discourse we are trying to describe. Readers who are familiar with the work of Michel Foucault will need no introduction to discourse. For those who have yet to encounter him, it is recommended that the reader start with his later interviews (for instance, Foucault, 2019) or with Veyne's (2010) summary of his thought, or Macey's (1993/2019) biography, rather than Foucault's books, which can be challenging.

For the purposes of this paper, discourse can be thought of as a heterogeneous system of ideas, beliefs, and practices that shape and govern knowledge and social relations within a particular historical context. Its rules, norms, and practices determine what can be said, thought, and understood within a given society or institution. Discourse plays a crucial role in the construction and regulation of social reality, but it is not conscious, and can, in Veyne's view, be compared to the psychoanalytic unconscious, though operating not just at the level of the individual subject, but subjectifying large groups, even entire societies.

Discourse limits the categories of our thought, applying *type* to people, groups, and many phenomena. The idea of non-Christian, for instance, referring to an obviously heterogeneous set of groups, becomes a distinct homogeneous set under a Christian discourse, a way of determining the important social dualism of *them* and *us*. In the primary author's original home, Northern Ireland, a place where the distinction between Roman Catholic and Protestant is vitally important, there is a joke: a dark-skinned person is asked their religion, and responds that they are a Buddhist, resulting in some confusion in the questioner, who then asks whether they are a Protestant Buddhist or a Catholic Buddhist. The humour is heightened by the reality of a discourse which sets out and limits available categories, determining what can and cannot be thought, and by the questioner's ignorance of the unconscious actuarial script that determines what can and must be asked, what can and cannot be thought, what can be known, what is acceptable.

Discourses, in Foucault's philosophy, are shaped by power relations. Discourse and power are two aspects of the same schemata. In the example above, power relations exist between the church(s) and their members, between the priests and parishioners, between secular political and military power and that of the church, and it is a two-way influence. The priest only has power as long as the parishioners permit it, and many a politician has been ousted by dissatisfied voters and revolutionaries. Secular government and military authority co-exist in often uneasy alliances, with, in a seemingly increasing number of cases internationally, the paramilitaries (revolutionaries or terrorists, depending on one's point of view) adding a third, fourth, and fifth authority, while the churches maintain an equally uneasy series of partnerships with them.

The everyday influence of such power relations is discourse, a mostly invisible, out-of-awareness script operating through language, knowledge, and social practices, shaping our understanding of ourselves and the world around us. The institutions, disciplinary practices, and social norms we take for granted are expressions of both power relations and discourse. Neither power relations nor discourse are fixed or homogeneous. They can be contradictory and multiple. Finally, we must accept that one cannot be outside of power (Foucault, 1978). Similarly, we cannot examine discourse except from within discourse. We might mention here, anticipating questions about clinical or rehabilitative work, that if one asks, how can we change the discourse that determines us as individuals, the question itself is determined by the discourse on individualism that determines us.

Discourse and the self

In her memoire, Kim Chernin (1995) writes:

> the sequence of provisional selves through which we pass in the course of our lives, each lived for its season then sloughed off, leaving behind fossil traces (memory), but no immediate, felt sense of the living being who once occupied one's life… This sense of fragmentation, this discontinuity, may or may not be a condition peculiar to me. (p. 10)

Examining a past in which we were never, or are no longer, involved, is difficult, because we can only do so from within a discourse affecting us in the present. One can perhaps get an idea of how discourse operates, however, by asking certain questions about one's own past, as Chernin was doing. For instance, if we focus on a decision we made 10 years ago, or, depending on one's age, 20, 30, or 40 years ago, a decision that at the time seemed reasoned and adult, we may today wish we had done it differently, made a different decision. We might be able to identify social forces, fashions, ways of thinking, particular people and institutions whose ideas or relationships with ourselves account for the decision. It can then be asked what were the influences, the powers, or power relations that created those social forces, fashions, ways of thinking and relationships, and which influenced the way the subjects in those relationships thought and felt. In the language of this paper, we might get a glimpse of the operation of discourse in the creation of those power relations, social forces and fashions, and the way we have been subjectified by it, the way we become subjects.

In other words, we can consider the sense of self, to use a formulation proposed by Stern (1985), as a *sense* rather than imagining the self as a reified object, if not entirely a consequence of discourse, as being significantly influenced by it. Veyne (2010) puts it quite definitively:

> Whatever a person's social or individual motives and motivations that, as we say, 'push' him or her, that person has to be free to allow himself/herself to be thus 'pushed' to create something new, instead of remaining trapped inside his/her discursive fishbowl… far from being sovereign, a free subject is constituted in a process that Foucault dubbed 'subjectivization': a subject is not 'natural'; in each age he is modelled by the 'discourses' and set-up of the day, by the reactions of his individual liberty and by whatever 'aestheticizations' he may undergo. (pp. 141–148)

Foucault (1984/1994) himself is considerably more cautious, suggesting that while we can work on ourselves as 'free beings', the possibilities are 'limited and determined' (p. 54), because there is no *outside* to subjectifying power relations. In saying that we can work on ourselves in a manner reminiscent of freedom or individual agency, Foucault is clear that we cannot know the extent to which what we are doing is already determined. Some, like Sapolsky (2023) would go further, suggesting that we should consider everything we do, think, or feel as determined. The argument in this paper does not go quite so far, but Sapolsky's view is useful, it can keep us humble, keep us wondering, what if …?

In answer to Chernin, then, we can fairly confidently respond, no, the sense of fragmentation and discontinuity is not peculiar to her, or to anyone. We could even argue that a sense of coherence and continuity, perhaps experienced or claimed by some, is as much a consequence of discourse as its opposite. Memory, we know, and as Chernin intimates, is a fragile thing, an unreliable archive at best (Genova, 2021) and deeply indebted to discourse. The question that arises, then, is, to what extent is the way we are, our sense of self, our range of feeling, the way we think – things we feel to be deeply personal, perhaps even original – to what extent is all this a creation of discourse? The ways we have understood ourselves and the world throughout our lifespan to date provides one lens through which we can observe and speculate.

The way we see ourselves over historical eras is another. There is good reason to consider, for instance, that the centrality we give to our phenomenology, our inner experience of ourselves, others, and the world, though foreshadowed by a small and largely ignored cadre of psychoanalysts and by philosophers such as Husserl, Heidegger, and Habermas, was not much in our awareness until about 1960. Prior to that, few people considered the inner world to have any importance at all until Bowlby (Kahr,

2015). The notion of childhood as it is widely understood today as extending at least until the teen years, and a picture of the family as responsible for the emerging nature of children is arguably just as recent (Ariès, 1960/1962). Foucault's (1966/1989) *The Order of Things* describes how each historical era is governed by what he called an *épistémè*, a concept overlapping with discourse, a set of conditions that define what is considered knowledge and truth, so that what is true in one era is not necessarily true in others. We tend to think of a kind of historicity of progress, such that truth advances from one era to another, but Foucault cautioned against this idea, suggesting that change is discontinuous and somewhat random, so what we think of as truth today is different, but not necessarily more correct, than what was truth in previous eras.

Looking at our own experience, then, and also taking a long historical perspective, we can see that our experience, our sense of what is, our definition of what is true, is defined, wholly or in part to a much greater extent than our neoliberal sense of individual autonomy (Harvey, 2005; P. Kelly, 2013) would predict. As Veyne (2010) puts it, '"Discourse" cannot be sidestepped, even if we are particularly fortunate, we cannot perceive the true truth or even a future truth, or what purports to be one' (p. 40).

Criminality, prison, and discourse

Two observations underpin this paper. They are not exactly the starting point because this body of work with criminality began before these two events occurred (Manning, 1995, 1997), but they seem like the departure point for the current Foucauldian approach, so we briefly describe them here.

A psychotherapist was talking with a man in prison. They had been working together for almost a year, and both psychotherapist and inmate looked forward to the visits. On the occasion in question, the man was dressed in the regulation uniform for the Visits facility, a one-piece bright orange heavy cotton garment fastened at the rear of the neck by a plastic tie that could only be removed by the cutter kept in the officers' station across the hall. They were in a glass-walled room with a camera in the ceiling, observed by the officers, visitors, and other prisoners as they passed. After a moment's silence, the inmate said to the psychotherapist, 'There is something you do not understand. There are two worlds out there, and in mine, I'm normal.'

The second event took place shortly afterwards, on another visit. A man who was scheduled for a visit from the psychotherapist could not be found. He was not on the muster (the list of resident prisoners). This was not a frequent event, but also not unusual. Prisoners were, and are, are transferred between facilities for a number of reasons – available programmes, space, discipline – at short notice, for security reasons. An officer indicated a number of orange-clad men sitting in the visits area just down the hall from the allocated glass-walled room, and said, 'It's OK, look, they are all the same. Just pick another one, any one.'

The clumsy attempt at humour notwithstanding, from that point on, two things came into focus; there was a *sameness* among the inmates, and they were in some way, common to all or most, *different from us*, from the world of officers and professional visitors. There was a way of walking, a way of holding the body, a set of gestures using the head, a way of looking, a tone of voice, a series of rapid, jerky salutes using the hands and arms, involving at times signals indicating allegiance to a particular gang. These phenomena and their effects are described at greater length elsewhere (Manning et al., 2024; Manning & Nicholls, 2020; Manning et al., 2025), so we will not elaborate further on the details, save to say that the impression, confirmed by many conversations, is one of rebellious pride, of functional roles, of, borrowing a term from Judith Butler (1990), *performativity*, a statement of identity, a *criminal subjectivity* defined and created by its own discourse. There is an important distinction in this. It is not that the men *perform* a certain subjectivity. It is not some kind of act. The discourse precedes them, and the subjectivity *performs them*. These men, arguably existing on the lowest tier of socioeconomic status, having lost their basic freedoms, many of them having lost much more, have adopted a stance toward their experience that is functional. These are men who have nothing, yet, because of a set of behaviours, mannerisms, ways of talking, gestures that are practised every day, have achieved friendships, many of which will last a lifetime, they have a society which welcomes them, they have a career of sorts, and they have mentors who will help them perform it better. If they were ever afraid of retribution, of punishment, they have lost that fear, so that it will be easier to return to prison than it was to go there the first time, just one reason why prison does not function well as a deterrent. The chances of return are high. For first offenders, 30% will be re-imprisoned within four years of release; after that the figure rises to 60%, and keeps on rising the longer the follow-up period (Nadesu, 2008, 2009).

In order to understand these phenomena on such a large scale, we need another Foucauldian concept. The *dispositif*, often translated, as in the title of a recent essay by Agamben (2023) and in a translation of a 1977 interview with Foucault (1980), as *apparatus*, is the way things are organised – an assemblage of discourses, ideas, institutions, and customs including 'the said as well as the unsaid,' (p. 194), which is responsible for what he calls a 'strategic elaboration' (p. 195) which can have unexpected consequences. Although an assemblage like the prison can be consciously designed for a specific purpose, the emergent *dispositif* has a completely different strategy. Foucault (1980) suggested that the prison is designed as 'the most efficient and rational method that could be applied to the phenomenon of criminality', which may be how many, or most, subjects in society think about it, but, as Foucault adds, it results in 'the constitution of a delinquent milieu' (pp. 195–196). That prisons create, rather than reduce, crime, has been suggested by others (Newbold, 2000, 2007, 2008; Reiman & Leighton, 2020), and the statistics on recidivism lend support to that conclusion (Manning & Nicholls, 2020; and below).

So here, in the prison, we have a very clear picture of lives driven by discourse – in this case the discourse about imprisonment and criminality *from the inside* – from the perspective of the *subject*, a term we use for an individual to suggest that we are the creation of *discourse* and *dispositif* – as opposed to the discourse about imprisonment and criminality among people who support tough-on-crime policies (for instance, Hanly, 2025), in which imprisonment is thought to be useful as punishment, rehabilitation, and/or deterrence.

As intimated above, there is good reason to believe that prisons do not deter. They do not rehabilitate, they do not serve victims (Courtney & Pelletier, 2016), they do not reduce crime and they are expensive (Gluckman, 2018). Aotearoa New Zealand has a high rate of imprisonment, and we seem to have a liking for locking up Māori, the poor, the dyslexic, the mentally unwell, the abused, the traumatised, and the neglected (Gluckman, 2011, 2018; Lambie, 2018a, 2018b, 2020). In Aotearoa New Zealand about 52% of prisoners, and a scandalous 69% of women prisoners (Johnston, 2020) are Māori, compared to 16–18% of the population.

The overall *dispositif* surrounding prisons produces conflicting discourses. One operates to drive the sentencing, particularly of young men and more particularly young Māori men, to prison, in the name of the victim and the public approval that accompanies such sentencing. Another operates in prison to turn those young men from troublesome boys into gang members and repeat offenders (Manning et al., 2024). The transition of Māori through educational institutions, through a child welfare system which has always disproportionately removed Indigenous children from their families, placed them in abusive institutions, and subsequently sent them to prison, has been convincingly and horrifyingly documented (Gluckman, 2011, 2018; Little, 2023). The persistence of such an illogical and ineffectual system can only be explained by a racist discourse so deeply embedded in the apparatus of government that it can be denied over the entire colonial history of Aotearoa New Zealand. Such is the power, and, in this case, the malignancy, of discourse.

It is important to note that, although in the latter example it underpins an oppressive apparatus, there is nothing inherently positive or negative about discourse. Racist discourse that creates the *pipeline* (Gluckman, 2018) known as *care to cages* (People Against Prisons Aotearoa, 2024) is clearly oppressive, but in prison, the transition from misfit to criminal is a move from powerlessness to identity, to a sense of place, a status among peers. Perhaps at this point it is clear why the idea of discourse seems apt to describe the lives of prisoners, and why it illuminates our observations about them. The rest of this chapter will explore the extent to which transactional analysis theory can incorporate this kind of thinking.

Discourse and TA

Tempting though it is to review transactional analysis theory in the light of discourse theory, the task would be enormous, and probably not very functional, so we will confine the discussion here mainly to two foundational concepts: ego state theory and the idea of contractual treatment.

Ego state theory

There is no difficulty in identifying discourse with the Parent ego state. Drego's (1983) *Cultural Parent* makes this clear, even extending the notion to second order structure, with internalised Parent in the Parent equivalent to cultural values, the Adult in the Parent to cultural technologies or practices, and the introjected Child to culturally supported patterns of emotional expression. (The idea that felt emotions, rather than being somehow universal or natural, are a product of culture is supported in literature on affective economies [Ahmed, 2014] and, with a particular eye on the carceral, affective arrangements [Wüschner, 2017].) Discourse, which prescribes values, technologies, and means of expression that are permitted and not permitted, adds depth to Drego's model, extending the idea of the Parent beyond defining it as introjected aspects of an actual person.

The Child ego state(s) similarly can be seen, not only as the remnants of the child's responses to the world, but as responses within the limits prescribed by discourse. We might need to set aside the Natural Child, described as an archaic ego state which is free from Parental influence (Berne, 1961), as it implies that there is a 'natural' way to be a child, an idea that is questioned by discourse theory and by literature on affect (Barrett,

157

2017; Emre, 2021; Leerkes et al., 2020). The functional Adapted Child becomes, then, the only possible model for a Child ego state.

Concerning the Adult, in his first book on transactional analysis, Berne (1961) writes, perhaps cautiously: 'Typically, there was one ego state characterized by reasonably adequate reality-testing and rational reckoning (secondary process), and another distinguished by autistic thinking and archaic fears and expectations (primary process)' (p. 28).

Subjectification by discourse, as described above in the prison example, is essentially a functional process. Criminal subjectivity works, it is functional in the sense of being a useful adaptation, in a similar sense to the way transactional analysis theory speaks of personality adaptations (Joines & Stewart, 2002; Ware, 1983). Even though we might recoil at the idea that criminality can be functional, we must see it as neither good nor bad, but simply adaptive, given a certain context. The prison is a signifier for this context, referred to by Foucault (1975/1995) as the *carceral* – the network of mechanisms that operate as surveillance, that serve to discipline, categorise, and correct, encompassing operations in schools, workplaces, services, at the table and the club, and in the workplace, which prescribe acceptable behaviour, thoughts, and feelings, and exclude that which deviates from a norm. The prison, which has a real presence in its concrete and razor wire, serves as a symbol for the carceral, a threat of what can happen if one deviates.

Foucault was influenced in this by his mentor, Georges Canguilhem (1966/1991), who, beginning with physiology, discussed the establishment of norms and normative practices, the processes by which we learn and decide what is normal, what is acceptable, and therefore what is *not* acceptable. 'Every preference for a possible order is accompanied, most often implicitly, by the aversion for the opposite possible order' (p. 240) suggests Canguilhem. A few lines later he adds that there can be an inversion, 'as the ethical norm, where sincerity prevails over duplicity, can be inverted into a norm where duplicity prevails over sincerity' (p. 240). Thus, the norm changes radically, depending on the point of view. Those who, for whatever reason, cannot or will not inhabit what we might call the mainstream normative world can discover that rejection of it might seem a reasonable alternative, and the most available kind of rejection in the surrounding world of discourse will be the most obvious choice. From the prisoner's perspective in the carceral, the most available discourse is a normative criminality. Borrowing again from Butler, the discourse will perform the prisoner, producing that sameness among prisoners mentioned earlier, and since it is functional, it forms a kind of *intoxicating performativity* (Manning & Nicholls, 2020).

The carceral not only reinforces society's prevailing normative practices, but, for those on the receiving end of its discipline, especially those who are imprisoned, there is an alternative, Canguilhem's inversion, a criminal subjectivity which rejects society's norms and enthusiastically embraces their opposite. As Foucault (1975/1995) observes, 'Delinquency is the vengeance of the prison on justice' (p. 255).

A criminal subjectivity provides a way of being, a sense of self, an Adult ego state, to people who are regarded as an inconvenient problem which needs to be locked away for a while. One source writing from a United States prison uses the metaphor of 'warehousing' people (Case, 2019), suggesting that prison is really not much more purposeful. This is supported in criminological literature, where claims of intent and design behind it are critiqued (Newbold, 2007, 2008, 2016; Reiman & Leighton, 2020). Adopting an identity as a criminal changes a man's status, resulting in a self-esteem hitherto unavailable. Accepting its functional nature, then, we must accept that it satisfies Berne's (1961) observation of an Adult ego state, characterised by 'reasonably adequate reality testing' (p. 28). It is a challenge to accepted theory to do so, since Adult functioning is implicitly (that is to say, within discourse) conformist, a function that assists the subject to fit in with societal norms. Even rebellion from an Adult perspective is driven by societal expectations of the rebel.

If we step sideways and look for evidence from other versions of the self, there are several immediately available from philosophy and neuroscience, and from combinations of the two. Damasio (2011) and Graziano (2010, 2013) provide a neuroscientist's picture of how an image of the self is constructed by the human brain. We create an image of ourselves from neural maps of the body in escalating order of complexity, starting with physiological homeostatic mechanisms and then making maps of maps of maps until consciousness is achieved (Damasio), and we construct images of the self in the same way, and with the same neural machinery, as we create images of others (Graziano). Edelman and Tononi (2000) present a convincing argument suggesting that images of the self – consciousness – arise as a quality of complexity and connectivity. In a beautifully poetic illustrated work describing how Galileo is given a tour of the brain and its functions by a guide named Frick (presumably a reference to the Nobel Prize winning Francis Crick, who concerned himself with consciousness in his later years [Koch, 2012]), Tononi (2012) explores the same mystery in fiction.

All of these illustrate cleverly how our subjectivity emerges, and all of them, with varying nuances, describe an illusion, a picture, and like all other pictures, it is something made up, something imagined. The twin ideas of authenticity and autonomy do not have much traction in this landscape. The self is a construction. From a more philosophical perspective, Metzinger's (2009) *Ego Tunnel* is a construction of the self that imagines events as actions, creating a mythical attribution of self. Sampson's *Assemblage Brain* (Sampson, 2017) attributes cognition to a construction arising from a co-operative assemblage of brain, body, technology, and relationship. These elegant models have one thing in common – the self is something constructed, made up from available material. It is not a given, it changes, and it makes meaning of things and of itself out of whatever material comes to hand. These models are far more aligned with discourse theory than with the individualistic theories of autonomy and agency which underpin much psychotherapeutic theory, and which cause some psychotherapists to reject postmodern ideas (Frie, 2003).

Because subjectivity does not assume individual autonomy or agency, this broad theoretical agreement from philosophy and neuroscience might be considered antipathetic to transactional analysis, with the latter's emphasis on individuation. In these models, we see that the subject could not have acted otherwise. Were we to adopt a much older metaphor, that of Plato's cave – in which we are like people imprisoned in a cave, compelled to face the rear wall, where we see only shadows of the world outside – the absence of personal agency would not seem strange. A modern version of the metaphor is given by Metzinger (2009):

> If we take our own phenomenology seriously, we clearly experience ourselves as beings that can initiate new causal chains out of the blue… The unsettling point about modern philosophy of mind and the cognitive neuroscience of will… is that a final theory may contradict the way we have been subjectively experiencing ourselves for millennia… There will be a conflict between the biological reality tunnel in our heads and the neuroscientific image of humankind. (p. 127)

It is startling to consider such a worldview, but, as Metzinger (2009) continues: 'If one takes the scientific worldview seriously, no such things as goals exist, and there is nobody who selects or specifies an action' (p. 130).

There are, of course, critics of this view. Sampson (2017), in his *Assemblage Brain*, argues for cognition as a consequence of an interaction between internal and external, which avoids the criticism of Plato's cave-like models such as Metzinger's. As Sampson (2017) puts it:

> This is seeing with eyes closed, without windows. It is an outside imagined as a phantom representation, separated from the body, the other, and the environment… The projections of the world on the walls of the cave are a relation to interiority. Unlike assemblages, they have no *relation to exteriority*. (p. 165)

Both Metzinger and Sampson, despite their differences, present models that are congruent with discourse theory. That Sampson sees more relationship between the internal world and an exterior, by including relationships and technologies as determinants, does not mean he is suggesting anything like autonomy. If anything, his model is all the more congruent with Foucault because the exterior world of discourse is explicitly part of the assemblage of consciousness.

Later in his 1961 text, Berne sets in motion the identification of Adult functioning with autonomy, though his formulation is still careful: 'The Adult ego state is characterized by an autonomous set of feelings, attitudes, and behavior patterns which are adapted to the current reality.' (Berne, 1961, p. 82).

Here we can detect an ambivalence in TA theory. 'Reasonably adequate reality testing' (Berne, 1961, p. 28) is not the same as autonomy as defined in this quotation. In Steiner's model of the script matrix, which extends ego state theory in the service of understanding the origins of script, all three ego states (or groups of ego states, depending on one's theoretical preference) are programmed, and the influence from parents which forms the Adult in the child is actually called the 'program' (Steiner, 1966, 1974/1995). In Berne's (1961) second order structure of the Adult, Ethos and Pathos suggest programming of Adult functioning by Parent and Child, with Logos between them surviving as a kind of logical functioning, a core of the self that might be capable of autonomous functioning.

The contract

The contract is arguably the defining concept in transactional analysis philosophy. In a carefully crafted article situating TA among the phenomenologist philosophies of Husserl, Heidegger, Binswanger, and May, Rotondo (2020) reminds us that it is a requirement of the ethical code of the European Association for Transactional Analysis, yet there are differences of opinion about whether it is necessary for change in therapy. For Berne, contracting expressed the bilateral nature of therapeutic dialogue, a subject–subject relationship, as opposed to the Cartesian subject–object paradigm typical of psychoanalysis as practised at the time Berne was writing. Rotondo suggests that it was his inclusion of the patient in clinical discussions – for instance, the staff–patient conferences he initiated on a psychiatric ward – that alienated him from his psychoanalytic community.

There was a secondary price paid in many popular writings following Berne, in which the process of contracting was oversimplified, and in Rotondo's description, 'impoverished'. The deeper philosophical meaning of the two-person dialogue may have been lost for many, becoming formulaic as in the procedural nature of redecision therapy (Goulding & Goulding, 1979) with its 'contact, contract, change, encore' (Hoyt, 1995), where identification of early decisions, redecision, and anchoring are usually accomplished within the same session. Contract became defined as *task*, supported by literature on task completion (for instance, Gellert & Wilson, 1978), and by Berne's (1972) definition of contract as an expression of an Adult-to-Adult partnership aimed at cure rather than progress. Cure and contract completion became conflated. In the interests of the patient, of clear, goal-directed therapy and simple language that would improve the bilaterality of therapeutic dialogue, contracting became increasingly structured, as in de Saint-Pierre's (2004) four-stage model.

Rotondo (2020) suggests that the appeal of simplified models hid potentially rich dialogues and differences within the method. One of the authors of redecision therapy, Mary Goulding (1995), revealed in a guest editorial, three years after her husband Bob's death, that she would argue over the universal necessity for contracting and anchoring.

Some writers have argued against the use of the contract as a measure of cure (for instance, Drye, 1980), suggesting that un-contracted outcomes such as an improved ability to deal with conflict, to be capable of loving and developing mature relationships with others, to have a 'firm sense of self' (p. 124), the development of self-awareness, and personality change are likely outcomes of therapy.

Two issues arise when TA-style contracting is considered alongside discourse. First, there is the practical matter of the therapist's discourse-driven inclination. The very notion of bilateral contractual treatment (Berne, 1966/1994) is driven by a certain discourse that is apparent in widespread changes in the way we thought about ourselves dating roughly from the end of the Second World War. Phenomenology and psychoanalysis had been around for about half a century, the former in narrow academic philosophical circles, the latter among a small group of men and women, both largely ignored or ridiculed by the wider society. By 15 years after the end of the war, perhaps as a spontaneous interest in ourselves following years of deprivation and discipline, the inner world had become interesting, not just among a few professionals, but in society at large. During the 1960s, people en masse enrolled in encounter groups, experiential psychological training, feminist consciousness raising groups, and what became known as humanistic therapies. We were not just openly interested in ourselves, in a way previously thought to be self-indulgent, we wanted a say in how this exploration was carried out. The notion of contracting was Berne's unique and brilliant way of combining this inward movement with phenomenology. We could not see at the time that a discourse on the self was driving this movement, but hindsight, as always, is clearer.

Discourse about psychotherapy had continued to shift with the emergence of self psychology, relational psychoanalysis, and attachment theory. Lamenting the decline of contractual regressive therapy, Jonathan and Laurie Weiss (1998) point to: (1) a backlash in the media; (2) conservative trends in acceptable practice, particularly concerning touch; and (3) managed care funding (relating to health insurance in the USA). Discourse theory would suggest that a widespread change in the ideas, beliefs, and practices that determine our social reality, neither better nor worse than the ideas, beliefs, and practices that gave regressive therapy such energy, are responsible for the change. Changes in funding strategies and media caution regarding touch are influenced by the same shift in how we define reality that caused us to move away from regressive therapy. The one did not cause the other; they are all parts of a change in discourse. In psychotherapy, for example, a fundamental idea behind regressive therapies was that early scenes can be located in which decisions, made in childhood, drive script in adulthood. Today we are much more likely to look for attachment strategies and complex patterns of trauma that result in adult patterns of inner experience and relationship.

The beliefs that drive the therapist's ideas of what works, what is good for people, and therefore the kind of contract that is acceptable, is profoundly influenced by current discourse in psychotherapy in general and in TA in particular. That is the first difficulty with contracting seen from the perspective of discourse.

The second issue with contracting is specific to the particular context being considered here, the prison, or, more broadly, what Foucault (1975/1995) calls the *carceral archipelago*, the physical and psychological assemblage which culminates in and sustains the prison, that is, the system of ideas, professions, institutions, and buildings necessary to create the idea of the prison in society at large. Its methods include surveillance, examination, categorisation, and correction. It includes policing, the criminal courts, the idea of delinquency, of corrections, of punitive consequences as retribution, as well as the physical prison itself.

Within this carceral, the therapist exists not as an independent, autonomous professional, but as a flesh-and-blood expression of an idea of criminality as a kind of disorder, an idea and a subject who is her/himself as much a part of the carceral as the walls and razor wire. Since the purpose of the carceral is to produce, in Foucault's (1975/1995) words, *docile bodies*, the therapist is unwittingly enlisted in working toward this end. Despite the therapist's protests of independence, it is virtually impossible that they should not wish to contract with the subject to *stop offending*. One might argue that every code of ethics applying to therapists insists upon it, but clearly it would be pointless. The odds are that every prisoner we might meet has had conversations with dozens of people, many of them professionals – teachers, social workers, psychologists, judges, corrections staff – trying to persuade them to stop offending. There is no reason to suppose that the psychotherapist's contracting strategy would be more effective.

If, however, we return to the original meaning of contractual therapy as formulated by Rotondo, starting with the idea of bilateral dialogue, or a subject–subject conversation, the idea of a contract can be a philosophical position from which to start a conversation. This position is stated well by Berne, and cited early in Rotondo's article:

> Since contractual treatment is bilateral rather than unilateral, the next step is for the therapist to say something like: 'Well, why don't you come a few times and that will give you a chance to look me over and you can see what I have to offer'. (Berne, 1966/1994, p. 88)

In the same work, Berne introduced the idea of the Martian attitude, a position from which pre-existing ideas are set aside. While in a literal sense, following Foucault, this is not a possibility, since one cannot operate outside of power relations or outside of discourse it is a useful metaphor for careful listening.

What if this becomes a position from which to conduct therapeutic conversations, not just a starting point? What if we decide that a contractual conversation is defined by bilaterality, which can be merely an agreement to meet and talk, perhaps to listen to each other, rather than by an 'explicit bilateral commitment to a well-defined course of action' (Berne, 1966/1994, p. 362), a definition that appears in a glossary, and is not, as Tudor (2025) points out, discussed in the text? In his provocative, and perhaps somewhat tongue-in-cheek 1971 article, Berne wrote:

> So a real psychotherapist's problem is: What do I do when I'm in a room with a person who is called a patient if I am called the therapist? Absolutely no gadgets – no note papers, no tape recorders, no music, nothing. That's how you learn to do psychotherapy. (Berne, 1971, cited in Rotondo, 2020, p. 13)

How to proceed

In the above examples, Berne seems to explore various positions. If he is taken as doing this, adopting a philosophically bilateral stance rather than as preaching a doctrine of explicit agreement, the idea of bilaterality becomes congruent with discourse theory. If we regard later, more prescriptive writings as appropriate only in their specific time and place, and not for every time or situation, and as Tudor (2025) teases out in the case of contracts, as contextual, contestable, and restrictive, it is relatively easy to find commonality between Foucault and TA. Other metaphors not explored here, but certainly including Moiso's (1985) transference diagrams and O'Reilly-Knapp and Erskine's (2010) script system, can contribute and perhaps benefit from partnering with discourse theory. All that is necessary is to substitute *discourse* for *script* and to see ego states as their individual expressions. These are useful and aesthetically attractive metaphors. What I am advocating is just adding another layer of thought. We know just how stubborn script can be. This is what one would expect if we allow the possibility that personal script is the creation, not of early decisions, but of discourse, arising outside the subject.

Though Foucault was not writing about psychotherapy, there have been many psychotherapeutic applications of his work, particularly in the field of narrative, which is advanced as an antidote to psychotherapy's structuralist pretensions (Besley, 2002; Epston & White, 1990). These ideas have their critics – that the change emerging is often in a predictable direction, that of neoliberal-style autonomy (Kurz, 2009) or feminism (Law, 1999). Foucault, especially his later work on the self, is misunderstood in such therapies as implying the freedom of the individual to shape their own narrative (Luepnitz, 1992). The exploration of 'discursive regimens' (Kaye, 1999) gives a privileged position to the therapist, on whose ability discourse analysis depends (Manning et al., 2025), with the difficulties mentioned above in discussing the therapist's inclinations in contracting.

Transactional analysis emerged as an expression of neoliberalism, a view of the self as self-created, as decisional. But truth changes – Foucault referred to the past as 'a cemetery of truths' (Veyne, 2010, p. 59). So, while there is much to gain from incorporating discourse theory, there is a sacrifice to be accepted. Relational (Hargaden & Sills, 2002) and co-creative (Summers & Tudor, 2000) models allow for cognition, patterns of feeling (both in intensity and content), and repeated behavioural and experiential sequences and their consequences as created in dialogue. Both, however, rest on an assumption, or seek to create, an autonomous or dialogic, relational self. Meantime, the literature that critiques the notion of free will (Sapolsky, 2023), which broadly supports deterministic discourse theory rather than the hypotheses of an autonomous or relational self, is set aside rather than incorporated.

From this perspective, when a man (or anyone, though I am here concerned with men) is talking in therapy, we are not listening to his words, or his experience; they are taken from the cultural discourse(s) in which he participates. Of course, what he is describing may have happened to him, at least in some form, that is not in question, but the way he describes it, the words he uses, the kind and degree of emotion accompanying the spoken language, are all governed by influences of which he is unlikely to be aware. As Kaye (1999) puts it, therapy 'privileges an exploration of the discursive regimes by which people are positioned' (p. 29).

Personal change is of course possible, but is not either predictable or entirely within our control. In the last year of his life, Foucault (1984/1994) writes:

> It is true that we have to give up hope of ever acceding to a point of view that could give us complete access to any complete and definitive knowledge [*connaissance*] of what may constitute our historical limits. And, from this point of view, *the theoretical and practical experience we have of our limits, and of the possibility of moving beyond them, is always limited and determined*; thus, we are always in the position of beginning again. (p. 54, emphasis added)

In this view we can work on ourselves, in a manner reminiscent of freedom, or individual agency, but we cannot know the extent to which what we are doing is determined. We can know that we are capable of something, but not of what we are capable. There is, in an earlier work, a hint of how personal change takes place, not by changing the self, but by putting pressure on discourse by talking.

> Is it not a historicity proper to man… that enables him to exercise upon language, with every word he speaks, a sort of constant interior pressure which makes it shift imperceptibly upon itself at any given moment in time… he not only 'has history' all around him, but is himself, in his own historicity, that by means of which a history of human life… [is given its] form. (Foucault, 1966/1989, p. 403)

Change takes place in the context of certain kinds of conversations, including those we normally think of as psychotherapy, but perhaps not as we are taught. If discourse is identified with language (M. G. Kelly, 2020), then when we enter into dialogue, there will be pressure toward small shifts in the discourse. The dialogue must therefore involve two voices, though there may be more, and group discussion may in some ways be more effective in the business of shifting discourse, as the culture of the group becomes the vehicle by which discourse goes about the business of subjectification In studies of how group psychotherapy works (for example, Yalom & Leszcz, 2020), change appears to be effected, as in individual therapy (Miller & Moyers, 2021) by processes and characteristics rather than by actions or theoretical approaches. It is always important, though, when discussing discourse and how it might change, to be aware that we can only effect such change from within discourse. This is a long way from a neoliberal idea of freedom. We can never quite know what effect we have or in what direction. It is the operation or two voices – the theme of the Conference at which this paper was originally presented – that pushes discourse, not the intention or the action of one voice. Since history is all around us, in everything we do, feel, think, and say, given form by language, its impact can be assumed to produce change. However, the idea that discourse shifts under pressure from language does not imply that we can do it deliberately, anticipating what change *will* occur. We can suggest that change will occur, but not in what direction, or when or with what effect. This may be a difficult concept for psychotherapists, whose theoretical understanding generally tries to predict and deliberately manage change.

We may say, 'I know myself, I know my clients, my friends, the people who surround me, I know that life is decisional, I am in control of my life because I feel it to be so', but this belief is also a consequence of discourse. Our phenomenology, our way of interpreting our own experience is hugely influenced by discourse. Our ideas of justice, imprisonment, crime, and punishment are likewise more a consequence of discourse than of reasoned argument. Metzinger (2009) puts it thus:

> The assumption that something like free agency exists, and the fact that we treat one another as autonomous agents, are concepts fundamental to our legal system and the rules governing our societies—rules built on the notions of responsibility, accountability, and guilt… if accountability and responsibility do not really exist, it is meaningless to punish people (as opposed to rehabilitating them) for something they ultimately could not have avoided doing. Retribution would then appear to be a Stone Age concept, something we inherited from animals. (p. 128)

We can look back and wonder at how people thought in the past, how they interpreted their inner worlds. There have been entire populations who experienced emotion as physical, bodily sensations, or who experienced thoughts as the voices of gods. Julian Jaynes' (1982) reflections on the bicameral (two-chambered) mind suggest that up to a certain point, possibly around 600–500 BCE in European history, inner voices were those of the gods, and only then did the notion of human consciousness and inner reflection emerge. There are current societies who find the centrality of individual experience repugnant. Thus, an audience member in a Teaching and Supervising Transactional Analyst Teaching exam pointed out that in Japan, '*They are OK* comes first, then *You are OK*, and only then *I am OK.*' (M. Aonuma, personal communication, November 2024). My experience with Indigenous Māori people is similar. One of the reasons why Māori psychotherapists are not so common – an estimate of about 4% of the membership of the Association of Psychotherapists Aotearoa New Zealand (formerly the New Zealand Association of Psychotherapists [NZAP], 2023), compared with 18% of the total population – may be that a basic assumption of most psychotherapies gives the individual a central role. It is disturbing to imagine that our treasured autonomy is a neoliberal illusion. All that is asked here, without changing anything that you do, is that the reader considers the possibility.

References

Agamben, G. (2023). What is an apparatus? In G. Bird (Ed.), *Dispositif: A cartography* (pp. 251–262). MIT Press.

Ahmed, S. (2014). *The cultural politics of emotion* (2nd ed.). Edinburgh University Press.

Ariès, P. (1962). *Centuries of childhood: A social history of family life* (R. Baldick, Trans.). Jonathan Cape/Vintage. (Original work published 1960)

Barrett, L. F. (2017). *How emotions are made: The secret life of the brain*. Pan Macmillan.

Berne, E. (1961). *Transactional analysis in psychotherapy*. Grove Press.

Berne, E. (1994). *Principles of group treatment*. Shea Books. (Original work published 1966)

Berne, E. (1971). Away from a theory of the impact of interpersonal interaction on non-verbal participation. *Transactional Analysis Journal, 1*(1), 6–13. https://doi.org/10.1177/036215377100100103

Berne, E. (1972). *What do you say after you say hello?* Bantam.

Besley, A. C. (2002). Foucault and the turn to narrative therapy. *British Journal of Guidance and Counselling, 30*(2), 125–143. https://doi.org/10.1080/03069880220128010

Butler, J. (1990). *Gender trouble: Feminism and the subversion of identity*. Routledge.

Butler, J. (1993). *Bodies that matter: On the discursive limits of 'sex'*. Routledge.

Canguilhem, G. (1991). *The normal and the pathological*. Zone Books. (Original work published 1966)

Case, B. (2019, February 14). *The surprisingly nomadic lives of prisoners*. The Marshall Project: Nonprofit journalism about criminal justice. https://www.themarshallproject.org/2019/02/14/the-surprisingly-nomadic-lives-of-prisoners

Chernin, K. (1995). *A different kind of listening*. Harper Collins.

Courtney, L., & Pelletier, E. (2016, August 5). *What do victims want from criminal justice reform?* Urban Institute. https://www.urban.org/urban-wire/what-do-victims-want-criminal-justice-reform

Damasio, A. (2011). *Self comes to mind: Constructing the conscious brain*. Random House.

de Saint-Pierre, C. (2004). The contract for change: An original model. *Transactional Analysis Journal, 34*(1), 46–51. https://doi.org/10.1177/036215370403400106

Drego, P. (1983). The cultural parent. *Transactional Analysis Journal, 13*(4), 224–227. https://doi.org/10.1177/036215378301300404

Drye, B. (1980). Psychoanalytic definitions of cure: Beyond contract completion. *Transactional Analysis Journal, 10*(2), 124–130. https://doi.org/10.1177/036215378001000210

Edelman, G. M., & Tononi, G. (2000). *Consciousness: How matter becomes imagination.* Allen Lane, Penguin Press.

Emre, M. (2021, April 19). *The repressive politics of emotional intelligence.* The New Yorker. https://www.newyorker.com/magazine/2021/04/19/the-repressive-politics-of-emotional-intelligence

Epston, D., & White, M. (1990). *Narrative means to therapeutic ends.* Norton.

Foucault, M. (1978). *The history of sexuality. Vol. 1: An introduction (The will to knowledge)* (R. Hurley, Trans.). Pelican Books.

Foucault, M. (1980). The confession of the flesh. In C. Gordon (Ed.), *Power/knowledge: Selected interviews and other writings, 1972–1977* (pp. 194–228). Routledge.

Foucault, M. (1981). The order of discourse: Inaugural lecture at the Collège de France, 2 December 1970. In R. Young (Ed.), *Untying the text: A post-structuralist reader* (pp. 48–78). Routledge and Kegan Paul.

Foucault, M. (1989). *The order of things: An archaeology of the human sciences.* Routledge. (Original work published 1966)

Foucault, M. (1994). What is enlightenment? In P. Rabinow & N. Rose (Eds.), *The essential Foucault: Selections from essential works of Foucault, 1954–1984* (pp. 43–57). The New Press. (Original work published 1984)

Foucault, M. (1995). *Discipline and punish: The birth of the prison.* Vintage Books. (Original work published 1975)

Foucault, M. (2002). Discussion of truth and subjectivity. In H.-P. Fruchard & D. Lonenzini (Eds.), *About the beginning of the hermeneutics of the self: Lectures at Dartmouth College, 1980* (pp. 93–126). University of Chicago Press.

Foucault, M. (2010). *The government of self and others: Lectures at the Collège de France 1982–83.* Palgrave Macmillan; St Martin's Press.

Foucault, M. (2019). The subject and power (1982 interview). In J. D. Faubion (Ed.), *Power: Essential works of Foucault 1954–1984* (Vol. 3, pp. 236–348). Penguin Books.

Foucault, M., Martin, L. H., Gutman, H., & Hutton, P. H. (1988). *Technologies of the self: A seminar with Michel Foucault.* University of Massachusetts Press.

Frie, R. (2003). *Understanding experience: Psychotherapy and postmodernism.* Routledge.

Gellert, S. D., & Wilson, G. (1978). Contracts. *Transactional Analysis Journal, 8*(1), 10–15. https://doi.org/10.1177/036215377800800103

Genova, L. (2021). *Remember: The science of memory and the art of forgetting.* Harmony.

Gluckman, P. (2011). *Improving the transition: Reducing social and psychological morbidity during adolescence: A report from the Prime Minister's Chief Science Advisor.* https://www.dpmc.govt.nz/sites/default/files/2021-10/pmcsa-Improving-the-Transition-report.pdf

Gluckman, P. (2018). *Using evidence to build a better justice system: The challenge of rising prison costs.* NZ Government. https://www.dpmc.govt.nz/sites/default/files/2021-10/pmcsa-Using-evidence-to-build-a-better-justice-system.pdf

Goulding, M. (1995). Letter from the guest editor. *Transactional Analysis Journal, 25*(4), 298–299. https://doi.org/10.1177/036215379502500401

Goulding, M., & Goulding, R. (1979). *Changing lives through redecision therapy.* Brunner/Mazel.

Graziano, M. S. A. (2010). *God soul mind brain: A neuroscientist's reflections on the spirit world.* Leapfrog Press.

Graziano, M. S. A. (2013). *Consciousness and the social brain.* Oxford University Press.

Hanly, L. (2025, May 5). *Mark Mitchell wants short prison sentences scrapped in hope of reducing reoffending.* RNZ. https://www.rnz.co.nz/news/national/559975/mark-mitchell-wants-short-prison-sentences-scrapped-in-hope-of-reducing-reoffending

Hargaden, H., & Sills, C. (2002). *Transactional analysis – A relational perspective.* Brunner Routledge.

Harvey, D. (2005). *A brief history of neoliberalism.* Oxford University Press.

Hoyt, M. F. (1995). Contact, contract, change, encore: A conversation with Bob Goulding. *Transactional Analysis Journal, 25*(4), 300–311. https://doi.org/10.1177/036215379502500402

Jaynes, J. (1982). *The origin of consciousness in the breakdown of the bicameral mind.* Penguin.

Johnston, P. (2020). *Prison monthly snapshots from 1983 (Report no. RA4502).* NZ Department of Corrections Ara Poutama Aotearoa.

Joines, V., & Stewart, I. (2002). *Personality adaptations: A new guide to human understanding in psychotherapy and counselling.* Lifespace Publishing.

Kahr, B. (2015). 'Led astray by their half-baked pseudo-scientific rubbish': John Bowlby and the paradigm shift in child psychiatry. *Attachment, 9*(3), 297–319.

Kaye, J. (1999). Toward a non-regulative praxis. In I. Parker (Ed.), *Deconstructing psychotherapy* (pp. 19–37). Sage.

Kelly, M. G. (2020). Foucault and the politics of language today. *Telos, 191*, 47–68. https://doi.org/10.3817/0620191047

Kelly, P. (2013). *The self as enterprise: Foucault and the spirit of 21st century capitalism.* Taylor and Francis.

Koch, C. (2012). *Consciousness: Confessions of a romantic reductionist.* MIT Press.

Kurz, J. J. (2009). Tina (A.C.) Besley and Michael A. Peters, Subjectivity and Truth: Foucault, Education, and the Culture of Self (New York: Peter Lang Publishing, 2007), ISBN: 978-0820481951 [Book review]. *Foucault Studies, 7*, 148–153. https://doi.org/10.22439/fs.v0i7.2643

Lambie, I. (2018a). *Every 4 minutes: A discussion paper on preventing family violence in New Zealand.* NZ Government. https://bpb-ap-se2.wpmucdn.com/blogs.auckland.ac.nz/dist/f/688/files/2020/02/Every-4-minutes-A-discussion-paper-on-preventing-family-violence-in-New-Zealand.-Lambie-report-8.11.18-x43nf4.pdf

Lambie, I. (2018b). *It's never too early, never too late: A discussion paper on preventing youth offending in New Zealand.* NZ Government. https://www.dpmc.govt.nz/sites/default/files/2021-10/pmcsa-Its-never-too-early-Discussion-paper-on-preventing-youth-offending-in-NZ.pdf

Lambie, I. (2020). *What were they thinking? A discussion paper on brain and behaviour in relation to the justice system in New Zealand.* NZ Government. https://www.dpmc.govt.nz/sites/default/files/2022-04/PMCSA-20-02_What-were-they-thinking-A-discussion-paper-on-brain-and-behaviour.pdf

Law, I. (1999). A discursive approach to therapy with men. In I. Parker (Ed.), *Deconstructing psychotherapy* (pp. 115–131). Sage Publications.

Leerkes, E. M., Bailes, L. G., & Augustine, M. E. (2020). The intergenerational transmission of emotion socialization. *Developmental Psychology*, *56*(3), 390–402. https://doi.org/10.1037/dev0000753

Little, R. J. (2023). *Royal commission of inquiry into abuse in state care: Daniel Gaffey statement.* Eagles, Eagles & Redpath, Barristers and Solicitors.

Luepnitz, D. A. (1992). Nothing in common but their first names: The case of Foucault and White. *Journal of Family Therapy*, *14*(3), 281–284. https://doi.org/10.1046/j..1992.00459.x

Macey, D. (2019). *The lives of Michel Foucault.* Verso. (Original work published 1993)

Manning, S. (1995). The FU decision: Reflections on antisocial role development. *Journal of the Australia and New Zealand Psychodrama Association*, *4*, 1–11. https://aanzpa.org/wp-content/uploads/ANZPA_Journal_04_art01.pdf

Manning, S. (1997). Working with antisocial personality disorder. *Forum: Journal of the New Zealand Association of Psychotherapists*, *3*(1), 110–128. https://doi.org/10.9791/ajpanz.1997.09

Manning, S., Day, E., & Nicholls, D. A. (2024). Troublesome boys, prison and intimate partner violence. *Psychotherapy and Politics International*, *22*(1), 1–24. https://doi.org/10.24135/ppi.v22i1.04

Manning, S., Felton, T.-L., Boreham, C., & Ashdown, J. (2017). *Increasing the effectiveness of Stopping Violence Dunedin Programmes.* Report to the Lottery Grants Board, New Zealand, July 2017.

Manning, S., & Nicholls, D. A. (2020). The assembly of a criminal self. *Ata: Journal of Psychotherapy Aotearoa New Zealand*, *24*(2), 43–61. https://doi.org/10.9791/ajpanz.2020.11

Manning, S., Nicholls, D. A., & Day, E. (2025). Throw away the manual! Reflections on psychotherapy and crime. *Aporia*, *17*(2). https://doi.org/10.18192/aporia.v17i2.7271

Metzinger, T. (2009). *The ego tunnel: The science of the mind and the myth of the self.* Basic Books.

Miller, W. R., & Moyers, T. B. (2021). *Effective psychotherapists: Clinical skills that improve client outcomes.* The Guilford Press.

Moiso, C. (1985). Ego states and transference. *Transactional Analysis Journal, 15*(3), 194–201. https://doi.org/10.1177/036215378501500302

Nadesu, A. (2008). *Re-conviction patterns of released offenders: A 48-months follow-up analysis.* Ara Poutama Aotearoa | Department of Corrections. https://www.corrections.govt.nz/resources/research/reconviction-patterns-of-offenders-managed-in-the-community-a-48-months-follow-up-analysis

Nadesu, A. (2009). *Reconviction patterns of offenders managed in the community: A 60-months follow-up analysis.* Ara Poutama Aotearoa | Department of Corrections. https://www.corrections.govt.nz/resources/research/reconviction-patterns-of-offenders-managed-in-the-community-a-60-months-follow-up-analysis3

Newbold, G. (2000). *Crime in New Zealand.* Dunmore.

Newbold, G. (2007). *The problem of prisons: Corrections reform in New Zealand since 1840.* Dunmore Pub.

Newbold, G. (2008). Another one bites the dust: Recent initiatives in correctional reform in New Zealand. *Australian and New Zealand Journal of Criminology, 41*(3), 384–401. https://doi.org/10.1375/acri.41.3.384

Newbold, G. (2016). *Crime, law, and justice in New Zealand.* Routledge.

New Zealand Association of Psychotherapists. (2023). *Report of the Administrative Officer.*

O'Reilly-Knapp, M., & Erskine, R. G. (2010). The script system: An unconscious organization of experience. In R. G. Erskine (Ed.), *Life scripts: A transactional analysis of unconscious relational patterns* (pp. 291–308). Karnac.

People Against Prisons Aotearoa. (2024). *Care not cages.* https://papa.org.nz/tag/care-not-cages/

Reiman, J., & Leighton, P. (2020). *The rich get richer and the poor get prison: Ideology, class, and criminal justice* (12th ed.). Pearson/Allyn & Bacon.

Rose, N. S. (1998). *Inventing our selves: Psychology, power, and personhood.* Cambridge University Press.

Rose, N. S. (1999). *Governing the soul: The shaping of the private self* (2nd ed.). Free Association Books.

Rotondo, A. (2020). Rethinking contracts: The heart of Eric Berne's transactional analysis. *Transactional Analysis Journal, 50*(3), 236–250. https://doi.org/10.1080/03621537.2020.1771032

Sampson, T. D. (2017). *The assemblage brain: Sense making in neuroculture.* University of Minnesota Press.

Sapolsky, R. (2023). *Determined: The science of life without free will.* Bodley Head.

Steiner, C. (1966). Script and counterscript. *Transactional Analysis Bulletin, 5*(18), 133–135.

Steiner, C. (1995). *Scripts people live.* Bantam. (Original work published 1974)

Stern, D. (1985). *The interpersonal world of the infant: A view from psychoanalysis and developmental psychology*. Basic Books.

Summers, G., & Tudor, K. (2000). Cocreative transactional analysis. *Transactional Analysis Journal, 30*(1), 23–40. https://doi.org/10.1177/036215370003000104

Tononi, G. (2012). *Phi: A voyage from the brain to the soul*. Pantheon.

Tudor, K. (2025). *Transactional analysis proper—and improper: Selected and new papers*. Routledge.

Veyne, P. (2010). *Foucault: His thought, his character*. Polity.

Ware, P. (1983). Personality adaptations: Doors to therapy. *Transactional Analysis Journal, 13*(1), 11–19. https://doi.org/10.1177/036215537830130010

Weiss, J. B., & Weiss, L. (1998). Perspectives on the current state of contractual regressive therapy. *Transactional Analysis Journal, 28*(2), 45–47. https://doi.org/10.1177/036215379802800110

Wüschner, P. (2017). Shame, guilt, and punishment. *Foucault Studies, 23*, 86–107. https://doi.org/10.22439/fs.v0i0.5343

Yalom, I., & Leszcz, M. (2020). *Theory and practice of group psychotherapy* (6th ed.). Basic Books.

Goldmine and minefield: Humour in transactional analysis and psychotherapy

John Evans

Abstract

This chapter explores the dual nature of humour in transactional analysis (TA) and psychotherapy, drawing on research, theory, and clinical experience. The author examines how humour can foster connection, insight, and psychological wellbeing, but also how it can be knowingly or unknowingly misused, causing harm or reinforcing shame. The chapter outlines three classic theories of humour – superiority/inferiority, incongruity, and relief – and links them to TA concepts such as ego states, life positions, and psychological scripts. Through practical examples and references to key TA thinkers like Eric Berne, the chapter highlights both the 'goldmine' of benefits and the 'minefield' of risks when using humour in therapeutic contexts. The author advocates for a nuanced, empathic approach, encouraging practitioners to integrate humour thoughtfully, with awareness of its potential to both heal and harm.

When I received the encouragement to present a workshop at the 2024 international TA Conference, it provided a timely opportunity to bring together some of my research around humour, and how it relates to TA and psychotherapy. This chapter is based on my presentation.

The Conference theme was 'Karangarua – Unity Through Diversity in Relationship', which was particularly poignant. For many years I have been interested in the diversity and potency of humour, and its ability to facilitate connection and intimacy, both in my TA psychotherapy practice and beyond.

I have been fortunate to share humour with pre-verbal infants, military personnel, prisoners, refugees, psychiatric patients, terminally ill adults, and people with whom I share no spoken language. Although many of them were strangers I often felt a powerful sense of unity as we powerfully felt the humorous irony or absurdity of what we were experiencing together.

In my early life I developed an awareness that loss, trauma, and painful experience could often be lightened by fun and laughter, and also keenly aware that humour and laughter could be weaponised with aggression and power.

As an adult I sought the help of a psychotherapist, troubled by a sense that life was intolerably harsh, unfair, and futile. The task of transforming my nihilism felt deadly serious to me, so I left my humour at the door – only for the therapist to frequently use humour as a means of connecting with wounded and confused parts of me. I am indebted and deeply grateful to him.

Eric Berne mentions humour and laughter frequently in his writings. The following quote sets the scene:

> The transactional analyst is well aware of the biological and existential function of humor, and does not hesitate to exploit it. It is only necessary for him to distinguish Parent, Adult and Child humor, and that is not always easy. (Berne, 1966, p. 288)

I am curious about Berne's assertion that transactional analysts readily exploit humour, as this is not often reflected in TA literature or teachings. His challenge around identifying ego states in humour is one example of how humour can be explored in relation to TA concepts, and why it is simultaneously a goldmine and a minefield.

In this paper, firstly, I offer a brief introduction to the three classic theories of humour and touch on how they correlate to TA concepts; secondly , I explore some of the benefits and possibilities, as well as risks and limitations, of using humour in psychotherapy; and lastly, I examine some TA concepts of humour and offer ideas on applying them.

The psychology of humour

How do we define humour? Here is one dictionary definition: 'a mental quality which apprehends and delights in the ludicrous and mirthful: that which causes mirth and amusement.' (Davidson et al., 1986, p. 468).

There are three classic main theories of humour. These are:

Superiority/inferiority humour
In superiority humour, motivation and power are important, and the 'funny' part results from someone or something being relatively better, smarter, more successful, more attractive, more powerful – than someone or something else, and this can be inverted into inferiority (Martin & Ford, 2018).

This form of humour can be experienced as aggressive when applied to others, or self-deprecating when applied to self. The TA concept of life positions (Ernst, 1971) is relevant in relation to superiority (I'm OK – You're not OK) and inferiority (I'm not OK – You're OK) humour, and I believe that as transactional analysts we can learn a lot about a person's internal process from analysing their humour, e.g., *'I've got an inferiority complex – but it's not a very good one.'*

Incongruity humour

Eysenck (1942) describes incongruity humour as being when 'laughter results from the sudden, insightful integration of contradictory or incongruous ideas, attitudes, or sentiments which are experienced objectively.' (p. 307).

In this form of humour we experience mirth and laughter when our perception of a situation changes, highlighting a mismatch between our expectations and reality. The TA concept of frame of reference (Schiff & Schiff, 1975) is relevant to congruent and incongruent experiences, e.g., *'I spent the whole morning building a time machine, so that's four hours of my life that I'm definitely getting back.'* (*The Guardian*, 2022, para. 6).

Relief humour

In relief humour, the humour acts as a pressure valve for releasing pent-up nervous energy or psychological tension. Sigmund Freud (1905) went further along this trajectory when he wrote a book about jokes and developed a theory that laughter allows momentary relief from repression of sexual and aggressive drives.

I consider that the TA concepts of psychological hungers and script relate well to relief humour, e.g., *'I phoned a call centre today, and the message said all the advisors were engaged. I was delighted for them, but my fridge is still broken.'*

Some jokes and humorous experiences work in relation to one of the theories of humour, some to two, and in some cases all three can be seen as operating. When all three forms are operating simultaneously in a humour situation, we can experience high levels of amusement. I describe this as bullseye humour and provide two examples later.

Goldmine: The benefits and possibilities of humour

Varied claims have been made about the physical and mental health benefits of humour and laughter; some being more evidence-based than others.
In a medical conference keynote address Fry (1979) states:

Mirthful laughter has a scientifically demonstrable exercise impact on several body systems. Muscles are activated; heart rate is increased; respiration is simplified... Stress is antagonized by humor both in its mental or emotional aspect and its physical aspect. Emotional tension, contributing to stress, is lowered through the cathartic effects of humor... If mirth is experienced, rage is impossible. (p. 1)

Martin and Ford (2018) note that recent studies show a generally positive yet complex link between humour and physical health. For instance, they found that certain types of humour appeared to reduce blood pressure and that people with greater levels of humour may perceive their health as being better, thereby having a different subjective experience.

Regarding the psychological benefits of humour, Martin and Ford (2018) summarise three main aspects shown by their review of the research literature: 'First, it appears to directly relate to self-reported psychological wellbeing. Second, it affects psychological wellbeing by helping people cope with stressful events. Third, humor relates to psychological wellbeing by facilitating healthy interpersonal relationships.' (p. 284).

When considering humour from a psychotherapeutic perspective, some writers advocate strongly for the use of 'healthy' humour. Lachman (2008) celebrates the use of humour in psychotherapy from a self-psychology perspective:

When applied appropriately, judiciously and sparingly, humor is a social lubricant and equalizer... in addition, through humor, we can circumvent anxiety, express a challenge, or reply to one that we might not get away with had we been more direct... Most important, however through humor and spontaneity we can also achieve an incomparable degree of intimacy that is hard to match through other avenues.' (p. 93)

Winnicott (1971) applauds the amusement of a child he was working with:

This sense of humour is evidence of a freedom, the opposite of a rigidity of the defences that characterises illness. A sense of humour is the ally of the therapist, who gets from it a feeling of confidence and a sense of having elbow room for manoeuvring. It is evidence of the child's creative imagination and of happiness. (p. 32)

McWilliams (2011) recognises that 'The emergence of humor in a previously dour or anguished patient is often the first sign of significant internal change.' (p. 184).

Minefield: The risks and limitations of humour

Most of us can recall painful experiences when humour is targeted towards us or against us. Difficult experiences are often made more humiliating or traumatic if we feel that we are laughed at in a judgmental way; insult is thus added to injury. Being the target of aggressive humour, such as sexist, racist, or homophobic jokes, can also be seen as a form of objectification. Jean-Paul Sartre (1943) writes about how judgement – and here I include forms of humour such as mockery and sarcasm – can result in a loss of personal subjectivity. In such instances we may experience shame associated with being the object of ridicule.

Some people develop patterns of difficulty in relation to humour; they may avoid humour or freeze when exposed to it. With symptoms similar to post-traumatic stress disorder, gelotophobia is a social phobia that involves a fear of being laughed at. This can result from 'repeated experiences with disparaging forms of laughter that took place over the course of socialization.' (Titze & Kühn, 2014, p. 1)

Some types of humour are more likely to be unhealthy or damaging than others. Mockery, ridicule, and sarcasm are the most common forms of humour that can be weaponised in attacking, controlling, or sadistic ways. Interpersonal relationships, and intra-group and inter-group processes can be strongly influenced by aggressive forms of humour (Martineau, 1972).

Sometimes, when challenged, those who bully or demean others will respond by saying 'I was only kidding'. 'The humiliation of ridicule serves as a social corrective, while the humor of ridicule creates ambiguity about underlying intentions. Thus, if one challenges ridicule, he or she risks further castigation for "not having a sense of humor"'. (Martin & Ford, 2018, p. 262)

Studies, including Janes and Olson's (2000), illustrate that the power of ridicule is such that merely *observing* ridicule in social situations, e.g., at school – creates peer pressure and conformity around behaviour and norms.

Psychoanalytic theory has a double-edged attitude to humour. It is sometimes celebrated as being insightful and liberating, whilst at other times derided for being problematic.

Those familiar with Sigmund Freud's (1905) work will understand that humour is defined as a defence mechanism against painful emotions. Nancy McWilliams (2011) writes about humour as negative as well as positive: 'the compulsion to be funny can be extremely defensive; most of us know someone who, when invited into a sincere conversation cannot stop making jokes.' (p. 148)

Some writers have been highly sceptical about using humour in psychotherapy, Kubie (1970), for example, was staunch in rejecting humour as too risky, defensive, and unhealthy a process in the therapy room. 'Humor has its place in life. Let us keep it there by acknowledging that one place where it has a very limited role, if any, is in psychotherapy.' (p. 866)

In my own professional experience, amongst countless examples of humour being helpful in therapy, there are examples of humour being painfully counterproductive. On one occasion early in my career as a psychotherapist, when working in my first session with a client, I smiled with amusement at one point when the client laughed. There was a brief pause before the client stopped laughing and changed the subject.

I slowly realised – with a guilty, sinking feeling – that I had not recognised their 'gallows' laugh (Berne, 1972) for what it was, and that my smile had most likely stroked their script beliefs. I awkwardly apologised, and although the client replied with 'No problem', the damage was done. At the end of the session the client politely agreed to schedule another session, but they did not attend, nor respond to my follow-up email. This painful experience helped to fire my interest in humour's complex role in psychotherapy.

Humour in TA

I now highlight some of the material relating to humour in TA, before making some suggestions for increasing our understanding and application of humour in our practice.

Eric Berne mentioned humour, or more frequently, laughter, on numerous occasions in his writing. Clearly Berne had an appreciation of the helpful and unhelpful aspects of laughter in relation to ego states, cautioning the analyst that: 'Parental laughter is indulgent or derisive and the Child laugh in the clinical situation is irreverent or triumphant.' (Berne, 1966, p. 288). Whereas 'the Adult laugh, which is therapeutic, is the laugh of insight, which arises from the absurdity of circumstantial predicament and the even greater absurdity of self-deception.' (p. 288)

For me this is a highly significant statement that points towards how profoundly healing humour can be when experienced in helpful ways, in and outside the therapy setting. Berne (1966) then switches his vocabulary from laughter to humour – suggesting:

> The biological or survival value of humor is to deal summarily with predicaments, thus releasing the individual to go about the business of living as effectively as he can in the circumstances. Since most psychogenic problems arise from self-deception, Adult humor has a most rightful place in the materia medica of the psychotherapist.' (p. 289)

As much of the TA literature is concerned with understanding and dealing with painful experiences, difficult emotions, confusions, imbalances of power, trauma, and oppression, it is to some extent understandable that humour is not widely referred to. Perhaps there is fear of amusement being seen as frivolous, insensitive, or mocking. I see this as unfortunate, as by avoiding the negative or destructive areas of humour, we often forgo the priceless resources found in helpful, healing forms of humour.

TA is not alone in this, as humour appears to be under-represented in theory and practice of non-TA fields of psychotherapy as well. Considering how often we smile, laugh, roll our eyes, or sigh at the ironic or absurd, or share a knowing glance with a colleague or friend, I believe there is much to gain from integrating humour into our work.

The humour in this provocative quote from Berne (1966) adds to its impact:

> There is no evidence that solemnity in psychotherapy leads to sounder or more rapid clinical improvement… Hence therapeutic solemnity arises from a folie à deux, which may have its place in some kinds of therapy but is inconsistent with a rational approach. (p. 288)

Having identified Adult humour as having a rightful place in TA psychotherapy, Berne (1972) suggests: 'There are several kinds of laughs which are of interest in script analysis.' (p. 338). Muriel James wrote a humour-focused article for the *Transactional Analysis Journal (TAJ)* to illustrate Berne's thinking, substituting 'unhealthy' laughter for Berne's 'scripty' laughter.

James (1979) differentiated Berne's descriptions of these two forms of laughter within Parent, Adult, and Child by diagramming two sets of the three ego states, one unhealthy and the other healthy. Unhealthy laughter in the Parent is a scripty, mocking, derisive form; the unhealthy laugh from the Adult ego state is 'the Adult's chuckle of rueful humour. It signifies a superficial insight. This the gallows laugh' (p. 247). Unhealthy Child humour is described as 'pull[ing] a fast one' and '*gamey*' (p. 247).

The 'healthy' forms of laughter identified in James' summary of Berne's thinking around humour and ego states are firstly in Parent, where the laughter is 'patronizing, benevolent and helpful … this is the grandad or Santa Claus laugh' (p. 247). Next is the healthy Adult laugh, who 'realises he has been conned, not by external figures, but by his own Parent and Child … This is the laugh of insight' (p. 247). Lastly is the healthy Child laughter – defined as spontaneous, and coming from those who are 'script-free or can put their scripts aside for the occasion' (p. 247).

James then gives a brief case example of 'laugh therapy', in which members of a therapy group are encouraged to learn about healthy and unhealthy forms of laughter focusing on emotional and bodily responses.

Interestingly, in this model there are healthy AND unhealthy forms of laughter in all three ego states, and I was intrigued to note that in this three-ego state model, healthy laughter can originate in the Parent or Child as well as the Adult. Also, the unhealthy gallows laugh originates in the Adult, and Berne (1972) suggests that this 'is the Adult's chuckle of rueful humour. It signifies a superficial insight.' (p. 388)

Berne (1972) defines gallows laughter as 'scripty' and writes:

> The gallows laugh (which results from a gallows transaction) means that if the patient laughs while recounting a misfortune, and particularly if the other group members join in the laughter, that misfortune is part of the catastrophe of the patient's script. (p. 377)

Stewart and Joines (2012) offer useful guidance around spotting and working with gallows laughter. Noting the presence or absence of driver behaviour in transactions prior to laughter is key. 'Did the person engage in driver behaviour just before he laughed or just before she expressed the feeling? If the answer is "no", then you know that the person has not moved into script.' (p. 167)

As suggested by Berne earlier, Stewart and Joines (2012), as well as McNeel (2024a), note the significance of gallows laughter and how we respond to it:

> Whenever someone gives a gallows laugh, smile or chuckle, he is making a non-verbal invitation to the listeners to reinforce one of his script beliefs. The invitation is accepted on the psychological level if the listeners join in the gallows laughter. (Stewart & Joines, 2012, p. 198)

I consider that the psychological level invitation described here casts doubt on whether gallows laughter – as suggested by Berne – is an Adult phenomenon, as this invitation (at the psychological level) would be communicated from Parent or Child.

In John McNeel's (2024a) revision of redecision work, he focuses on injunctive messages and advises us to notice, and also to sensitively and compassionately confront, unhealthy humour such as gallows laughter:

> When someone says with great mirth, 'I am just a failure and always have been (ha ha)', it is our obligation to tell the person what we hear and to refuse to laugh at what is not funny. This is an act of empathy. (p. 5)

McNeel (2024b) also places humour – along with other 'Impasse Allies' including empathy, acceptance, and invitation – in an important bridging position on the pathway from the restrictive 'believable falsehood' of injunctive messages towards healing in his expanded redecision therapy model.

Without specifically mentioning humour, in their two articles on play as time structuring that leads to fun and positive payoffs, Cowles-Boyd and Boyd (1980a) argue: '"games" and "play" are structurally very similar… Upon closer examination, it is also evident that "games" are an inverse of "play" as if a game were a form of play that had somehow gone sour.' (pp. 6–7)

Interestingly Cowles-Boyd and Boyd (1980a) then suggest that:

> If the therapist knows techniques for changing games into play, as opposed to confronting a patient's games head on, s/he can make use of the available energy to speed up the therapy, make it less painful for the patient, and make it more fun for both therapist and patient. (p. 7)

In the second of their articles Cowles-Boyd and Boyd (1980b) describe 'the Game/Play shift' as a potent way of 'accessing the Child-level concerns and problems of the patient.' (p. 8) They caution against discounting or making fun of the patient and emphasise the importance of the I'm OK – You're OK life position.

Gopakumar (2021) contributes an impressive *TAJ* article in which play is channelled as a healing force that brings forth humour, thereby evolving meaning in the narratives of the people she is working with. Gopakumar expands Cowles-Boyd and Boyd's work to include the integrating Adult, along with the Child in ego state terms. This is a very useful contribution that offers a potent way of working with script. She includes impactful examples of clients moving from having previously been shamed by humour, to being freed by it, through a process of playful experiment and empathic exchange.

'Humor can relieve the immense tension the client faces, and incongruity and surprise make the process engaging and enjoyable.' (Gopakumar, 2021, p. 373) This suggestion emphasises the relevance of the incongruity and relief forms of humour in the psychotherapy space.

In Berne's (1966) 'therapeutic operations' and Hargaden and Sills' (2002) 'empathic transactions', the use of humour is encouraged. In the therapeutic operation of Confrontation, Berne suggests the therapist works with the patient's uncontaminated Adult when confronting an inconsistency – one outcome of this can be:

> The insightful laugh, on the other hand, is pathognomic of a decisive cathectic shift, with the release of psychic energy previously bound up in maintaining the inconsistency that the confrontation attacks; it therefore marks a therapeutic success of some stability. (p. 235)

Building on Berne's original concept, Hargaden and Sills (2002) offer an empathic transaction of 'illustration'. 'This is a more whimsical transaction and can involve jokes, lyrics, stories, references to soap operas, the news and anything else that emerges as supporting the healthy direction of treatment.' (p. 126)

'It can also be a very economical use of time as a perhaps confrontative point can be made by a humorous remark or an anecdote that might take hours of painstaking specification and explanation.' (Hargaden & Sills, 2002, p. 126)

In discussing healthy laughter, my view is that Tudor's (2003) concept of the integrating Adult offers us a helpful and flexible space to explore humour as a process. Tudor argues that: 'This present-centred state of the ego has the ability and capacity to act autonomously (with awareness, spontaneity and intimacy), to laugh, have fun and be silly' (pp. 201–202). Considering this in relation to Berne's humour model, the integrating Adult is where the 'laugh of insight' can comfortably sit.

In the three-ego state model, 'being silly' is viewed as taking place in the Child – 'the Child's laugh of sheer fun' (Berne, 1972, p. 338). However, in the integrating Adult model (Tudor, 2003), this spontaneous aspect of Child humour is integrated into the Adult, as is the benevolent 'Grandad' laughter of the Parent, to form a healthy integrated or integrating sense of humour. It seems clear that as more of a person's energy moves into their integrating Adult ego state, their sense of humour will evolve into a more potent force for insight and relatedness.

For instance, irony as a form of humour usually requires a painful realisation or recognition. For the humour to be healthy and constructive in a relational sense, we need to fully resonate with the painful aspects of the ironic situation to ensure we are laughing 'with', rather than 'at' the other person. This could be defined as the humour of shared or co-created insight and represents a space where growth and healing can emerge.

I have found Widdowson's (2008) concept of meta-communication helpful in tuning my approach towards humour in the therapeutic space – using intuition and 'shuttling awareness' between myself, the client (or group), and the intersubjective space to support my awareness of what might be a good time to lean in towards providing a humorous stimulus or response.

As transactional analysts we can support the healthy and effective use of humour in a variety of ways. Avoidance or minimising use of humour out of our fear of harming our clients is understandable, and yet so often represents a missed opportunity. Eusden (2023) encourages us to 'dare' by taking risks in our work. Provided we have enough 'care' in the relationship (we could define this as empathic contact or attunement), our use of humour will likely have a helpful impact overall.

There is a need to take the emotional world of our clients seriously, and how this relates to our own pain, shame, and grief – but this does not preclude humour, and, as Berne suggests, insight can be very funny in the darkest of places. Our challenge is to be attuned, empathic, and sufficiently aware in the intersubjective space to consider what meanings are possible, and to have a sense of when we can safely lean towards amusement. I often feel touched and blessed when I recall how often a client, or member of a group, feels and names the ironic or the absurd spontaneously, and does this regardless of what I do, or do not do.

A very fine ironic humour transaction is articulated by Marco Mazzetti (2012). Mazzetti's intention is to reduce his trainees' anxiety about making mistakes, and prior to what I assume is a practice exercise, he makes the following appeal to his trainees: 'Please, make at least a couple of mistakes! I still make mistakes after more than 25 years of practice. Do not humiliate me by working perfectly at the beginning of your career. Do it for me!' (p. 47)

Mazzetti is toying with his trainees and himself – how ironic it would be if his trainees practiced perfectly on their first attempt, whilst after so many years he remains fallible. This is an example of what I call a humour bullseye transaction in which incongruity, superiority, and release all play a part, in response to Mazzetti's (2012) plea: 'They laugh and the energy flows where it is needed, that is, toward the amygdala, hippocampus, and limbic lobe, which needs to be relaxed and possibly happy in order to learn.' (p. 47)

Healthy humour is a relational, or co-created experience, as well as an internal integrating process. Many of us will spontaneously start smiling or laughing when another person is smiling or laughing – humour can be infectious. One way to understand how humour works as a shared experience with implicit agreement is to consider the philosopher Simon Critchley's (2002) understanding of jokes:

> There is a tacit social contract here, namely some agreement about the social world in which we find ourselves as the implicit background to the joke… I recognize that a joke is being told and assent to having my attention caught in this way. (pp. 4–5)

I am interested in the concept of a 'tacit' contract from a TA perspective – perhaps the tacit contract for shared humour is established, sometimes subtly, via metacommunication, as mentioned in relation to Widdowson's concept mentioned earlier.

Transactional analysis of a joke

I finish this article with a Bill Hicks joke that can be diagrammed into a simple ego state transaction exchange, with a crossed transaction representing the 'punchline'. I hope that this will help illustrate the transactional nature of 'jokes' and humorous exchanges.

Bill is at work late one afternoon. He is holding a sweeping brush and standing motionless, staring into space in an empty warehouse. Observing from his balcony office, Bill's supervisor notices Bill's lack of activity and angrily shouts down: 'Hicks, how come you're not working?'

To which Bill responds: 'There's nothing to do boss.' Indignant, the supervisor yells: 'Well – pretend you're working!' After a brief pause, Bill retorts: 'Why don't YOU pretend I'm working?!'

The exchange:

Boss: 'Hicks, how come you're not working?'

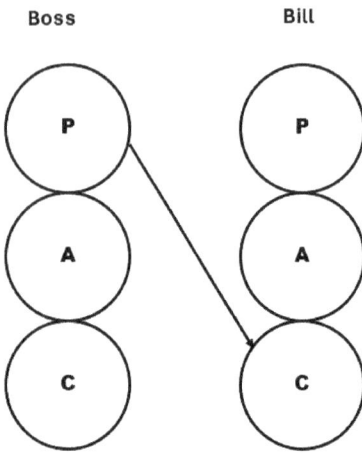

Boss   Bill

Bill: 'There's nothing to do boss.'

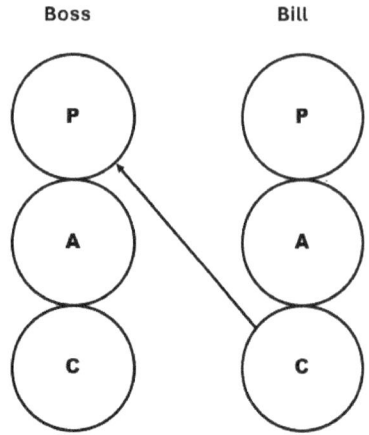

Boss   Bill

Boss: 'Well – pretend you're working!'

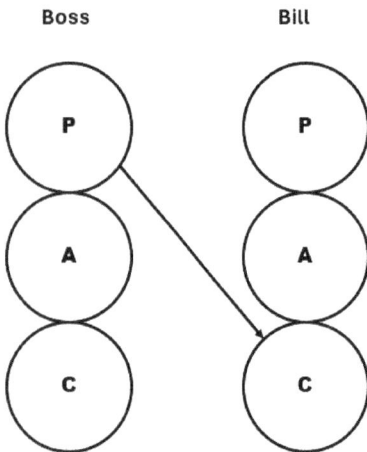

Boss   Bill

Bill: (pause) 'Why don't YOU pretend I'm working?!'

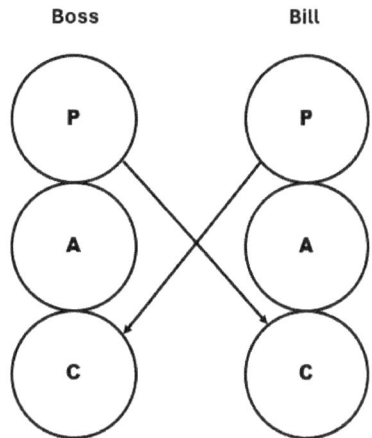

Boss   Bill

We don't find out what happens next... However, in this 'bullseye' example, all three theories of humour are represented. There are the three forms of humour – incongruity, superiority, and release forms of humour combined simultaneously.

As I said in the introduction to this chapter, humour in the context of my own therapy as a client has been immensely helpful over the years, and I am particularly grateful for my good fortune with my first therapist.

As a younger man I held a cynical, negative view of myself, people, and the world, and found my therapist's often humorous approach confronting and intriguing. In an early exchange I was avoidant – defending against exploring painful experiences and he reassured me it's OK to be vulnerable. With a furrowed brow I said: 'Hm. I don't like the idea of being vulnerable.' After a long pause my therapist stood up, started putting his jacket on and said:

> OK. Well, if you don't like the idea of being vulnerable today, we could finish this session early and reschedule. How about we come back in 200 years and talk about being vulnerable. So that will be 4 pm on the 5th of May 2200. The session will probably cost more due to inflation.

Initially baffled, I gave a confused smile and a brief laugh and replied: 'Oh. I hadn't thought about it like that.' My therapist used grandiose absurdity to imply that whether or not I liked the idea of being vulnerable, I *was* vulnerable, as a mortal being. In doing so, he (an American man in his 60s) invited me (a British man age 30) into a shared intimate space that I found hilarious as well as challenging and liberating. When I see him at the session in 175 years' time, I will tell my former therapist he was right – it *is* OK to be vulnerable.

References

Berne, E. (1966). *Principles of group treatment*. Grove Press.

Berne, E. (1972). *What do you say after you say hello?* Grove Press.

Cowles-Boyd, L., & Boyd, H. S. (1980a). Play as a time structure. *Transactional Analysis Journal, 10*(1), 5–7. https://doi.org/10.1177/036215378001000102

Cowles-Boyd, L., & Boyd, H. S. (1980b). Playing with games: The game/play shift. *Transactional Analysis Journal, 10*(1), 8–11. https://doi.org/10.1177/036215378001000103

Critchley, S. (2002). *On humour*. Routledge.

Davidson, G. W., Seaton, M. A., & Simpson, J. (1986). *Chambers concise 20th century dictionary*. Chambers.

Ernst, F. H. (1971). The OK corral: The grid for get-on-with. *Transactional Analysis Journal, 1*(4), 33–42. https://doi.org/10.1177/036215377100100409

Eusden, S. (2023). High dare/high care compass: A guide to transforming trouble and ethical disorientation in psychotherapy. *Transactional Analysis Journal, 53*(3), 207–221. https://doi.org/10.1080/03621537.2023.2213952

Eysenck, H. J. (1942). The appreciation of humour: An experimental and theoretical study. *British Journal of Psychology, 32*, 295–309. https://doi.org/10.1111/j.2044-8295.1942.tb01027.x

Freud, S. (1905). *Jokes and their relation to the unconscious*. Standard Edition Volume 8. Vintage.

Fry, W. F. (1979). *Using humor to save lives* [Speech]. Annual Convention of the American Orthopsychiatric Association.

The Guardian. (2022, August 16). From time machines to threesomes: 12 of the funniest jokes from the Edinburgh fringe. (2022, August 16). *The Guardian* https://www.theguardian.com/culture/2022/aug/16/from-time-machines-to-threesomes-12-of-the-funniest-jokes-from-the-edinburgh-fringe

Gopakumar, A. (2021). Story options: A technique for transforming narrative through playful emotional exploration. *Transactional Analysis Journal, 51*(4), 364–378. https://doi.org/10.1080/03621537.2021.1975080

Hargaden, H., & Sills. C. (2002). *Transactional analysis: A relational perspective*. Routledge.

James, M. (1979). Laugh therapy: Theory, procedures, results in clinical and special fields. *Transactional Analysis Journal, 9*(4), 244–250. https://doi.org/10.1177/036215377900900404

Janes, L. M., & Olson, J. M. (2000). Jeer pressures: The behavioral effects of observing ridicule of others. *Personality and Social Psychology Bulletin, 26*(4), 474–485. https://doi.org/10.1177/0146167200266006

Kubie, L. S. (1970). The destructive potential of humor in psychotherapy. *The American Journal of Psychiatry, 127*(7), 861–866. https://doi.org/10.1176/ajp.127.7.861

Lachman, F. M. (2008). *Transforming narcissism: Reflections on empathy, humor and expectations*. Analytic Press.

Martin, R. A., & Ford, T. E. (2018). *The psychology of humor*. Academic Press.

Martineau, W. H. (1972). A model of the social functions of humor. In J. H. Goldstein & P. E. McGhee (Eds.), *The psychology of humour* (pp. 101–125). Academic Press.

Mazzetti, M. (2012). Teaching trainees to make mistakes. *Transactional Analysis Journal, 42*(1), 43–52. https://doi.org/10.1177/036215371204200106

McNeel, J. (2024a). *Dear friends of the injunctive message charts*. https://static1.squarespace.com/static/5b5a2d76b40b9d0ca1148654/t/62cc8765d93c203dd110ec3d/1657571173985/FRIENDS+OF+THE+IM+CHARTS.pdf

McNeel, J. (2024b). *Injunctive message master tables*. https://static1.squarespace.com/static/5b5a2d76b40b9d0ca1148654/t/68240ee19a2c7c77309c016f/1747193569949/CHART+EVOLUTION.pdf

McWilliams, N. (2011). *Psychoanalytic diagnosis*. Guilford Press.

Sartre, J. P. (1943). *Being and nothingness*. Atria Books.

Schiff, J. L., & Schiff, A. (1975). Frames of reference. *Transactional Analysis Journal, 5*(3), 290–294. https://doi.org/10.1177/036215377500500320

Stewart, I., & Joines, V. (2012). *TA today* (2nd ed.). Lifespace.

Titze, M., & Kühn, R. (2014). When laughter causes shame. In K. G. Lockhart (Ed.), *Psychology of shame: New research* (pp. 141–156). Nova Science Publishers.

Tudor, K. (2003). The neopsyche: The integrating adult ego state. In C. Sills & H. Hargaden (Eds.), *Ego states* (pp. 201–231). Worth Publishing.

Widdowson, M. (2008). Metacommunicative transactions. *Transactional Analysis Journal, 38*(1), 58–71. https://doi.org/10.1177/036215370803800108

Winnicott, D. W. (1971). *Therapeutic consultations in child psychiatry.* Basic Books.

Transactional Analysis Proper – and Improper: Selected and New Papers by Keith Tudor (Routledge, 2025), 320 pages, with 20 black and white illustrations. ISBN 9780367027216

Deepak Dhananjaya

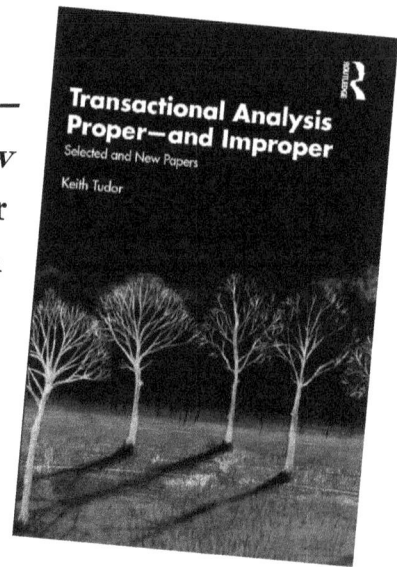

First impression

As I began reading the introduction to this book, what immediately stood out was the author's rationale for writing it and the way he highlights Zalcman's (1990) critique of the development of transactional analysis (TA) theory and practice, which she believed had slowed down and become misdirected due to four emerging trends. I was particularly struck by one of these trends – the tendency to reframe TA either as an analytical or psychodynamic approach to gain professional respect, or as pop psychology to make it more marketable – both of which still feel strikingly relevant today.

This, in turn, led me to reflect on the very birth of TA: its departure from psychoanalysis. Berne's (1961) earlier stance that TA was sufficient up to the point of deconfusion but that severe regressions required psychoanalysis for structural change; his later position (Berne, 1972) was that TA itself was sufficient for structural change.

The introduction serves as a powerful opening, drawing attention to the original thinking behind TA as well as the author's personal connection with the theory. What I found stimulating was the way original ideas are presented alongside relevant references and a clear rationale. The author's style – an objective critique of theory, consistently grounded in reasoning – runs throughout the book and keeps the reader engaged. It builds a solid sense of TA's origins, its critiques, and contemporary relevance.

My focus in this review

My review can be seen as illustrating that 'the whole is greater than the sum of its parts' (Aristotle, ca. 350 BCE/n.d.; Wertheimer, 1923), with a focus on the flow of the different sections – Basic Assumptions (Part I), New Wine from Old Roots (Part II), Looking Back, Looking Forward (Part III) – and the weaving of chapters within these parts, which together form a fabric depicting the evolution and robustness of the theoretical framework, much like the intricate thread count of a fine cotton cloth.

In reviewing this book, I want to bring to the reader the nuances of each chapter, its relevance within the order it is positioned, while also holding the thread of transactional analysis theory and its subtleties. I have read many of the chapters in their original form as standalone papers, and while they carried meaning on their own, reading them in the sequence in which they are placed in the book weaves a far more nuanced storyline – one that traces the evolution of transactional analysis theory itself. In tracing the evolution, the author also extends the theory to contemporary situations without losing the rigor of its theoretical basis; in a way, this seems to safeguard against falling into one of the trends that Zalcman (1990) explicitly identifies at the beginning of the book.

The storyline

Part I: Basic assumption

This part has three chapters out of 13 chapters in the book. This section lays the conceptual foundation of the book. It revisits the philosophical and theoretical bases of transactional analysis, grounding it in relational and ethical principles. The chapters in this part re-examine foundational ideas – such as life positions, contractual method, and the three Ps (permission, protection, and potency) – not as fixed techniques, but as evolving relational processes that shape the very essence of TA.

Positioning the 'We Are' paper (Tudor, 2016) as the opening chapter underscores its current relevance. I was particularly drawn to the author's nuanced clarification of Berne's idea of life positions, which some have connected to Klein's 'paranoid-schizoid' and 'depressive' positions. Tudor clarifies that Berne's concept was more about *conceptual stances of self and other* rather than developmental positions (Klein, 1946/1997). This level of clarification exemplifies the richness of the book.

The argument that 'We Are' is the core, fundamental position – that we are all born embedded in relationships – shifts the focus away from Berne's (1961) earlier idea that

191

one decides the life position based on early experiences to an emphasis on the inescapable collective dimension of existence. This is also a useful lens for understanding systemic 'othering' and the splitting seen in today's world.

The following chapters continue two threads: the intricacies of how theory is presented, interpreted, and extended. Chapter 2 offers multiple threads for the reader to follow, each giving a different flavour yet leading to the same essence – like viewing a world map from different perspectives and still arriving at a full sense of the whole. One thread I particularly enjoyed was the exploration of epistemology, ontology, and ethics of TA practice, especially the author's treatment of *methodology of the method itself* – in this case, the contractual method – and its links with various approaches in TA.

The chapter on 'Permission, protection, and potency: The three Ps reconsidered' provides a fresh orientation to Crossman's (1966) original ideas, reframing them from 'things to be done' in therapy to relational qualities co-created in the therapeutic encounter. I did, however, wonder whether its placement belonged in Part I (Basic Assumptions) or in Part II (New Wine from Old Roots), as it bridges the shift from one-person psychology to two-person psychology (Stark, 1999).

Part II: New wine from old roots

This part comprises seven of the 13 chapters in the book, making it the largest section. It reflects the author's emphasis on developing contemporary ideas that evolve from the original foundations of TA. Here, the author extends classical TA theory into present-day contexts, exploring how enduring concepts such as ego states, scripts, and relational dynamics can be reinterpreted through modern lenses. The focus moves from one-person psychology to two-person and two-person-plus perspectives, integrating social, cultural, and ethical dimensions of practice while remaining true to Berne's original spirit.

This part begins by arguing for a shift in focus from the *therapeutic relationship* to *relationships that can be therapeutic*. In Chapter 4, the author highlights the complex realities of living in a world of multiple and overlapping roles, inviting readers to consider the potential advantages of dual therapeutic relationships, while also cautioning against the risks of harm.

I found myself reflecting on the radical idea that dual relationships can sometimes be therapeutic. Yet I could not ignore the reality of power differentials inherent in such dynamics. For instance, is it truly possible to sustain a dual role – such as trainer–trainee and therapist–client – without the imbalance of power affecting the relationship? While

I appreciate the author's perspective that issues of relating surface across all roles, the boundaries differ depending on whether one is acting as therapist, trainer, or supervisor. For me, this chapter left a lingering question about whether the radical proposition is fully rooted in the reality of these power differences. Still, I could see the author's shift of focus – from *therapeutic relationship* to *therapeutic relating* – as an invitation to live TA principles in practice (Stark, 1999).

Chapter 5 felt like a continuation of this argument, extending the emphasis to present-centred exploration of relationships in therapy. I found this chapter particularly fascinating, as it drew on Stern's (2004) focus on the present moment, Rogers' (1959) client-centred perspective, Stark's (1999) two-person psychology, and Mitchell's (1988) relational psychoanalysis, before extending to what Tudor (2011) describes as a *two-person-plus* psychology. This addition of a *fourth* mode introduces the social context, recognising that current interactions are shaped not only by early relational experiences but also by present social realities. I will refrain from unpacking all the nuances here – each of which could easily become its own commentary – but I want to highlight how this chapter deepened my appreciation of the book's flow: it situates new ideas within old perspectives, making them both fresh and relevant.

In Chapter 6, the author revisits the concept of ego states (Berne, 1961). He raises important questions about the theory's consistency, presenting two perspectives: Berne's idea that ego states are fixed and must be restructured through processes like decontamination, deconfusion, or reparenting, versus the more fluid view of ego states where the Adult expands by integrating Parent and Child into the present. Rather than privileging one perspective, the author invites practitioners to let their practice inform their theoretical stance, ensuring congruence. I found this invitation particularly powerful – it continues the theme of revisiting old theory in light of decades of practice and encourages readers to fill in the gaps.

Chapter 7 extends this dialogue, engaging the reader with a deeper exploration of ego states. Here, the author provides a rich historical context, linking the concept to ego psychology and beyond, while also connecting the Adult process to *physis*, the inherent force of growth. I found the style of this chapter engaging – it felt less like being instructed and more like being invited to a dance. If this book were a drama, this chapter would be the perfect act where the concept of ego states becomes concrete and expansive, synthesising academic rigor with the practitioner's voice.

Chapter 8 shifts to the phenomenon of shame, explained through TA concepts such as transactions, impasse theory, and scripts. At first, I questioned its placement within the flow. Yet, when I reached Chapter 9, I realised that Chapter 8 acted as a prelude to script theory, easing the transition between ego states and script analysis. In retrospect, its placement made sense: it provided a lived experience application of TA concepts before leading into the more structured theoretical work on scripts.

In Chapter 9, the author explores 'Growth: Old Scripts, New Narratives', weaving together TA's concept of scripts with a broader view of human growth – social, physical, psychological. I was especially intrigued by the idea that evidence of growth should be demonstrable in the practice of transactional analysts themselves, including in credentialing processes such as written exams and Teaching and Supervising Transactional Analyst (TSTA) evaluations. Drawing on physis as the inherent force of growth, the author shows how clients can work through scripts and protocols to move toward autonomy. The references to Berne's original writings and subsequent expansions and critiques enriched this chapter, and for me it captured the spirit of 'new wine from old roots'.

Chapter 10, on regulation and registration, brings TA into the wider context of national and international practice. The author surfaces the complexities of practicing TA psychotherapy in countries where it may not be officially recognised, raising the question of whether TA credentials alone are sufficient. His appeal is for plural existence: for transactional analysts to find legitimacy both within and outside of national regulations. He also underscores the International Transactional Analysis Association's emphasis on compliance with local laws and regulations. I did wonder if this chapter might have fit more naturally into Part III, given its forward-looking concern with sustainability of TA. Still, I appreciated its honesty about the identity struggles of transactional analysts navigating recognition.

The final chapter of this section, Chapter 11, revisits game theory. I enjoyed tracing the trajectory of references to games from Berne's original work to their relative decline by the 2020s. The chapter offers both a historical overview and a fresh link to play and gaming in the Winnicottian sense of unconscious creative space. This insight – that games can provide a space for clients to articulate what cannot otherwise be spoken – justified the placement of this chapter in the flow. It rounded off Part II by reconnecting to Berne's foundational ideas of games while contemporary ideas of examining the unconscious playing.

Part III: Looking back, looking forwards
This part includes the final two chapters of the 13, inviting the reader to look ahead while remaining grounded in a solid theoretical foundation. It reflects on the evolution

of TA and gestures toward its future directions. The section honours the diversity of approaches that have emerged over the decades and encourages readers to maintain theoretical integrity while embracing innovation. Its tone is integrative and forward-looking, inspiring curiosity, critical reflection, and a renewed connection to TA's group and social roots.

I experienced Part III as an invitation to pause, digest the origins of TA, and then step forward into critique and expansion while keeping practice at the centre. It felt like the author wanted to ground innovation firmly in the roots of the theory, ensuring continuity and coherence.

Chapter 12 focuses on honouring the evolution of TA from 'schools' to 'approaches'. The author maps out the different approaches available today and provides a helpful scheme for analysing them according to function, logic, and underlying thinking. This framework allows both readers and practitioners to clarify where a given approach fits and what it offers. I found the examples particularly illuminating, as they turned abstract classification into something concrete. By situating contemporary approaches in relation to Berne's original categories, the author also invites readers to see this diversity as part of TA's vitality rather than fragmentation.

Chapter 13, the final chapter, struck me as both reflective and forward-looking. The author invites readers to adopt two imaginative mindsets – that of the 'Martian' and the 'Vulcan' – as a way of ensuring that TA continues to evolve without losing its foundations. These perspectives allow practitioners to view TA from the outside, maintaining curiosity, rigor, and a sense of distance. Importantly, the author reminds us of Berne's five rules for theory-making, emphasising the need for clarity, testability, and clinical relevance (Berne, 1961, 1972). The chapter also renews the call for group therapy to regain prominence in TA practice and credentialing processes. This reminder felt timely: group work was one of the original attractions of TA, yet it has sometimes receded into the background of individual psychotherapy.

For me, Part III served as a kind of consolidation. It offered both a summation of TA's evolution and a vision for how the field might continue to develop without losing its coherence. The emphasis on approaches, meta-analysis, and group therapy provided a fitting close to the book's narrative arc.

Conclusion

Reading and reviewing this book was a dual task. On the one hand, I found myself immersed in the flow of the arguments and the richness of the theory; on the other hand, I had to step back and evaluate how each chapter fit into the larger structure. This sometimes felt like what the author describes as a 'Martian' task – checking whether I was grasping not just the content of each chapter but also the logic of the book's overall flow.

What impressed me most was how the book consistently balanced honouring Berne's original formulations with critiquing, extending, and recontextualising them. It reminded me that TA is not static; it is a living theory that continues to grow.

As Berne (1966) famously said, 'symptomatic cure first and analysis later' (p. 209). I would echo a parallel message to contemporary transactional analysts: Apply first and write later. That, for me, is the one-line crystallisation of reading this book – a reminder that TA is most alive when it is practiced with integrity, then reflected upon and written about.

References

Aristotle. (n.d.). *Metaphysics* (W. D. Ross, Trans.). https://classics.mit.edu/Aristotle/metaphysics.html (Original work published ca. 350 BCE)

Berne, E. (1961). *Transactional analysis in psychotherapy: A systematic individual and social psychiatry*. Grove Press.

Berne, E. (1966). *Principles of group treatment*. Grove Press.

Berne, E. (1972). *What do you say after you say hello?* Grove Press.

Crossman, P. (1966). Permission and protection. *Transactional Analysis Bulletin, 5*(19), 152–154.

Klein, M. (1997). Notes on some schizoid mechanisms. In J. Mitchell (Ed.), *The selected Melanie Klein* (pp. 176–200). Free Press. (Original work published 1946)

Mitchell, S. A. (1988). *Relational concepts in psychoanalysis: An integration*. Harvard University Press.

Rogers, C. R. (1959). A theory of therapy, personality, and interpersonal relationships, as developed in the client-centered framework. In S. Koch (Ed.), *Psychology: A study of a science* (Vol. 3, pp. 184–256). McGraw-Hill.

Stark, M. (1999). *Modes of therapeutic action*. Jason Aronson.

Stern, D. N. (2004). *The present moment in psychotherapy and everyday life*. W. W. Norton.

Tudor, K. (2011). Three modes of transactional analysis. *Transactional Analysis Journal*, *41*(1), 5–25. https://doi.org/10.1177/036215371104100103

Tudor, K. (2016). We are: The fundamental life position. *Transactional Analysis Journal*, *46*(3), 208–222. https://doi.org/10.1177/0362153716654855

Wertheimer, M. (1923). Untersuchungen zur Lehre von der Gestalt [Laws of organisation in perceptual forms]. *Psychologische Forschung, 4*, 301–350. https://doi.org/10.1007/BF00410640

Zalcman, M. J. (1990). Four trends in transactional analysis. *Transactional Analysis Journal*, *20*(1), 31–34. https://doi.org/10.1177/036215379002000106

Paper 13

Karangarua – Tētehi whakaaroaro | A reflection

Jemma Dymond (Te Ātiawa)

Abstract

This paper is a personal reflection following attendance at the international TA Conference in 2024 as a response to the organisers, presenters, and contributors to this book. In it, the author reflects on her Conference experience; expresses her gratitude for the protocols that were honoured; admits to her still developing embrace of diversity; and shares her thoughts about the Conference theme that she sees as organically embedded throughout the process of this book coming to be.

As a ten-year-old, my nan told me off for describing my new lunchbox as 'wicked'. To ten-year-old me, I was at the height of my coolness using that word, following the zeitgeist of the 1990s and not expecting Nan (at her age) to get it. She told me that 'wicked' meant evil and the dictionary would not disagree with her. That's language though; it can be open to interpretation, be reimagined, reclaimed, and shaped by location, perspective, and time. The gifting of a name for a conference theme, I imagine, is no easy feat. I appreciate whaea Shirley (Rivers) for the time and consideration she put into arriving at 'Karangarua' for our international TA Conference, held in Te Whanganui-a-Tara | Wellington in 2024.

Just as my use of 'wicked' did not translate across the generational divide between me and Nan, karangarua, or karanga rua, as it can also be written, will not mean the same to everyone. By definition, it can refer to 'standing in a double relationship' and also to 'someone related through different lines'. In a more literal sense, it describes karanga (to call, summon), and rua (two, both). Depending on the time and space you occupied as you attended the Conference or as you read of the experience here, this calling will evoke in you what is ready to be evoked. I am grateful to the varying Conference presenters and authors who have generously shared what it evokes in them – ngā mihi ki a koutou | acknowledgements to you all. I hope the absence of a singular translatable definition of this word continues to invite reflection, dialogue, debate, and choice.

I attended the Conference with the hope of reconnecting with colleagues unseen for some time and to rekindle the sense of belonging I have felt at TA events in the past. As the sole TA practitioner in my region (Taranaki), I stand to gain so much from these interactions. To start the Conference with pōwhiri added to my 'homecoming', in part because we were hosted by my own iwi so the tikanga was my norm and partly because I'm still learning that the discomfort I can feel at times can often be attributed to tikanga not being followed. The ritual of being welcomed by mana whenua prevents the familiar discomfort felt in occasions where it hasn't occurred. I find the discomfort hard to describe; suffice to say, I've been socially conditioned to ignore it, which makes requesting or advocating for it a challenge. To have someone else recognise the value and honour the importance of saying hello 'our way' was meaningful to me and I am grateful to the Conference organisers for making it happen – whakawhetai e hoa mā | my appreciations to you, my friends.

Witnessing matua Seán in the role of kaikōrero was inspiring. This was my first experience of meeting him and I perceived his command of reo Māori as a demonstration of a deep respect and commitment to te Ao Māori. It did also spark a moment of fear in me as I wondered if this is sustainable? Too often I've been in workplaces or groups that have honoured our cultural practices purely on the backs of the select few with the mātauranga and pūkenga to carry it out only for it to be lost when those people move on. I sat there in that pōwhiri feeling such gratitude for the efforts of our community with an almost sense of impending doom that it won't last and a pressure to help carry the mantle, which I don't feel ready or able to bear – tēnā koe matua Sean. I recognise that your ability to perform that role as well as you did comes from years of dedication.

Reflecting on the tag line of the Conference theme 'Unity through Diversity in Relationship', I questioned how open and embracing of diversity I really am. I was there to connect with the like-minded, others that choose TA; to feel kinship, nurture bonds, and form new ones, so I wondered if that's me preferring sameness over difference: unity *over* diversity, rather than *through* it? How comfortable or even willing am I to explore difference and embrace diversity? Then as I would expect, I had such delight in connecting with Conference colleagues from around the world. The playful ice-breaker exercise determining who had travelled the furthest to be there sparked a real joy.[3] My genuine interest to engage with those from faraway places reaffirmed that I needn't worry; I have always and I'm sure will always continue to be curious to learn and explore the diversity amongst our community, and that will continue to foster unity. While it feels easy and natural in the TA setting, I am aware that I'm still grappling at times to sit with professionals of different theoretical persuasions and hold an I'm OK, You're

[3] From Bergen op Zoom, The Netherlands, 18,668 kilometres; Ljubljana, Slovenia 18,347 kms; Bohus-Björkö, Sweden 17,830 kilometres; York, UK 14,403 kms.; Coimbatore, India 11,462 kms; Tokyo, Japan 9,274 kms; and Sydney, Australia 2,226 kms; as well as from far and near in Aotearoa New Zealand.

OK stance. Getting to spend time amongst the TA crowd feels a bit like the relief of wearing comfortable trackpants when I'm too often feeling forced into stiffly ironed dress pants. We might all wear trackpants of different styles, colours, and fabrics, but we're still distinguishable as a group when put next to those in suits and ties.

At the Conference, the challenge of deciding which presentations to attend felt like choosing between mislabelled lollies. It was a bit of a gamble not knowing exactly what you were going to get: some titles were direct and to the point, others more playfully obscure. Either way, I went, having some confidence knowing that it's rare to find a TA lolly I don't like – and the calibre of presenters was equally sweet. Nevertheless, it took some strategy to make the most of the experience, so I'm grateful to those that agreed to go to different presentations than me to then swap notes during the lunch times.

From the hands-on experience demonstrating the metaphor of tukutuku (Paper 4 in this book) to the vulnerability of describing a want to change an aspect within the national character of the Japanese (Paper 7). From reflecting on the discursively constructed criminal self (Paper 10) to exploring what is humour and where it fits in TA theory and practice (Paper 11); and from burnout (in two presentations at the Conference) to creativity (Paper 8): the presenters themselves represented the Conference theme, karangarua: we are always standing in the double relationship in which and whereby these apparently opposite topics are valid and meaningful, occupying the same space, time, and audience.

The Conference was held in an urban marae; a dual-purpose building that transforms to fit its purpose. The open space at the front was the marae ātea during the pōwhiri, a sacred area governed by the atua Tūmatauenga, the god of war and people because it's where speeches occur which can be highly contested debates. After the ceremonies were complete, its status was restored to that of a standard courtyard, allowing for a space to eat our lunch outside (which is not permitted on a typical marae ātea). The very building we met in stands in a double relationship of marae and Conference room, meeting the diverse needs of our people so we could be united in relationship.

TA theory and practice not only brought us all together for those inspiring days of challenge and connection, they also give us a foundation to explore, reflect, question, and develop our ideas and then ultimately to share them with one another and the world.

Accepting the invite to read the collection of papers provided for the making of this book, I imagined the authors sitting in their homes, transferring their spoken presentations into written form. I enjoyed seeing how even this part of the process exemplifies karangarua: standing in the double relationships of being colleagues attending the Conference side-by-side, and then as presenter and participant, knowing that others would likely include supervisors and supervisees, trainers and trainees, and now authors and readers. Seeing the presentations and articles as the authors' karanga or call, shared for a second time equating again to the more literal translation of karangarua. Karanga on marae are responded to; so this reflection is my response to the authors. In honour of them calling twice, I vowed to listen twice. Reading the articles over, hearing and feeling something different each time, I am moved by our opportunity, resources, and willingness to take individual thoughts and expertise, formed in various parts of the world to share them collectively. A cohesive whole, made up of individual parts, unity through diversity.

E koekoe te tūī, e ketekete te kākā, e kūkū te kererū | The tūī, the kākā, and the kererū each make their own unique sound.

Kuputakanui – Glossary

Compiled by *Keith Tudor, Maria Haenga-Collins (Ngāti Porou, Te Aitanga a Māhaki, Ngāi Tahu), Raewyn Knowles, and Angie Strachan*

As indicated in the Introduction, this glossary provides a brief dictionary to ngā kūpu Māori (the Māori words) used in the text of this book. However, given the international audience of the book, we have taken the opportunity to expand the glossary by adding footnotes – for the most part, originally compiled by Raewyn and subsequently expanded and edited by Keith – in order to provide more background to the context that informs the words, language, and concepts used and referred to in the book.

te Ao Māori	the Māori world
Aotearoa[4]	New Zealand
āta haere	to go slowly; to take it easy; to go cautiously
atua	deity
awa whiria	braided rivers
awhiowhio	whirlwind, tornado
hapū[5]	sub-tribe; to be pregnant
harakeke[6]	flax
hau	a person's spiritual essence; wind; breath
hau kāinga	the local/home people
hauora	health
hauora Māori	Māori health
hīkoi	march; demonstration
Hīkoi mō te Tiriti[7]	(the) March for Te Tiriti [o Waitangi]

---

[4] Although this generally refers to the landmass of New Zealand, there are also separate words used for the main islands of the country, i.e., Te Ika-a-Māui – the North Island, Te Waipounamu – the South Island, and Rakiura – Stewart Island.

[5] Also, kinship group or clan, a section of a large(r) kinship group (iwi) and the primary political unit in traditional Māori society, consisting of many whānau sharing descent from a common ancestor, usually being named after the ancestor, though sometimes from an important event in the group's history.

[6] New Zealand flax (*Phormium tenax*) – an important native plant with long, stiff, upright leaves, seed pods, and dull red flowers, found in lowland swamps throughout Aotearoa New Zealand.

[7] A nine-day march that took place in November 2024 from Cape Reinga at the top of the North Island, and from Bluff in the far south of the South Island to Wellington, which included a series of meetings and protests along the way, against what was referred to as 'the Treaty Principles Bill' (2024).

hinengaro	two flowing waters of the mind; thought; intellect; consciousness
hongi	pressing of noses [verb and noun]
horopaki me karanga	context and call
iwi Māori	Māori tribe(s); Māori people
ka mua, ka muri	(literally) go in front, go behind; (metaphorically) the idea of walking backwards into the future
kai	food
kaiako	teacher
kaikaranga	the caller (usually female)
kaikōrero[8]	speakers; orators
kaitiaki	guardian(s)
kapa haka	a traditional Māori performing art form
karakia	chant; incantation; prayer
karakia wairua	opening to the divine
karanga[9]	(the) call
karanga rua	related through two different lines; standing in a double relationship
karangarua	standing in a double relationship; unity through diversity
karu	eye(s)
kaumātua	elder(s)
kaupapa	the reason for an encounter; purpose
kete	basket(s)
ngā kete o te wānanga[10]	the baskets of knowledge

---

[8] Although orators are usually male, some iwi (e.g., Ngāti Porou and Ngāti Kahungunu) allow women of mana to whaikōrero. However, this is not common across iwi due to the tapu nature of women as the whare tangata (literally, the house of mankind), i.e., mothers. The general prohibition on women as kaikōrero is to provide protection for them from physical and/or spiritual harm.

[9] To call, call out, shout, summon; a formal call, ceremonial call, or call of welcome to visitors onto a marae, or equivalent venue at the start of a pōwhiri. The term is also used for the responses from the manuhiri (or visiting group) to the tangata whenua. Karanga follow a format which includes addressing and greeting each other and the people they are representing; paying tribute to the dead, especially those who have died recently; and addressing the purpose of the meeting or occasion.

[10] The three baskets of knowledge obtained for humankind by the god Tāne, known primarily as the god of the forests and all that dwells within them. In order to acquire the baskets of knowledge, Tāne had to ascend to the twelfth heaven, Te Toi-o-ngā-rangi, and there be ushered into the presence of the Supreme

ko wai au?	who am I?
koha	gift (usually money)
kōrero	speech; talk; talking
kotahitanga	interwoven narratives; unity; togetherness; solidarity
kupu	word(s)
mā te wā	it takes as long as it takes; time will tell
mahi	work
mana	authority; prestige; control; power; influence
mana motuhake	autonomy and self-defined wellbeing
mana whenua	host(s)
manaakitanga	reciprocity; care; hospitality
manuhiri/manuwhiri	visitor(s)
māori	normal; usual; natural; ordinary; native
Māori[11]	indigenous person/people of Aotearoa
Māoritanga	Māori culture, practices, beliefs
marae	a communal, sacred place
marae ātea	courtyard; the open place in front of the wharenui
mātauranga	knowledge
mātauranga Māori	Māori knowledge, systems
ngā mate ō te wā	the recently deceased
Matike Mai Aotearoa	an independent working group on constitutional reform[12]

God, Io-matua-kore, to make his request, which was granted, and hence the knowledge humans have in our possession and at our disposal. The three baskets of knowledge are usually called te kete tuauri (the basket of life), te kete tuatea (the basket of darkness), and te kete aronui (the basket of pursuit).

[11] Since the 18th century (Common Era), a new use of the word resulting from Pākehā contact in order to distinguish between people of Māori descent and settlers/colonisers.

[12] The Independent Working Group (the Group) on Constitutional Transformation was first promoted at a meeting of the Iwi Chairs' Forum (the Forum) in 2010. The terms of reference given to the Working Group were deliberately broad, and included:

> **To develop and implement a model for an inclusive Constitution for Aotearoa based on tikanga and kawa, He Whakaputanga o te Rangatiratanga o Niu Tireni of 1835, Te Tiriti o Waitangi of 1840, and other indigenous human rights instruments which enjoy a wide degree of international recognition**. (Mutu & Jackson, 2016, p. 7; original emphasis)

A Forum representative, Professor Margaret Mutu, was appointed as the Working Group's Chair and Moana Jackson was invited to be its Convenor. Members of the Working Group were nominated by iwi, and other organisations or were co-opted. The Chairperson and Convenor facilitated 252 hui (meetings) between 2012 and 2015. The rōpū rangatahi convened by Veronica Tawhai presented 70 wānanga. The Working Group also invited written submissions, organised focus groups, and conducted one-on-one interviews. The views they received canvassed a number of topics such as the relationship between *Te Tiriti* and democracy, what is meant by a treaty relationship, what is a constitution, and other related issues (see Mutu & Jackson, 2016; Tudor, 2021).

matua	adult; chief; father; parent
Mehana	Mason
Mehana model	a clinical assessment model named after Sir Mason Durie[13]
mihi	speech (of greeting)
mihimihi	greeting(s)
moko/puna	grandchild/ren (an abbreviated form of mokopuna [see entry below])
moko kauae	traditional chin tattoo for Māori women
mokopuna	grandchild/ren
ngā	the (plural)
ngākau	heart
noa	ordinary; unrestricted; void; transported out of sacredness
Pākehā[14]	non-Māori
Papatūānuku (Papa)	Earth mother
pepeha	a traditional Māori introduction
poi	a light ball on a string of varying length[15]
pono	true
poroporoaki	ending
pou	post
pounamu	greenstone
poutama	stepped pattern of tukutuku panels and woven mats symbolising genealogies, also the various levels of learning and intellectual achievement
pōwhiri	welcoming ceremony

[13] A framework for clinical assessment that integrates Māori perspectives to improve healthcare for Māori patients (Pitama et al., 2007). It emphasises a holistic approach, considering the interconnectedness of physical, mental, spiritual, and social wellbeing, as well as the impact of societal factors such as colonisation and racism. The model utilises the concept of a waka (canoe) with its crossbars representing different dimensions of health, and ngā hau e whā (the four winds) representing historical and current societal influences.

[14] From pakepakeha (imaginary beings resembling humans), a term generally used to refer to non-Māori of white, European descent, but a concept in flux (Tudor, 2025; Wevers, n.d.).

[15] These are usually swung or twirled rhythmically to sung accompaniment; traditionally made of raupō leaves.

puku	abdomen; gut instinct; intuition; to swell; very[16]
pūkenga	skilled; versed in
pūrākau	narrative
rangatira	chief(s)
rangatiratanga	chieftainship; chiefly autonomy
Ranginui (Rangi)	Sky father
i raro	from below
raupatu	the stealing or confiscation of land
te reo Māori	the Māori language
te reo Pākehā	English (language, speech)
rongo	to listen; to know or to get to know[17]
Rongo	the god of peace
rōpū	group
Te Rōpū Whakamana i Te Tiriti o Waitangi	Waitangi Tribunal[18]
i roto	from inside
i runga	from above
rua	two; both
taha Māori	Māori identity; Māori characteristic
ngā Tama-ā-rangi	the children of Ranginui and Papatūānuku
tamariki	children
Tāne	the son of Papatūānuku and Ranginui
Tāne mahuta (Tane)	Māori god of the forest and bird life
Tangaroa	Māori god of the ocean(s) and water
tangata whaiora	client(s)

---

[16] As a modifier, it means very, e.g., riri = angry; pukuriri = very angry/furious; also, as a modifier after a word, it means something done on the quiet, e.g., haere puku = to go secretly, nohopuku = to remain silent.

[17] Not only by hearing but also by touching, feeling, seeing, intuition, or any other means.

[18] The Waitangi Tribunal was established by the *Treaty of Waitangi Act 1975*. Since te Tiriti was signed in 1840, Māori have made many complaints to the Crown that the terms of te Tiriti have not been upheld. By establishing the Waitangi Tribunal, the New Zealand Parliament provided a legal process by which Māori Treaty claims could be investigated. Tribunal inquiries contribute to the resolution of Treaty claims and to the reconciliation of outstanding issues between Māori and the Crown. The Tribunal has reported on many issues, from te reo Māori and the radio spectrum, to fresh water, fisheries, the foreshore and seabed, and Māori heath and homelessness. Many of the recommendations contained in its reports have been implemented by governments, and have contributed to many initiatives and new institutions, including reo irirangi (Māori radio), te Taura Whiri i te Reo Māori (the Māori Language Commission), te Māngai Pāho (the Māori Broadcasting Funding Agency), and te Aka Whai Ora (the Māori Health Authority). At first, the Tribunal could only hear claims about current government actions. In 1985, Parliament allowed the Tribunal to investigate events dating back to 1840.

tangata whenua	people of the land; people of the marae
taonga	precious object
tapu	restriction; sacredness
taringa	ear(s)
tauiwi	(literally) new tribe; (metaphorically) non-Māori
tauparapara	incantation; beginning
Tāwhirimātea	Māori god of the weather and, specifically, winds
te	the (singular)
tēnā koe	hello; greetings to you (an individual)
tēnā kōrua	hello; greetings to you (two)
tēnā koutou katoa	hello; greetings to you (three or more)
tikanga	customary practices; practice guidelines; ways of being; cultural norms
tinana	the physical aspect of self; body
tino rangatiratanga	self-determination; Māori sovereignty[19]
tipuna/tupuna, tīpuna/ tūpuna	ancestor(s)
te Tiriti o Waitangi[20]	the Treaty of Waitangi
tohunga	healing practice; Māori healers
toitū	to be undisturbed, untouched, permanent, entire
Toitū te Tiriti[21]	respect te Tiriti
tomokanga	entrance; gateway, e.g., the gate of the marae gate
tūī	parson bird (*Prosthemadera novaeseelandiae*)[22]
tukutuku	a traditional Māori woven latticework that is both artistic and symbolic
tukutuku pae[23]	tukutuku panel
Tūmatauenga	the God of war
tūrangawaewae	(a) place to stand[24]

---

[19] Enshrined in *Te Tiriti o Waitangi* (Article 2).

[20] The founding document of the modern New Zealand nation, signed in 1840 between Māori rangatira (chiefs) and representatives of the British Crown (see Museum of New Zealand | Te Papa Tongarewa, 2025; Waitangi Tribunal, 2025).

[21] Is a movement inspired by the ancestors, is treaty led, driven by self-determination, and focused on future generations. Its stated intent is to 'demonstrate the beginning of a unified Aotearoa response to the Government's assault on tangata whenua and Te Tiriti o Waitangi' (Te Toitū te Tiriti, 2025, para. 1).

[22] A songbird that imitates other birds' calls; has glossy-black plumage and two white tufts at the throat.

[23] A form of Māori art and architecture; a traditional woven lattice that record various concepts and teachings, the panels consist of vertical stakes (traditionally made of kākaho), horizontal rods (traditionally made of stalks of bracken-fern or thin strips of tōtara wood), and flexible material of flax, kiekie, and pīngao, which form the traditional pattern, each of which has a name.

[24] A right to residence and belonging through kinship and whakapapa.

waewae tapu	a person who is new to the marae ātea, is here for the first time, and requires special acknowledgement and special attention
wahine	woman
wāhine	women
i waho	from outside
wai	water
waiata	song; sing
wairua	spirit; soul
wairuatanga	spirituality
wānanga	to meet; discuss; deliberate; consider; a forum; conference seminar
waka	seagoing vessel; canoe
wānanga	workshop
whāea	mother; aunt; elder (female)
whaikōrero	formal speech
whaiora/tangata whaiora	client[25]
whakaoranga	respect for life
whakaotinga	completion/new beginnings
whakapapa	genealogy; also blueprint and depiction of DNA[26]
whakapuaki	letting wellness flow
He Whakaputanga	The Declaration of the Independence of New Zealand
whakarata	expression; openness; trust
whakārongo	listen
whakatangi	emotional shift; expression
whakataukī	proverb/saying
whakawhanaungatanga	(the) process of establishing relationships
whānau	(extended) family(ies)
whanaungatanga	relationships; connecting
whāngai	to feed, nourish; adoption
Whanganui-a-Tara	Wellington
whare	house; ancestral house
te whare tapu whā[27]	the four sides or walls of the house

---

[25] Literally, a person seeking health.
[26] Deoxyribonucleic acid.
[27] A Māori model of health, advanced by Mason Durie (1994), that describes four dimensions of holistic wellbeing based on the image of the four walls of the wharenui (Māori meeting house) which, in the model, represent tinana (the physical), wairua (spiritual), hinengaro (mental and emotional), and whānau (family and social).

wharenui	the (Māori) meeting house
whare wānanga	house(s) of learning; university(ies)
te wheke[28]	the octopus
whenua	land; placenta

References

Durie, M. (1994). *Whaiora: Maori health development.* Oxford University Press.

Museum of New Zealand | Te Papa Tongarewa. (2025). *The full text of Te Tiriti o Waitangi | The Treaty of Waitangi.* https://www.tepapa.govt.nz/discover-collections/read-watch-play/maori/treaty-waitangi/treaty-close/full-text-te-tiriti-o

Mutu, M., & Jackson, M. (2016). *The report of Matike Mai Aotearoa – The Independent Working Group on Constitutional Transformation.* https://nwo.org.nz/wp-content/uploads/2018/06/MatikeMaiAotearoa25Jan16.pdf

Pere, R. R. (1997). Te wheke – *A celebration of infinite wisdom* (N. Nicholson, Illus.). Ao Ako Learning New Zealand.

Pitama, S., Robertson, P., Cram, F., Gillies, M., Huria, T., & Dallas-Katoa, W. (2007). Meihana model: A clinical assessment framework. *New Zealand Journal of Psychology, 36*(3), 118–125. https://www.psychology.org.nz/journal-archive/Pitamaetal_NZJP36-3_pg118.pdf

Principles of the Treaty of Waitangi Bill 2024. https://www.legislation.govt.nz/bill/government/2024/0094/latest/whole.html

Toitū te Tiriti. (2025). *Our kaupapa.* https://toitutetiriti.co.nz/pages/kaupapa

Treaty of Waitangi Act 1975. https://www.legislation.govt.nz/act/public/1975/0114/latest/whole.html

Tudor, K. (2021). Tūtira mai ahau. In *20/20 vision, 2020* (pp. 184–193). Tuwhera Open Access Books. https://ojs.aut.ac.nz/tuwhera-open-monographs/catalog/book/6

Tudor, K. (2025). S is for settler: A psychosocial perspective on belonging and unbelonging in Aotearoa New Zealand. In B. Lythberg, C. Woods, & S. Nemec (Eds.), *Settler responsibility for decolonisation: Stories from the field* (pp. 144–162). Routledge.

Waitangi Tribunal. (2025). *About the Treaty.* https://www.waitangitribunal.govt.nz/en/about/the-treaty/about-the-treaty

Wevers, L. (n.d.). *Being pākehā.* https://www.wgtn.ac.nz/wellington/pakehaha/being-pakeha

---

[28] Another Māori model of health created by Rangimarie Rose Pere (1997).

Editors' and contributors' biographies

Editors

Matt Bird, CTA (Psychotherapy) has a background in addiction treatment, primarily working in residential treatment settings and therapeutic communities, working as a clinician, leader, and consultant. He embarked on his TA journey in 2019 with the Physis Institute, Ōtepoti | Dunedin, having briefly stepped away from residential treatment settings after relocating there. Until recently he worked in a therapeutic community working with complex mental health and addiction issues, and is now developing a private practice working with individuals and groups. He was the co-chair of the scientific committee for the international TA Conference held in Wellington in 2024, and completed his CTA exam in 2025. Matt is passionate about group work and integrating socio-political theory in practice having been inspired and influenced by Radical Psychiatry early in his TA training. Email: mattbirdnz@gmail.com

Keith Tudor, PhD, CQSW, Dip. Psychotherapy, Certified and Teaching and Supervising Transactional Analyst (Psychotherapy), is professor of psychotherapy and co-lead of Moana Nui, a research group for psychological therapies at Auckland University of Technology, Aotearoa New Zealand. He has been actively involved in transactional analysis (TA) for 40 years and was co-chair of the scientific committee for the international TA Conference held in Wellington in 2024, and has recently been appointed as chair of the International Transactional Analysis Association's Conference(s) Committee. He has contributed extensively to thinking about TA theory and practice, and is the recipient, with Graeme Summers, of the 2020 Eric Berne Memorial Award (EBMA) for their work on co-creative transactional analysis, and of the 2025 EBMA 'for revitalising and advancing the critical and social edge of transactional analysis and critiquing TA from within and without'. He is also the recipient of the 2025 Carl Rogers Award (bestowed by the Humanistic Psychology Division of the American Psychological Association) 'in recognition of distinguished lifetime contributions to humanistic psychology'. Keith has a small private practice in West Auckland as a health care provider and transactional analyst, primarily offering online supervision and training. Email: keith.tudor@aut.ac.nz

Contributors

Masumi Aonuma is a Certified Transactional Analysis (CTA) in the educational field and is currently undergoing training as a Provisional Teaching and Supervising Transactional Analyst (PTSTA). She is qualified in Japan as a state-certified career consultant. Following experience in the human resources department of a private company, Masumi has worked as a freelance business trainer since 2001. She is engaged in human skills training for employees and specialised business education at contracted companies. She is well-regarded for expanding and supporting business careers by maximising use of TA. She has trained over 3,000 new recruits in total and continues to provide development programmes that contribute to workplace retention and reducing staff turnover. Currently in Japan, she has formed a TA continuing learning group to facilitate daily mutual learning among participating members. Email: f-voice@outlook.jp

Elizabeth Day is an Associate Professor in the Department of Psychotherapy & Counselling at Auckland University of Technology. She held the role of Head of Department from 2020 to 2023. She served as a Board Director of the Psychotherapy and Counselling Federation of Australia (PACFA) from 2012 to 2014, and was a past chair and member of the PACFA Research Committee, and editorial board member of the *Psychotherapy and Counselling Journal of Australia* (*PACJA*) from 2012 to 2023. Elizabeth was honoured with lifetime membership of PACFA in 2025 for her leadership and service to the profession in Australia. She supervises students in PhD, DHSc, and Masters research, and has published in the areas of field theory, mindfulness, gender and sexuality, identity and violence, ethics, human experiences of social Artificial Intelligence, the use of outcomes measures, Grounded Theory, telepsychotherapy, and professional practice. She spent many years in Melbourne studying and teaching at the University of Melbourne, Monash University, and ACAP University College. Elizabeth moved to Aotearoa in 2015 where, alongside her academic role, she has established a yoga and meditation studio with her wife, Willa. She teaches meditation at her studio in Kihikihi, as well as online, and internationally (Australia, India, the USA), and runs a private practice in integrative psychotherapy. In 2026 she is taking leave of absence from all commitments to undertake a year of meditation retreat. Email: elizabeth.day@aut.ac.nz

Deepak Dhananjaya is a psychotherapist and Agile-Leadership-Organisation Coach based in Bangalore, India. He is the co-founder of AgileSattva Consulting, an organisation development and transformation firm, and the founder of the Prabhava Institute of Inclusive Mental Health, which focuses on inclusivity in mental health education and services by engaging with the intersections of privilege and oppression across patriarchy, sexuality, class, caste, and religion. A CTA and a PTSTA (Psychotherapy), Deepak's grounding in a radical relational approach to TA deeply informs his clinical practice, teaching, and supervision. An engineer by training, he also holds master's degrees in Sexuality and Sexual Counselling. His work bridges psychotherapy, systems thinking, and leadership, exploring how socio-cultural-political dynamics shape personal and organisational narratives. Since 2012, Deepak has been actively associated with the TA community in various roles at both regional and international levels. Engaging with the group relations framework since 2019, he has participated in multiple conferences and workshops in both member and staff roles. Deepak's work is informed by TA, group relations, and a socio-cultural-political frame of reference, reflecting a deep engagement with authority, belonging, and transformation – both in the therapy room, within organisations, and in his writings. Email: deepak.dhananjaya@gmail.com

Jemma Dymond (Te Ātiawa) BN, PG Dip HSc, is a CTA, a registered psychotherapist, and clinical supervisor in New Plymouth, Aotearoa New Zealand. She started her career in health 25 years ago as a Defence Force medic, moving into Nursing for Child & Adolescent Mental Health Services (therapy, management, and education roles) both at home and in Australia before transitioning into psychotherapy where she now has a private practice. Email: jemldymond@gmail.com

John Evans is a TA psychotherapist, supervisor, and trainer based in Te Whanganui a Tara | Wellington for the last 15 years. Born and raised in the UK, John has worked in different settings around the field of mental health and addiction for approaching 30 years, previously as social worker and counsellor. Before this John played guitar in a heavy metal band. John has an independent practice in the Hutt Valley; he teaches and supervises trainees and therapists at the Wellington Transactional Analysis Training Institute. John has a particular interest in humour as a human phenomenon, and how it can be understood and applied in the therapeutic space as well as life in general. This interest has led him to research and write about the topic of humour. Ethics is another area of John's interests, and he is a member of the ITAA Ethics Committee. John lives with his partner and several animals in the Hutt Valley. Email: jevans883@yahoo.co.nz

Anna Hinehou Fleming (she/her/ia) has whakapapa connections to Ngāti Hine and Tūhoe through her mother and to London, England through her father. She has worked in social services for over 20 years, spending the last decade practicing as a psychotherapist in Tāmaki Makaurau, primarily working with whānau Māori through tertiary health services, private practice, and ACC Sensitive Claims. Anna is a Lecturer in the Department of Psychotherapy & Counselling at Auckland University of Technology and works on both the Graduate Diploma and the Master of Psychotherapy programmes. Her clinical practice and academic mahi is supported and informed by Indigenous models of health care, social justice movements, and the consistent work of Māori clinicians in establishing a kaupapa Māori based psychotherapy in Aotearoa. In 2024, Anna co-founded Awatea Therapy, a kaupapa Māori therapy practice comprising psychotherapists, counsellors, and creative arts therapists based in Mauinaina (Panmure) in Tāmaki Makaurau. Email: email@annafleming.co.nz

Bev Gibbons – I am a TSTA in the field of psychotherapy. I have an MA in TA Psychotherapy and BA(Hons) in Integrative Counselling. I live in North Yorkshire in the United Kingdom (UK), and work as a trainer, supervisor, and psychotherapist in private practice with individuals, groups, and organisations. I worked for many years as a psychotherapist clinical lead working with schools and universities and in the not-for-profit sector. Mutuality, curiosity, and anti-oppressive practice are central in my way of working. My professional passions include working to share power; to connect with and understand other cultures through lived experience conversations; to make meaning with other/s in the intersubjective 'space between' and working in ways that draw from all fields of application in TA. I am a current member of the EATA PTSC, and a member of the Training and Accreditation Standards Committee of the United Kingdom TA Association. Email: bgcp@bevgibbons.co.uk

Te Amokura Griggs
Ko Puketoi rātou ko Kupukōkore, ko Maungatautari ngā maunga
Ko Owahanga rātou ko Mataikona, ko Waipa, ko Waikato ngā awa
Ko Matawhaurua rātou ko Takitimu, ko Kurahaupō ngā waka
Ko Te Hika O Pāpāuma rāua ko Ngāti Apakura ngā iwi
Ko Te Amokura taku ingoa
Tēnā koutou katoa. My name is Te Amokura, and I am an Addictions Clinician and Clinical Supervisor. I have also completed three years of study with the Wellington Transactional Analysis Training Institute Ltd (2016–2019) and continue to work towards the CTA exam. I reside in Waipawa in the region of Kahungunu ki Tamatea, in Aotearoa New Zealand. I currently work as an addictions clinician on the Opioid Substitute Treatment program in the Te Mata-A-Maui (Hawkes Bay region). I am also a clinical supervisor of individual practitioners and groups who work in therapeutic communities. I am also a member of the Addictions Practitioners Association Aotearoa New Zealand (DAPAANZ), and of Waka Oranga (the National Collective of Māori Psychotherapy Practitioners). Email: te.amokura@xtra.co.nz

Rhae Hooper, LSDA, CTA(E), MSc, is an educator, facilitator, and visual artist whose career spans more than four decades across education, organisational development, and the arts. She is a CTA (Education) and holds a Master of Science degree, with her work grounded in the psychology of learning, communication, and leadership. Hooper is a contributor to *Educational Transactional Analysis* (Routledge, 2016), in which she examines the application of TA principles to professional and organisational training

213

environments. Her professional background includes ownership of a management recruitment and training consultancy for 16 years and co-founding a major direct-marketing enterprise in home shopping, catalogues, internet, and television retailing that employed more than 700 staff. Earlier, she held senior management roles with Xerox Corporation and IBM, specialising in systems training, staff development, and organisational support. Rhae designs and facilitates leadership, communication, and professional development programmes for corporate and community organisations, and provides communication skills training for several charity groups. She is trained in Neuro-Linguistic Programming, DSC, and the Belbin Team Roles model, and is a qualified Speech and Drama teacher. In addition to her educational and organisational work, she is an exhibiting artist whose abstract and landscape paintings explore colour, movement, and emotion. Her lifelong commitment to adult learning and creativity reflects a belief in human potential, relational learning, and the transformative power of both art and education. Email: Rhae@Interfine.com.au

Raewyn Knowles is a CTA(P), psychotherapist, and clinical supervisor based in Auckland, Aotearoa New Zealand, with over three decades experience in mental health, addiction, and psychotherapy. Her professional background includes clinical roles in substance use treatment and mental health services, with a sustained focus on psychotherapeutic practice in both public and private sectors. She holds a Diploma in Occupational Therapy and qualifications in alcohol and drug studies. Her theoretical orientation is integrative, primarily drawing on relational and psychodynamic approaches, with a particular focus on developmental and systemic contexts. Her clinical interests include complex trauma, addiction, grief and loss, identity formation, and interpersonal dynamics. She actively engages in clinical supervision, offering reflective practice and professional development for practitioners across disciplines. Her supervisory work is guided by a commitment to ethical inquiry, bicultural competence, and fostering practitioner resilience. Her practice is grounded in a profound engagement with issues of culture, identity, and personal narrative. Her heritage encompasses Celtic, Nordic, French, Portuguese, Croatian, and North African influences, which inform her sensitivity to cultural identity and the intergenerational transmission of experience. She is registered with the Psychotherapists Board of Aotearoa New Zealand, a member of the New Zealand Association of Counsellors, the Association of Psychotherapists Aotearoa New Zealand (APANZ), and the DAPAANZ. Email: raewyn.knowles@gmail.com

Mandy Lacy, PhD, is a counsellor, coach, supervisor, and educator based in Aotearoa New Zealand, with over 25 years' experience working across mental health, education, leadership, and organisational development. Her practice integrates TA, positive psychology, and creative methods to support individuals and groups in personal and professional growth, communication, and transformation. Mandy's professional focus is on the intersection between creativity, wellbeing, and relational development, exploring how personal and professional evolution occur most powerfully in unison. A TSTA in both organisational and counselling fields, Mandy has contributed to the advancement of TA through her writing, teaching, and development of experiential learning frameworks. Her work, epitomised in *Ignite Your Creativity* (www.mandylacy.nz) weaves TA theory, metaphor, and neuroscience into accessible tools for creative reawakening, including workshops, reflective practices, and individual personal development. Her PhD research examined group memory, and she also continues academic work within a tertiary business school as a master's supervisor. Mandy is passionate about reimagining creativity as an innate human force for inclusion, resilience, and connection. Through her writing, teaching, and practice, she invites people to rediscover their 'secret garden' – a metaphor for the generative, diverse, and life-affirming essence of self. Email: mandy@mandylacy.nz www.mandylacy.nz

Seán Manning, MSc, DipGrad, DipSW, TSTA, MNZAP, DAPAANZ. Raised in Belfast, Northern Ireland, Seán has lived in Aotearoa New Zealand since 1975. He has three adult children and two grandchildren. Seán is a registered psychotherapist in private practice, a tutor on the degree-level addictions counselling programme Te Taketake, and a group facilitator and one-to-one therapist in a stopping violence programme. He has a long history working with crime, violence, and drug use in psychiatric hospitals, therapeutic community, prison, and mandated services in the community. He has performed multiple roles in professional associations, has served on the Board of the ITAA, and has twice been president of the APANZ. Between 1993 and 2011 he taught TA and still contributes as a guest trainer, examiner, and presenter. Seán has qualifications in psychology, social work, Māori studies, and psychotherapy, and is currently promising to finish a Doctorate in Health Science on the assembly of criminal subjectivity. He studies Spanish in a desultory manner and although his command of Māori language is deteriorating, it is still more functional than his Irish. He plays some stringed instruments, including the Irish harp, just well enough to have company. Seán has published regularly over the past three decades and intends to continue as long as he is able. Now in his 81st year, he regards retirement as probably a bad idea. Email: seanmanning120845@gmail.com

Dave Nicholls is a Professor of Critical Physiotherapy in the School of Clinical Sciences at Auckland University in Auckland, Aotearoa New Zealand. He is a physiotherapist, lecturer, researcher, and writer, with a passion for critical thinking in and around the physical therapies. Dave is the founder of the Critical Physiotherapy

Network, an organisation that promotes the use of cultural studies, education, history, philosophy, sociology, and a range of other disciplines in the study of the profession's past, present, and future. David's own research work focuses on the philosophy, sociology, and critical history of physiotherapy, and considers how physiotherapy might need to adapt to the changing economy of healthcare in the 21st century. He has published numerous peer-reviewed articles and book chapters, many as first author. His first book, *The End of Physiotherapy* (Routledge, 2017), was the first book-length critical history of the profession. A second sole-authored book, *Physiotherapy Otherwise*, was published in 2022 as a free pdf/eBook (available from https://ojs.aut.ac.nz/tuwhera-open-monographs/catalog/book/8). He was co-editor on the first collection of critical physiotherapy writings, *Manipulating Practices* (Cappelen Damm, 2018), and was the lead editor for the follow-up *Mobilising Knowledge* (Routledge, 2020). In early 2023 he established a new site specialising in post-critical healthcare (paradoxa.substack.com). He has taught in physiotherapy programmes in the UK and New Zealand for over 30 years and has presented his work around the world. Email: david.nicholls@aut.ac.nz

Shirley Rivers was born in rural Hokianga (Ngāi Takoto, Ngāpuhi) however grew up in Auckland (Te Waiōhua, Te Kawerau ā Maki) and Hamilton. Shirley has worked in iwi social services, community development, career development and counselling, as a tertiary educator for social work and counselling, and more recently, as a missioner supporting faith-based social service provision. She has developed and taught tertiary programmes specifically for Māori who aspire to work from a Māori-centred approach. Email: lnsrivers1106@gmail.com

Mariko Seki is a CTA in the psychotherapy field and PTSTA. Mariko is qualified in Japan as a nationally certified psychologist and clinical psychologist. Mariko works as a counsellor at a university's student counselling centre and at a non-profit organisation counselling education support centre, providing individual therapy and counselling, as well as education based on transactional analysis to interpersonal support professionals and those aspiring to become such professionals. Email: marisans66@gmail.com

Index[29]

Entries that appear in **bold** indicate Tables; entries that appear in *italics* indicate Figures; and entries that appear in ***bold italics*** indicate that they appear in the Glossary.

[29] Compiled by Matt Bird and Keith Tudor.

220

223

224

www.ingramcontent.com/pod-product-compliance
Lightning Source LLC
Chambersburg PA
CBHW052017030426
42335CB00026B/3179